Mrs. Evelyn Stefa... ...n

and

Mr. J...

announce the marriage

on Tuesday, the twenty-first of April

Nineteen hundred and sixty-four

Washington, District of Columbia

de nous Marc Chagall
Vava.

FINDING MY WAY

FINDING MY WAY

The Autobiography of an Optimist

EVELYN STEFANSSON NEF

THE FRANCIS PRESS

Washington, D. C.

Printed in the United States of America

FIRST EDITION

Credit for artwork on endsheets: Untitled drawing by Marc Chagall © 2002 Artists Rights Society (ARS), New York / ADAGP, Paris

Photograph of "Christopher Morley and Evelyn Baird Stefansson at the Gotham Book Mart on Christmas Eve in the early thirties" from *Wise Men Fish Here: The Story of Frances Steloff and the Gotham Book Mart*, Copyright © 1965 by W.G. Rogers and renewed 1993 by Stuart Cotton, reprinted by permission of Harcourt, Inc.

Library of Congress Cataloging-in-Publication Data

Nef, Evelyn Stefansson, 1913-
    Finding my way : the autobiography of an optimist / Evelyn
Stefansson Nef. -- 1st ed.
            p. cm.
    Includes index.
    ISBN 0-9665051-5-8 (hardcover)
    1. Nef, Evelyn Stefansson, 1913-   . 2. Nef, Evelyn Stefansson, 1913-
--Friends and associates. 3. Linguists--United States. 4. Psycho-
therapists--United States. 5. Philanthropists--United States.   I. Title.
CT275.N4237A3 2002
973.9'092--dc21
    [B]   2002001028

Book and jacket design by Dede Cummings

Published by The Francis Press
Washington, D.C.
www.francispress.com

For Marty and Bob Carswell
who made the romance of my life
with John Nef possible

CONTENTS

Washington, D.C.

NEW

YORK

CHAPTER I

A Brooklyn Childhood

*I*N 1916, WHEN I WAS THREE YEARS OLD, my little brother Myron was born. Following the birth of three girls, he should have been the cause of rejoicing and celebration for my Hungarian-born Jewish immigrant parents—the male heir at last. But my beautiful mother, still in her mid-twenties, did not rejoice. Instead, she developed psychotic postpartum depression and tried to kill herself by swallowing bichloride of mercury, an antiseptic precursor of iodine. Discovered in time to save her life, she was sent to a summer resort in Lakewood, New Jersey, "to rest and recover." When she returned home to Bensonhurst, Brooklyn, she was *not* better and was finally hospitalized at Zion Hospital in nearby Bath Beach.

No one explained anything to me, but I knew that my mother had disappeared, and I was left with feelings of deep sadness and abandonment that permeated my entire childhood until adolescence. I have never been able to discover how long my mother was in the hospital. Neither of my two older sisters, Julia, eighteen months my senior, or Rosalind, two years older than Julia, who might have known, could tell. We could only guess. Rosalind had no memory of the hospitalization at all. Julie thought it was a matter of months, though she confessed that she didn't really know. My guess is that it was at least two years, since my next memory of mother was from about the time I entered kindergarten. We three girls were taken for a visit to the hospital. Only Rosalind was admitted; Julie and I had to wait outside—we were too young, they said. All I remember of this time is being taken to the outside of a large building and told to wave through a window to a figure who didn't wave back. In those days mental illness, like cancer, was never discussed openly. Whispered about within the family, yes, but never "in front of the children." Because I couldn't understand what was going on around me, feelings of puzzlement and confusion joined the sadness and loneliness. When my mother eventually returned home, we were both changed. The two of us had lost our liveliness, our *joie de vivre*.

So while she kept house, sewed, baked, and went to the synagogue on Saturday, she did so on a reduced energy budget that eliminated fun, pleasure, and affection. Only Rosalind remembers my mother as lively; Julie and I remember no liveliness, only the lack of affection and even attention. It wasn't until my late teens that I learned with a shock from Rosalind that my mother had tried to commit suicide and that *that* was the reason for her disappearance. This news marked the birth of my long search for the reasons why. It took me more than half a century to figure out that we had both been suffering from depression.

U NDER the Austro-Hungarian Hapsburg monarchy, Hungarian Jews had been granted political freedom in 1867 and recognition of the Jewish religion in 1896. Though anti-Semitism existed in Hungary, Jews were not subjected to the kind of government-sponsored anti-Semitic propaganda, pogroms, and scapegoating that flourished in nearby Russia. Indeed, Jews played a large—some say dominant—part in the financial, economic, and intellectual life of the country.

Following the unsuccessful Kossuth 1848 revolution, prosperity arrived in Hungary, bringing with it the gradual industrialization of the country. But prosperity was unevenly dispersed, with the rich getting richer and many of the poor living in misery. These trends coincided with a huge population increase that almost doubled the country's inhabitants by the end of the century. The crowding resulted in a wave of emigration that started in 1890, in which my father, Jenö Schwartz, and his brothers took part.

In Hungary at the beginning of the twentieth century, Jews were divided into two broad groups: the orthodox religious Jews, and the richer, generally more educated, nonobservant Jews who thought of themselves as enlightened. My mother's family, the Kleins, belonged to the second group, which looked down on the Jews who retained their beards and side curls. They might attend a service on Yom Kippur or Rosh Hashanah, marry and name their children in the faith, and think little more about it. There were no Reform or Conservative synagogues. My mother, for instance, went to a Roman Catholic Convent School, Notre Dame de Sion, because it was the best school in Debrecen. There she learned to speak German, French, and English, to sew and embroider beautifully, and to cook.

Jenö Schwartz came from Szatmar, in northeast Hungary, a town that later became part of Romania. He came from an upper middle-class background and was probably trained as a furrier and tailor. He was said to have a merry temperament and could draw and paint and play the violin. Though he considered himself an orthodox Jew, he did not wear a beard or side curls or dress in the black suits and hats that marked the most orthodox Jews. My father arrived at Ellis Island in 1903, at the age of seventeen.[*] He was the youngest of three brothers who sought a better life in America. Sam, the eldest, was already established in Albany, and it was there that Jenö and Morris, a year older, went first when they arrived. In America, Jenö wore ordinary American dress, but he still prayed every morning in Hebrew wearing a prayer shawl and tefillin and kept a kosher house.

---

[*] I know this thanks to a recent project designed by Caroline Kennedy's husband Edward Shlossberg, called "Explore Your Family History at Ellis Island." Of the eleven Jenö Schwartzes who came between 1893 and 1911, my father was the only one who gave his "residence" as Szatmar, where I knew he had been born. Thus I was able to determine the year of his arrival and his age at the time.

Sometime after 1905 Morris and Jenö moved to New York and established a business partnership called Schwartz Brothers, Ladies Tailors and Furriers. Their business occupied the entire building, except for a ground floor linen shop, at 429 Fifth Avenue, between Thirty-seventh and Thirty-eighth Streets, across from Lord & Taylor. The brothers soon had a flourishing firm, manufacturing and selling ladies suits and coats on the premises. During this period, Jenö reconnected with a lovely young woman from his past.

My maternal grandmother, Serena Meyer, was one of three beautiful sisters. (Were there ever any plain Hungarian sisters?) She and Blanca and Csenny had grown up on the family estates in Madaras, about one hundred miles south of Budapest. The family was rich, and all three girls married wealthy landowners. They were well-educated and sophisticated. Serena married Kalman Klein, whose father received the title of Baron and estates from the Kaiser. The Kleins lived in Debrecen, 120 miles east of Budapest, and more than a hundred miles north of Madaras, where they summered.

In 1906 the Baroness Serena Meyer Klein suffered the loss of her husband. She decided to take her five children, Hella, Bella, Cornel, Irene, and Alexander, around the world and sold one of her houses to pay for the trip. On their way they stopped in New York to see the sights and renewed their acquaintance with Jenö Schwartz, whom they had known in Hungary.

Jenö Schwartz and Bella Klein, my mother, had played with each other as children in Madaras. In New York their childhood affection blossomed; they fell in love and decided to marry. The round-the-world journey stopped while the family resolved several important questions, a process that took two years, during which time wedding arrangements were made. Cornel decided to stay in New York, and Irene finished the school she was attending. Hella chose to go to Paris and study photography, and later became a successful photographer in both Paris and Debrecen. Beautiful Bella, then eighteen, slender, dark eyed, with thick reddish-brown hair and very white skin, was married to Jenö in a magnificent lace gown at a lavish wedding reception. The day after, the family, including Hella but minus Bella and Cornel, embarked on the *President Polk* for the return to Hungary.

When my parents married, they moved to Bensonhurst, Brooklyn, near where Morris lived. They found a house at Twentieth and Cropsey Avenues, where my oldest sister, Rosalind, was born. Soon afterward the little family—my mother already pregnant with her second child—went back to Hungary for a visit to show her to the family. They brought a bicycle for Alex, mother's younger brother—a gift that brought about tragedy. Alex, who was then fifteen, and a friend biked to a nearby river to go swimming, and Alex was accidentally drowned, casting a pall over the happy family reunion. Shortly after they returned from this trip, my parents moved to an apartment in Manhattan in an upper middle-class Jewish neighborhood, at 201 West 109th Street, near Amsterdam Avenue.

Not until I began doing research for this book did I learn about my mother's family—their wealth and their way of life. I couldn't recall a single family conversation about the old days in Hungary. When we had Hungarian visitors, there must have been talk about the past, but they spoke to each other in Hungarian, which I didn't understand. Now, with what I know about my grandmother's title and social position, I can begin to imagine how difficult it must have been for my mother, however much in love, to make the transition from a luxurious, sophisticated, worldly life to that of a middle-class, orthodox wife who kept a kosher house.

As was common in those days before widespread birth control, my mother had four children in quick succession. Following the birth of Rosalind, whom we called Rosie or Roz, on February 22, 1909, came Julia, called Julie, on January 7, 1912. I arrived eighteen months later, on July 24, 1913, and was named Evelyn and called Evvie. Three years later, on September 18, 1916, came my little brother, named and called Myron, the long-awaited male heir, completing the family.

My FIRST memory is of sitting in a high chair beside a thinly curtained window through which sunshine was pouring as a gentle breeze wafted the curtain. In this memory I seem to know that we are going to move from Manhattan back to Bensonhurst. My mother was probably pregnant with my brother, and I was two-and-a-half years old.

Strangely, I have almost no memories of my mother and me together after the age of three. I remember only one birthday present in my entire childhood (birthdays as a rule were not celebrated in our family), and this memory has a special poignance for me. On that occasion, my mother gave me a round woven sewing basket, about ten inches in diameter, made of sweet grass, whose delicious scent I can still conjure up at will. She and I were alone together on the porch, and she patiently showed me how to begin the embroidery. It is the only time I remember being alone with her, having her entire attention. Common sense tells me there must have been innumerable encounters between just the two of us, but they are all erased.

My sister Rosalind tells me that mother was lively and fun-loving in the early years of her marriage. She taught us to sing songs, do gymnastics, and dance the minuet. I did learn some Hungarian songs, which she must have taught us, but I have no clear memories of gay or merry times. Perhaps I was too young.

When I was around five, my father gathered all the children together and seriously cautioned us that we had to be good and gentle with my mother because she was nervous and fragile. When a small child is told to "look after" a parent, the reversal of roles places a burden on the child, who is ill-equipped to bear it. "What do I have to do? Will I be able to do it? What happens if I fail? Who will look after *me*?" are the unspoken, anxiety-producing questions that must have occupied us. I had no instruction or demonstrations from anyone about how to solve the problem of my mother's remoteness.

My parents never quarreled, at least in front of us, which is as unnatural as parents who quarrel all the time. We never learned that it was all right to disagree, that it was possible to resolve disagreements or handle or discharge sensibly our angry feelings. In that too-smooth, careful atmosphere, I must have wondered what went on secretly. Perhaps this early experience of secrecy was at the root of my permanent hunger to know, my curiosity about everything. Was this why I grew to be a careful listener, an intent watcher, a patient gatherer of every fragment of disparate information, someone who tried to make it all into some intelligible whole?

Because we knew we should not make waves or create scenes that might upset my mother, the ambience in and around our house was quiet. My mother was very muted in her ways. Unlike our neighbors, she never shouted for us when she wanted us to come in for supper. Instead, she would clap her hands in a very ladylike manner—perhaps a remnant of her convent schooling in Debrecen. We all understood the signal and responded. The house was pervaded by an unseemly calm and self-control. In our family there was none of the spontaneous hugging or kissing or touching common among orthodox European Jews. I have no memory of sitting on my mother's or father's lap, although I must have as an infant. No one ever read to me. We were taught to be polite to our parents and siblings, but there was no real affection among us until we were grown, after we had learned it elsewhere. I always believed my father and mother loved each other, but I never saw a demonstration of affection, never saw them embrace, beyond a formal hello or a goodbye kiss.

Mother never attempted to commit suicide again, as far as I know. But then I had the feeling I was never "in the know." This isolation may have been deepened by the language barrier. When my parents didn't want the children to know what they were saying, they spoke Hungarian. Rosalind learned Hungarian, but she was the only one of us fluent in the language. Julie knew some, and I could count to ten and sing a few songs. Otherwise we spoke English.

Mother never punished us. She reported our misdeeds to father when he came home from work, and he decided on the punishment.

I was usually a "good child" and remember being spanked only once, when I was around twelve. I have long forgotten the misdeed, but I do remember the pleasurable release of excitement in being chased and caught by my angry father—a demonstration of emotion in contrast to the controlled calm of our everyday life.

Our usual family punishment was to be made to stand in the cellar for fifteen minutes, half an hour, or at most an hour, depending on the seriousness of the offense. The cellar of our house contained many large pottery crocks of cucumbers in various stages of their development into dill pickles. Here, too, were the furnace and coal bins, the soapstone laundry tubs, and a clothes wringer that consisted of two rubber cylinders turned by a handle. A four-foot square platform just inside the basement door topped the steps leading downward. The few times I was punished I remember standing on top of the stairs in the dark. A thin rim of light outlined the door. On the other side I could hear the family life going on without me, as if I didn't exist. The time always seemed endless, and I was bathed in feelings of abandonment and loneliness.

During these early years, I often felt left out, solitary, and powerless. Being the third child, the third *girl*, followed by the darling brother, I was frequently overlooked. Roz, as first born, had the first choice of food, new clothes, and attention. Julie always seemed to know how to get attention or demand it by being bad. Defending myself against sadness, anger, and that most common of all childhood feelings, a sense of *unfairness*, I adopted a kind of emotional numbness, an "I don't care" attitude that masked intense feelings. My existence eventually admitted no highs or lows but seemed restricted to a narrow, safe path. I slept, woke up, ate meals, went to school, did my homework something like an automaton. I had no friends or playmates. I lived with an emptiness I was unable to name until many years later.

We had a maid and a nanny when we were young and for a time a strange Hungarian gardener named Lutzi, who had been shell-shocked in World War I. Since he knew no English, we never talked. He was completely bald, and always wore a cap. He lived in a corner of our large basement and worked only outdoors.

One of the reasons I remember World War I, though I was only five years old at its end, was the coal shortage. Because of it, in winter we hauled sacks of the scarce and precious fuel home from the coal storage depot on our Flexible Flyer sled. Rosalind told me that during the war mother was a member of a women's auxiliary of the Red Cross that met regularly and rolled bandages for wounded soldiers. That story revived a fleeting memory of her in a white nurses uniform with a large head scarf that had a bright red cross carefully appliquéd on the part covering her forehead.

I also remember the wild excitement of the armistice, with people running out into the streets amidst delirious laughter and screaming. After the war there was a great victory parade of returned soldiers, headed by General Pershing, marching down Fifth Avenue, where my father's place of business was. His showroom windows facing the avenue were lined with chairs, and family and friends gathered for a perfect view. Part of the parade was a huge block-long American flag carried by numerous soldiers in uniform onto which people threw coins for the Red Cross or some soldiers' benefit fund. I remember begging for a coin and wrapping it in a piece of paper (perhaps for better aim) and throwing it two stories down onto the flag.

All of us children came down at the same time with influenza during the terrible worldwide epidemic of 1918. We were confined in a single hospital-like room in the house, and I was given the first and only toy I can remember receiving, miniature doll furniture, which my father brought home from Manhattan.

I longed for a doll. I would cut out pictures of dolls from magazine advertisements, including those with outrageously high prices. I dreamt of schemes by which I could earn enough to buy one big enough to hold and hug, but it never happened. Neither of my older sisters had dolls, and I must have understood that dolls were not a part of life's possibilities, because I never actually asked for one. I remember drawing and cutting out Kewpie dolls and creating clothes for them with tabs that could be folded over and hung on their shoulders.

I have tried to understand why we weren't given dolls. Was it connected with the taboo against "graven images"? It certainly wasn't because we couldn't afford them. Despite our expensive clothes and servants, I felt distinctly deprived. My classmates had birthday parties, to which I was occasionally invited, but we didn't celebrate birthdays— perhaps in keeping with the unnatural quiet of the house, with not calling attention to oneself or being conspicuous. These deprivations must be filed in that strange attic of unsolved childhood mysteries.

WITH my father's business flourishing, we moved again, to a large, single-family, three-story house surrounded by a spacious yard, also in Bensonhurst, on Eighty-fourth Street between Nineteenth and Twentieth Avenues.

Mother's younger brother, Cornel, who had stayed in New York when my parents married, lived in Manhattan and worked at De Pinna's, the elegant Fifth Avenue clothing store. I remember him as a tall, light-haired young man who when he visited often brought us gifts of expensive clothing. My sister Roz tells me that he had a little automobile that had a side car like the World War I motorcycles, but I was too young to remember it. Oddly, I also cannot remember when he married a beautiful, blue-eyed, blond gentile girl named Tessie and they came to live with us in our house on Eighty-fourth Street.

The middle of three rooms on the top floor was fixed up with a bathtub, toilet, and stove to make a slightly primitive apartment for them. Among orthodox Jews, marrying a "shiksa" is considered to be a tragedy. The culprit is mourned as if he had died, his family sits "shiva" for him, and he is shunned for the rest of his life. Though Cornel's family was not orthodox, my father was, and I never knew how it was managed that he and his wife lived with us until they were able to afford a place of their own. This situation may have brought more tension into our family life. In any case, Uncle Cornel and Aunt Tessie moved out as soon as they were able.

After that we saw much less of them. Several years later, when I was ten years old, I was told that Uncle Cornel had had an accident and died. In my teens I asked my sisters what they knew about this accident and his death. Only then did I find out that he had thrown himself in front of a moving subway train. I was shocked and indignant that I had not been told the truth at the time, which deepened my sense of being an outsider. Perhaps every child feels something like this at some point. Perhaps, too, I was told about Uncle Cornel at the time but did not understand, or misheard or misinterpreted what I heard. But I was, in fact, very alone and isolated within my own family.

My oldest sister, Rosalind, was the object of my envy. Her beautiful auburn hair and hazel eyes and graceful, sunny social manner made her popular with both boys and girls of her age. It was her clear voice that usually started the sisters singing in the house. As senior sibling she was the leader in activities that required all of us participating, like marching to the synagogue, who played whom and when in the backyard croquet games, and the distribution of candy from the Whitman's chocolate box brought by the occasional visitor.

Julie had green eyes with sooty black lashes, the highest IQ of all of us, and a body that not only was perfectly proportioned but could dance and outperform us all in athletic contests. She was mischievous and musical and always sought and found the spotlight.

My little brother Myron was a mechanical wonder. He was always surrounded by strange multicolored wires and bits and pieces of plastic and metal, useless junk to the casual observer, but valuable and useful to him in some visionary way. He made his first radio set from those bits and pieces and other found objects.

All of us, in turn, went to Elementary Public School No. 128 on Eighty-fifth Street between Twentieth and Twenty-first Avenues, only three blocks from our home in Bensonhurst. In addition to learning the three Rs, the boys did shop work and the girls had cooking and sewing lessons called Home Economics. Strangely, it was not from my mother, the expert embroiderer, but at school that I learned to sew all kinds of seams when we made our graduation dresses entirely by hand out of white voile. Learning all the stitches for hand sewing and how to darn was not only interesting to me but turned out to be invaluable later in life.

When we were old enough, we were all sent to Hebrew school in the afternoons after public school. By the time I was seven, my father was prosperous enough to be able to stop working on the Sabbath. In 1920, the year President Harding was elected, we joined a synagogue in the neighborhood, and from then on we all attended services on Saturday. My sisters and I sat upstairs with our mother. My little brother, Myron, was allowed on the ground floor with the men. It never occurred to me that the women were being treated as second-class citizens by being separated from the main scene.

Going to the synagogue was a routine that left me unmoved except for the music. I loved the singing and as soon as I could joined in the singing part of the service. I was never filled with any religious feeling. I was taught about God and all the strict dos and don'ts of orthodox Judaism, and I never questioned any of it, but it wasn't invested with any emotion for me. I didn't pray or call on God for help, because I didn't believe he would help. Perhaps I had tried at some point and been disappointed.

In 1921, when I was eight, my maternal Grandma from Hungary visited us for the summer. Grandma was a "presence"—tall, handsome, very energetic. But she was also peculiar. I remember her walking down Eighty-fourth Street incompletely dressed and with her long hair unpinned, calling out my name like a street crier—something my own mother would never do—to my terrible embarrassment. Another sharp memory was of my mother following her with a bottle of red medicine (which I now know to be chloral hydrate) trying to get her to take it and to "calm down." By this time Grandmother Klein was married again to a rich spice merchant, also named Schwartz, and had moved from Debrecen to Niredhaza. In later years she used to "wander," and my stepgrandfather Schwartz built her a separate little house on the estate and locked her out of the main house.

ALTHOUGH my early childhood was characterized by feelings of sadness and isolation, certain aspects of family life proved quite rich and rewarding.

The smells and tastes of my mother's cooking were always a source of comfort and pleasure. She used to bake every Thursday in preparation for Friday night and the Sabbath, which began with the ritual of lighting the candles and a blessing. Coming home from school, I would often find the dining room table and chairs draped with bed linens and covered with the thinnest of thin sheets of rolled-out strudel dough. Later, when three or four sheets were combined, filled with nuts, spices, and apple, rolled, and baked, they would be transformed into the crisp *mille feuilles* of strudel.

My mother also made butter cookies that melted in the mouth, thin spicy cookies, and strips of pastry dough wound spirally around metal forms and later filled with whipped cream. Our house at such times smelled like an Austro-Hungarian pastry shop. Homemade egg noodles also appeared for the Friday night chicken soup, as well as thin crepe pancakes called *polachintas*, filled with jelly for dessert or eaten plain or with creamy cheese interiors for lunch or supper. Matzo ball soup alternated with noodle soup; the appearance of a chicken's foot in one's soup was a rare, highly prized special treat. With four children and only two feet to a chicken, someone was always disappointed.

One of my favorite tasks was to grind the coffee beans in a square wooden box that had an s-shaped handle with a wooden button on the end. Holding the machine tightly between my knees, I would turn the handle with all my might. The delicious smell was intensified as I opened the little drawer in the bottom of the box that caught the fresh grounds. Good smells of many varieties emanated from my mother's kitchen: The scents of the ever-present paprika (always the imported Hungarian kind), roasts and goulash, baking cakes and cookies often perfumed the entire downstairs. I looked forward to mealtime. The best and most delicious taste of all was a piece of Jewish rye-bread toast spread with chicken fat (which Hungarian cooks used in place of butter) and then rubbed with a cut clove of garlic—manna to a ravening school child.

I was often sent to a bakery on Twentieth Avenue, in a row of shops, to buy the still-warm rolls and delicious-smelling rye bread. Nearby, a delicatessen sold holiday treats like frankfurters, salami, smoked whitefish, sturgeon, and other goodies.

In addition to her talents in the kitchen, Momma's skills with a needle were legendary in the neighborhood. She made by hand filet lace curtains for the living and dining rooms. She embroidered many kinds of tablecloths and napkins, and her most elaborate semi-sculptured flower embroideries were framed and hung on the living room walls. She made silk lamp shades and sewed and embroidered our good dresses.

We always had new clothes for Passover and for Rosh Hashanah, the Jewish New Year. A cousin of mother's made our everyday clothes, supplemented with those Uncle Cornel brought us from De Pinna. Poppa made our best clothes. I remember pussy-willow-patterned silk piped in lavender, blue serge sailor suits with pleated skirts, gold linen summer frocks enhanced by a Greek key design embroidered by my mother around the waist. Another favorite of mine was an unbleached muslin dress with a sailor collar outlined in a double row of embroidered scallops, a line of blue and a line of red. We three girls were always dressed alike until Rosalind reached adolescence and rebellion.

I especially remember the new dress I wore on the first day of school: a grey flannel pleated skirt with large pearl buttons circling the waist of a white middy blouse. There was pleasure in the feel of the new dress and more pleasure in having the family spotlight on me for a few moments. Throughout my early childhood I suffered from my family's good taste. While I longed for yellow chiffon ruffled party dresses, I was dressed in handsome balbriggan tailored dresses. I was probably the only pupil in my class who was really chic, in my plain beautiful dresses, but like most youngsters I longed to look like everybody else. Not until my teens did I realize how marvelous my childhood clothes had been and how insufficiently I had appreciated them.

My father made Rosalind's first formal evening dress of white silk taffeta; its only decoration was a chartreuse silk handmade rose at the waist. I thought it disappointingly plain at the time, but because I retain such a full-color memory of it, I now know it was superb.

Some of my happier memories are connected with music and singing. We were a musical family, and in the days before radio and television, the big upright Hardman Peck piano in the living room was the center of the family's entertainment. Beautiful Rosalind had a pure soprano voice. She sang in the Glee Club and had solo roles in the Gilbert and Sullivan operas that were produced at New Utrecht High School, where she and Julie went. When Rosalind played the piano, Julie played the violin. (A neighbor gave me elementary piano lessons, but for reasons I don't understand, they never took, although I was just as musical as the rest of the family.) We sang the popular songs of the day, the songs we learned at school, and some of mother's store of Hungarian folk songs. We sang while doing the dishes and clearing up after meals, teaching each other any new songs we learned. We sang at the Passover Seder, and we sang in the synagogue. Singing was when I felt most a part of the family and that we *were* a family.

Music was also a diversion for me in lonely times. I would sing to myself to pass the time, and it had a soothing and comforting effect. One of my first chores was to sing my infant brother to sleep when I was three years old. I still remember the lullaby:

> Sleep, baby, sleep
> Father is watching the sheep
> Mother is shaking the dreamland tree

And down comes a little dream for thee
Sleep, baby, sleep.

There was a fourteen-foot-high swing in our backyard that my handy father built. We took turns pushing each other higher and higher, and when feeling really intrepid we would stand instead of sit on the board seat and with a kind of pumping-bending-and-straightening motion of our legs swing out until we were as high as the top of the swing. In summertime a croquet set would be set up in the backyard, and on weekends all the family would play. During the warmer months we would occasionally go swimming at nearby Bath Beach. My mother dressed in black stockings and a sleeved black cotton bathing dress. I was never comfortable in the water unless my feet could touch bottom, and I didn't learn to swim well until I was middle-aged.

Our quiet neighborhood streets were lit by gas lampposts set at regular intervals. Each evening a lamplighter would come by to light the white-netted cone that illuminated the street, its glow stretching slowly farther and farther along the way with each lamp he reached. In the daytime a knife grinder came by in a horse-drawn wagon and stopped every so often to sharpen knives and scissors. An old clothes buyer man on foot would interrupt the stillness with his repetitious shout of "I cash clothes, I cash clothes."

When friends of my parents came to visit in a pony cart, they would sometimes give us children a ride—very exciting. After cars became a more common sight, a large beige Pierce Arrow automobile would occasionally appear on our street on a Sunday, and while its owner was visiting someone, the chauffeur would give rides to all the kids on the block.

WHEN I was eleven, one day in a small group of girls an inevitable subject arose. A pale-faced, dark-haired girl, the daughter of a doctor, announced arrogantly, "I know where babies come from, and I'll tell you how it is done." Instant silence and rapt attention. "A man's penis gets big, and he puts it in his wife's vagina and plants a seed that grows into a baby. When the baby is big enough to be born, it comes out of her vagina." I didn't know the words penis or vagina, but I got the shocking message. With enormous indignation I retorted as many a child does, "Maybe that's what *your* mother and father do to get a baby, but *my* parents would *never* do such a dirty thing."

My father wore a thick mustache. His bright dark eyes sparkled below heavy eyebrows, and his pale skin marked him as a man who worked indoors. Throughout my childhood he rose early, made the oatmeal that we ate for breakfast, and drove off to work before I was up. He returned after I was in bed. Saturdays were devoted to going to the synagogue, and on Sundays, after working so hard all week, he would often sleep during the day.

Poppa and his brother Morris were close to each other and very successful in their Fifth Avenue business, netting a profit of around $30,000 per year, which would be something like $300,000 today. Uncle Morris was temperamental and high strung. In 1925 or '26 Aunt Margaret, his wife, decided to separate from him and seek a divorce. When Morris learned of this, he disappeared in order to avoid being served with the papers. One day while he was visiting us on Eighty-fourth Street, the sheriff came to serve the legal papers and to arrest him for nonpayment of support. He resisted arrest, making a loud and violent scene. I was home at the time and was frightened by the shouting and the hubbub. Uncle Morris was out of control, shouting crazily and flailing about. An ambulance was sent for, and he was placed in a straitjacket and taken to the hospital. My cousin Sydney, Morris' eldest son, whom he used to meet surreptitiously during his "disappearance," reached him at the hospital, and Uncle Morris died in his arms of cardiac arrest.

Uncle Morris's death, with its dramatic, noisy prelude in our usually too-quiet house, had to have had momentous emotional and physical consequences. Although I was about twelve at the time, no mention of it was ever made, and if my parents discussed it, they did so alone—"not in front of the children."

Sydney, who was six years older than I, was my favorite cousin, and it seems I was his. He used to come over and take me to the local Chinese restaurant on Eighty-sixth Street for what we called "Chinks." He thought I was pretty sophisticated for thirteen, and I loved having a grownup interested in me as a person—what a novelty and a joy! Sydney took me to a Philharmonic concert, my first, and regaled and enchanted me with tales of the Metropolitan Opera. I still remember his description of the magnificent costumes and setting of *Turandot*. He was articulate, and his vivid descriptions of music meshed with my own dreams and fantasies, providing me with pleasure and hope that somewhere there was a world of wonder and beauty that I might experience, too. Sydney had wanted to be an engineer and go to Cooper Union for training, but Jews were not admitted, and he was advised to study law. He became a very successful corporate lawyer, representing Pierre Cardin, Estee Lauder, and other international corporations. He was always willing to give the family free legal advice in his gentle, affectionate manner.

After Uncle Morris died, Poppa gave up the Fifth Avenue location, moved to Fifty-seventh Street, and became a well-known fur designer. He designed and sold patterns of fur coats to the most exclusive furriers and created one-of-a-kind coats for wealthy, fashionable ladies. He pioneered innovative ways to handle fur. He made the first tailored fur coats, using fur as if it were cloth material. He used braid to separate the skins and form interesting lines. I think he was also the first to use leather to pipe the edges of the tailored coats, sometimes matching but sometimes also contrasting with the fur color. I remember one black fur evening coat whose standing collar was lined with silver kid. Mother's wardrobe benefited from his creativity. In addition to the standard black seal coat that most women in our neighborhood favored, he fashioned a lightweight coat of caramel-colored summer ermine for her and, for a silk suit, lined the wide sleeve cuffs of black caracul with winter-white ermine. He also made all her evening clothes. One was blue lamé "like Mrs. Harding's," the president's wife.

My parents used to go to the opera, dressing up in evening clothes to hear Caruso and Galli-Curci sing at the Metropolitan Opera House. With a few exceptions all our records for the tall mahogany wind-up Victrola were operatic. I remember playing "funeral" to the Miserere of *Il Travatore*. We also had music appreciation classes in grade school, where Miss Murgatroyd, who had a huge bosom and wore pince-nez glasses, would wind up the phonograph and play Schubert's *Unfinished Symphony* and other gems. That was my introduction to symphonic music, for which I instantly developed a taste.

Halfway down our street, toward Twentieth Avenue, the glamorous Myerson sisters lived. They were identical twins and beautiful, each with a mole, or beauty spot, on her cheek. They gave ballet lessons, and one of the rooms in their house was set up as a dance studio with a beautiful polished floor and a bar. The three Schwartz girls all took ballet dancing lessons from the Myersons as we grew to a suitable age.

Comparing myself with my two older sisters, I felt not as pretty or as smart and had come to the conclusion that there must be something basically wrong with me. No one seemed to pay any attention to me, no affection was bestowed, no confidences shared. Both sisters, going to a co-educational high school, had many beaux. I had none. I was always trying to catch up to their level, without understanding that because they were older they knew more and that I never could "catch up." I eventually concluded that I wasn't good enough or worthy and retreated back into my neutral, early childhood of not allowing myself to have feelings.

One evening when I was about eleven, after finishing my homework I began to idly sketch a female figure in some detail on a blank sheet of my unlined writing tablet. As my father walked by, he stopped to see what I was doing and discovered I could draw. Poppa encouraged me to sketch and brought home copies of *Women's Wear*

Daily for me to examine and copy. All at once I felt the pleasure of his growing interest, pleasure in pleasing him, pleasure in drawing, and delight in being with someone who was interested in me. He began to talk of my becoming a designer, too, and told me that he envisioned our working together in his business. Suddenly I seemed to have a future, a career, and with my father! The empty, sad, and lonely feelings that had been the leitmotif of my childhood were slowly replaced by a new sense of belonging to someone.

My sister Julie tells me that Poppa had tried to interest her in the fashion business but that she had resisted his efforts. She didn't get along with my father, was often in trouble, and is still resentful as she tells how she was made to cut a switch from the huge lilac bushes beside the house for Poppa to use to hit her on the legs for punishment. This was news to me. I never saw it happen. But how much went on that I didn't see?

The possibility that with training I, too, could become a designer and go into my father's business and work beside him produced something like an emotional volcanic eruption in me. It was like a movie closeup of an eye that as the camera recedes grows larger and larger, until a whole city is in view. That he thought me talented was gift enough, but that he could see me working with him, learning the business, and eventually being a partner was the first memory I have of real happiness. Suddenly I knew the meaning of that word and could hardly believe my good fortune. Now I had something to work and strive for, now I had a purpose in life, and best of all I had been found worthy.

My self-esteem took a giant step forward. I came alive. I dared to feel good. I suddenly knew who I was: Evelyn Schwartz the artist. Evelyn Schwartz the designer. Evelyn Schwartz the daughter of Jenö Schwartz. It was as if the narrow pathway I trod previously was suddenly expanded from, say, 20 degrees to 180. Suddenly I noticed and was tuned into new feelings and sensations. Part of this was certainly connected with the onset of adolescence—that disturbing time that recapitulates past feeling and provides new and explosive ones. It felt like turning on a light in a darkened room. I was *aware* of color, land-scape, people, and interiors, and the world had a new, expanded mean-ing. I felt brighter, shinier, and more certain of myself. Was it possible that I could be *important* to someone or something?

My father was good with his hands, so I tried to become good with my hands, and succeeded. I developed a hunger to *make* things, to cre-ate something, which has lasted all my life. Making something from nothing or from something discarded was my pleasure, whether it was through sewing, knitting, painting, or carpentry. Making my father still prouder of me became a burning ambition. He decided I should go to summer art school at the Traphagen School of Fashion, which was only a block away from his business. So during the sum-mer of 1925, when public school was out, I drove into Manhattan with my good-looking father in our open-touring Maxwell car, feeling very grown up. We were shown around the Traphagen School and in the process entered a life class for which a middle-aged nude woman was posing. Glancing at my father, I saw him turning beet red, and then I was yanked out of the room, with Poppa mumbling something about my being a little too young as we left. But apparently he got used to the idea that studying art included life classes, and the next summer, when I was thirteen, I was enrolled.

The Traphagen School of Fashion had high-ceilinged studio class-rooms and wonderful bright light. The building is still there, on Fifty-seventh Street and Seventh Avenue. I was the youngest pupil—indeed, the only child. Surrounded by older, more experienced students, most of whom had had previous training, I had to work very hard to keep up, which I did most willingly. Comparing my work with theirs left me worried about whether I was sufficiently talented to merit the high tuition. It never occurred to me to make allowances for my youth and inexperience. Besides life classes, we had fashion illustrating lessons, where I felt I did better. My father was pleased with my efforts, which calmed my fears. He would show my sketches proudly to his cus-tomers. That was all the reward I needed.

One of the lovely memories of that happy period in my life was of buying my first art supplies. From the moment I took the list of required items given to me by the Traphagen School to the art supply store, I was in ecstasy. I loved the expensive, beautiful green Venus drawing pencils (I was to have eight) ranging from the hard 2H to the soft, soft 6B. The exquisite pleasure of sharpening them into long points with a knife and further shaping them perfectly with a little gadget that consisted of a pad of sandpaper sheets attached to a wooden holder made me feel like a genuine artist. To this day I prefer a sharp knife to the most modern electric pencil sharpener. Then came the papers: paper for pencil drawings, huge pads of it; watercolor papers; smooth papers; textured papers, some of them handmade; Bristol board; and colored papers to make collages. Contè crayons, charcoal sticks, tubes of Windsor and Newton's watercolors, sable brushes in several sizes—amazing riches and all mine! It was like an imagined scene from *Arabian Nights*.

I loved learning to look at everything in a new, careful way. Color, shape, texture, light became new sources of study and pleasure. I brought my best efforts home to show my father, who admired them and encouraged me. I tried to make every minute of the school day count. It was as if fresh blood were coursing through my veins, providing energy never before experienced. My world had expanded to include a million things I had never noticed before, all of them subjects for my new-found scrutiny. Now I knew how to look and appreciate. Going to an art museum was an exciting adventure. My life was changed forever, irrevocably.

Each day during that glorious summer we traveled into Manhattan together. Rising early, dressing hastily but neatly, I would breakfast with my father before the rest of the family was up. I imagine riding with him for the hour-long drive through Brooklyn, across the bridge into Manhattan. My sister Rosalind tells me it is unlikely that we went in the car; we would certainly have gone on the subway. In any case, having my father's sole attention was the beginning of a series of new pleasures. Shyly I learned to talk to him first about the weather, then about art school, then about his fur designer business and how it worked. "What is it I need to know in order to be helpful to you?" I asked. In several days, we were talking easily and enthusiastically with each other. He welcomed my inquiries and offered advice. He asked to see my drawings and often admired or corrected something.

My sisters, fifteen and seventeen, seemed too busy with school, dates, and clothes to be jealous or envious of what seemed to me a new favored status I had achieved in having this special relationship with my father.

After traveling into town together, I would leave my father at work and walk down Fifty-seventh Street to school. At noon I would pick him up and we would lunch together at a *restaurant*. That was normally a rare and special event, but now it happened every day. I was allowed to order anything I wanted, like a grown up, and just the two of us lunching was like having a date. When the afternoon school session was over I returned to his shop and investigated the various interesting fur skins that were nailed to boards and the finished samples of magnificent fur coats until it was closing time. I developed a taste for the smell, feel, and touch of beautiful furs that has never left me. Then there was the hour-long trip home together. As my initial shyness disappeared, so did the old feeling that there must be something wrong with me. I became certain that I would be an artist, that I would have a place in the world beside my father, a glamorous career.

After such a lonely childhood, that summer of twelve-going-on-thirteen was an oasis filled with many strange wonders. Much of the self-doubt that bathes adolescence was erased by my father's interest and pride in me. Suddenly I felt connected instead of separated.

I began to menstruate at last. My sisters had explained what it was about and instructed me in the dos and don'ts (at least half of the latter were incorrect). Someone must have told my father, for he made a kindly oblique reference to my being "grown up now." I cannot remember anything at all about my mother during that time. It may be that she withdrew from me even more during that summer, or perhaps more likely I withdrew from her into the rich involvement with my father. When I became thirteen on July 24, no notice was taken, as usual, but for once it didn't matter; I was happier than I'd ever been.

Shortly after this period, my father found that the making and selling of his design patterns to other furriers proved more profitable than doing one-of-a-kind luxurious wraps for the fashionable, so he moved from exclusive Fifty-seventh Street to Thirty-first Street, in the heart of the bustling fur district, considerably expanding his business.

That fall my father had decided that instead of going to nearby New Utrecht High School, where my sisters went, I was to go to Washington Irving High School for girls, in Manhattan, because it offered strong art courses. Despite the daily subway commute of one hour each way, it was an exciting prospect, since I could continue my preparation for the time when I would join my father's thriving designing business.

Washington Irving High School was unusual. Situated at Sixteenth Street and Irving Place, just south of Gramercy Park, it was a short and pleasant walk from the Union Square subway station of the BMT. The school building was handsome: One entered into a majestic, mahogany-columned foyer, where an excellent white marble sculpture framed a central fireplace. A dozen impressive murals depicting Washington Irving's view of New York's history graced the walls; only recently did I learn that they were commissioned by Mrs. E. H. Harriman and painted by Barry Faulkner, a distinguished muralist. Beyond the entrance hall was a large auditorium with an organ, whose gilded pipes decorated each side of the proscenium of the large stage. Instead of plain glass in the door panels leading to the auditorium, there were charming decorative stained glass panels. Someone had worked to make this building more than just a school building. It was an inspiring place for would-be artists and remains so to this day.

My happy delirium continued through the winter and the following spring of 1927, when a new and terrible drama began to unfold.

CHAPTER II

The Loss of My Parents

O N AN ORDINARY SPRING DAY IN MAY 1927, my sister Rosalind had a special-occasion date for which she needed a new dress. She traveled to Manhattan to shop and stopped in at Poppa's new work place on Thirty-first Street to get some money. Poppa said that he was not feeling well; he reported a heaviness in his chest, and Rosalind, wanting to be helpful, went to a drugstore to get him some bicarbonate of soda. When she returned, he said, "I'm going to the doctor; come with me." "Why?" Roz asked. "In case anything happens to me," he said. They returned to Brooklyn together on the subway and went directly to Dr. Simon Rothenberg's downtown office. By then Rosalind had begun to be frightened because my father had become very pale and appeared to have something seriously the matter with him.

Waiting their turn at the doctor's office, my father began to make struggling noises, had a seizure, and then was quiet. Rosalind frantically got the doctor, who gave Poppa a hypodermic injection, but it was too late. He was dead.

The doctor called Poppa's office to send someone to take Rosalind home. The boy who made deliveries came and escorted her to Eighty-fourth Street. As soon as she knew Poppa was dead, she had telephoned home to warn us, saying that he was "sick." Mother and children were gathered in the dining room waiting for the news when

Roz arrived to tell us that Poppa had died in Dr. Rothenberg's waiting room from a heart attack.

He was only forty-eight years old! We had had no preparation for this blow. He went to work in the morning and was brought home dead the same day. Rosalind had to tell her story over again several times until we could begin to believe it, sometimes adding a detail or two, such as the doctor giving her Poppa's gold watch and cash money for safe keeping.

Dr. Rothenberg came to the house to explain once more how Poppa died of angina pectoris and to sign the death certificate. We were all in a state of shock. I don't remember any crying or shrieking. What I remember is the silence and a feeling that the light of life had been turned off.

Julie remembers answering the front doorbell and finding two men bringing Poppa's body home in a raw pine casket, which was placed in the living room for the funeral. Ladies from the synagogue came to the house for the ritual washing of the body, the paring of the nails, and the preparation for burial. At the funeral I recall the shock of seeing my father, unembalmed according to orthodox Jewish custom, wrapped in his white prayer shawl, which covered the top of his head like a shroud but not his sweet face. Rosalind has told me that because Poppa was a Mason his Masonic regalia of apron and trowel were buried with him. He seemed a frightening stranger who merely resembled my father, his quick, sprightly manner stilled forever.

At one point during the Hebrew ceremony, which took place in our living room, a man with a knife cut my mother's beautiful black dress and then the dresses of all three of us girls in turn. At the time, I found this gesture incomprehensible. Many years later Rosalind explained that it represented the Biblical "rending of garments." *

I was struck by the fact that while everybody around me was crying, I remained dry-eyed. I was ashamed of not being able to cry, too. How

---

* This practice has recently been changed, no doubt in the interests of economy; today, mourners are provided with strips of ribbon to be cut, saving all those good black dresses.

could this beautiful, remarkable man—who had just begun to notice and appreciate me, who loved me and promised me a career at his side—just not *be?* I choked on my anguished feelings, but I could not cry—not even at the Sons of Israel Cemetery in Bath Beach as each of us ceremonially threw a handful of earth on the coffin before it was finally and permanently covered.

After the funeral we sat shivah for the required seven days, receiving visitors, many of whom brought food and would talk with us about my father. Shivah behavior is ritualized, and one is not supposed to be too comfortable. We sat on cushions or stools instead of chairs and wore no shoes. No hellos or goodbyes were said.

Someone, perhaps the undertaker, had neatly placed the shoes that my father had been wearing when he died under one of the larger living room chairs. I had to pass them several times a day going from the hall to the dining room. They remained there day after day, and each time I saw them I was frightened—of what, I didn't know. I didn't dare touch them.

From the moment Poppa died, my poor shocked mother did nothing but sit quietly and weep and stare ahead. At first she would sometimes answer yes or no to a direct question if one could somehow get her attention. But gradually even those monosyllabic responses stopped. She actually became mute and never really spoke again for the rest of her life. She behaved as though we didn't exist, as if only her fantasy world were real to her.

Pat Barker's remarkable book *Regeneration* (Penguin Plume, 1993) describes the treatment of mutism in shell-shocked World War I soldiers and offers what I consider the best explanation of the condition: "Mutism seems to spring from conflict between *wanting* to say something and knowing if you *do* say it the consequences will be disastrous. So you resolve it by making it physically impossible for yourself to speak."

My mother's sudden muteness felt like a repetition of her disappearance when I was three. She was physically present in the house, but since she never spoke it was as if she weren't really there. We knew her thoughts were somewhere, just not with the person speaking to her. Each of us tried to get her to talk, to rouse her into being her old self again, but none of us succeeded. Her face displayed a neutral expression that looked out at us calmly, unsmilingly, without change. It was as if she was using *my* no-feeling defense multiplied many times.

She eventually became almost catatonic; that is, she had periods of alternating stupor and activity. She would bathe for long periods, dress herself, and comb her hair. She fed herself, but no longer prepared meals for us. She slept in the bedroom she had shared with Poppa. She moved about the house occasionally, but my main, constant memory is of her seated in the dining room in a cotton house dress either weeping or with a sad look on her face. My mother was gentle and quiet and passive, but she clearly was not normal. In one sense we were deeply ashamed of her. We didn't have a familiar name for her illness, and we were afraid that the neighbors would think she was crazy. We wanted desperately to believe she wasn't crazy and told ourselves that crazy people were loud and violent. We tried to defend and protect her as much as possible.

All of this intensified the agony that followed my father's death. Death was final; it came to everybody eventually, and there was nothing to be done about it. But mental illness was different. Like many people in those days, I believed that mental illness was largely a matter of will. You either gave in or didn't give in to your emotions. You were supposed to pull yourself together and "manage" them. Having witnessed my mother's response to grief, I decided that I would make every effort to fight hard if anything like that ever happened to me. I believed my mother had a choice, and it angered me that she seemed to have chosen mute sorrow over being a mother to us.

Once, during a crisis in my young life, I wanted to know whether I should accept an invitation that sounded exciting but that I suspected harbored an unmentioned danger. Worried and confused, I went to my mother and pleaded for her help and guidance. Getting the usual passive, blank stare, I lost my temper and through my tears shouted at her, "You are my mother! You are supposed to help me and tell me what to do!" When this produced no change of expression on her face, I was left to finish my crying and resolve my problem, however ineptly, by myself. It seemed that if I needed the solution to a problem, I would always have to find it myself. The important and bitter lesson was learned, but I was plunged back into the lonely, solitary world I had lived in before my father "discovered" me.

As I think back on it now with more compassion, I am struck by the tragedy of a precious lifetime wasted. My mother was only thirty-six years old and still beautiful when Poppa died. It wasn't until many years later that I began to consider the connection between our family secrets: my mother's suicide attempt and later mutism, Grandma Meyer-Klein-Schwartz's aberrant behavior, and Uncle Cornel's suicide. I finally realized that there was something peculiar and scary about my mother's family—a strong genetic line of mental illness.

But at the time I didn't understand why my mother stopped behaving like a mother and became lost in her world and took no notice at all of mine. I did not know the word "depression." Antidepressant drugs were not available, nor did doctors offer effective help. Dr. Rothenberg, in whose office Poppa had died, was an early student of Freud's works and knowledgeable about psychological matters. He called mother's illness "hysterical mutism," but that label failed to help or to explain anything to our fatherless, frightened family. No treatment was available; Dr. Rothenberg said you couldn't treat someone who wouldn't talk. We continued to revolve around our mother, a familiar figure now deprived of all animation and personality.[*]

So when I lost my father, I lost my mother, too. Roz, Julie, Myron, and I were, in reality, orphans.

---

[*] Many years later, when she finally had to be hospitalized, the nurses loved her because she was never any trouble. She helped out with sewing and anything else she could do that didn't require talking. When shock treatment was discovered, they tried it with her, and for a short time her facial expressions were livelier. Indeed, her face then had a certain manic quality, but the only words she spoke were "yes" and "no" in answer to direct questions. Even these minor improvements turned out to be temporary, and she soon relapsed into her habitual silence and neutrality.

WHEN my father died, I lost any small remnant of religious faith I might have had. My anger at losing him had a paralyzing effect on me, and I never went into a synagogue again to pray. Without either father or mother to lead us, I don't think any of the children retained much religious feeling. As the male child, my eleven-year-old brother, Myron, was supposed to go to the synagogue regularly for a year to say the requisite prayers for the dead. I remember someone from the synagogue coming to the house looking for him and wanting to know why he wasn't doing his duty. He would not go.

I remember how silent the house became—the absence of people, the sudden cessation of music, noise, and laughter. Julie and Roz kept different hours because their school was nearby. I had to get up earlier to allow for the hour-long subway commute to Washington Irving.

My mother's muteness was the final blow that plunged our household into confusion. It was not long after my father's death that big changes took place. His particular creative talents were what had made his business a success. With no one to take his place, the business closed. We had been well off and then we were suddenly poor. We had to let the gardener go first, then the maid. None of us knew anything about running a household or cooking or handling what little money there was.

For a little while Mother would sign checks at our urging when we needed money to pay pressing bills or for school supplies like art materials or gym shoes. Eventually that stopped. Soon we understood that there wasn't any money left in the checking account and no more would be forthcoming. Mr. Berger, a friend of my father's, used to visit us occasionally with advice about money matters, but when my father's small insurance policy of $10,000 was spent he stopped coming. Roz left school and I started working Saturdays. Ten thousand dollars didn't go far toward supporting a wife and four children. When my father's estate was finally settled, each child received a check for $109, and mother just double that.

For a while, the bonds between my sisters and me became closer after my father's death. At first Rosalind, then seventeen, took on the role of our little mother and tried to keep some semblance of order. She went to work as a sales clerk at Franklin Simon's, a Fifth Avenue ladies' department store. Soon she began dating Maxwell Feller whom she later married, and her attention was diverted from home matters to love and the establishment of her family. Julie finished high school and almost immediately got a job in the chorus line of the Ziegfield Follies, overnight becoming in my eyes a glamorous showgirl. In the beginning we all rallied and were helpful to each other, but as time passed and we realized how serious our situation was, we often quarreled and thought each other selfish or unfeeling. Myron began to play hooky from school. No one was in charge to tell us to do our homework, wash our hands before meals, or shine our shoes before going to school. Myron bonded with me, his closest sibling, but I wasn't much help at the time, engrossed, as I was, in anger and sadness about my father's death. But I did listen to him. When he grew up and became an inventor I continued to be interested in his ideas and schemes, lending him money from my household funds, sometimes secretly, to make a model, or start up in business in a small way. He was eventually successful, but he never learned to spell. Slowly and painfully we learned to cook for ourselves, go to school or not as we pleased, mend our clothes as they began to wear out, and direct our own lives.

Crisis after crisis would arrive with none of us knowing what to do or how to fix things when they went wrong. I remember the first time the fire in the coal furnace in the cellar went out. We knew how to feed the fire once it was started, but how to make the fire in the first place was momentarily beyond us. We pooled what knowledge we had while the house cooled; finally we started a wood fire and slowly added coal a little at a time, eventually making it work. But our initial panic and helplessness was frightening. Meanwhile we were trying to protect our darling mother from the outside world and being thought "crazy." In the background was the constant sense of loss.

In the attic apartment where Cornel and Tessie had lived briefly, we had a tenant we called Aunt Rosie—not really our aunt but a distant cousin of my mother's. Like many Hungarian immigrants, she worked in the garment industry as a seamstress. Her presence in our house was part of the tradition common among newcomers to America of helping newer immigrants get a start. Aunt Rosie was shy but friendly; however, she was independent, making her own meals and eating them alone. We seldom saw her.

One day about a year after Poppa died, when my sisters and I were on the bedroom floor of the house, we smelt something terrible. We called Aunt Rosie to find out what it was, and after repeated calls with no answer we decided to investigate. "You go first." "No, you." Finally we decided to go in chronological order, Rosalind first, then Julie, with me trailing behind. Frightened, we crept slowly upstairs and with horror discovered the source of the smell: Aunt Rosie was lying dead on her bedroom floor. The hot summer sun was still streaming through the unshaded window, speeding the decay. Her skin was black and her slender body bloated, and flies and other insects were buzzing on and around her. We were terrified. She must have had a heart attack and died immediately, for we had heard no sound of struggle. Rosalind took charge and telephoned Dr. Rothenberg, who notified the authorities. The next thing I remember was two burly men coming with a wicker basket shaped like a mummy case. A while later they descended the stairs with the basket. It was heavy and they clumped clumsily down the stairs, maneuvering it along the narrow winding staircase with stops and bumps and heaving sounds, carrying off the ghastly remains of Aunt Rosie. She was the second dead person I ever saw.

The summer of my fifteenth year my sister Julie provided me with a gift. She had had a summer job waiting on tables at an elegant girls' camp in the Adirondack Mountains. She hadn't received a salary, but her expenses had been paid, and once her waitress chores were finished she had been entitled to take part in all camp activities. She was asked to come back again, but she had found a much better-paying job, so she sent me in her place. I was thrilled to be accepted—the prospect of a summer at an expensive girls' camp was unexpected and exotic. I knew that if my father had still been alive I would not have been permitted to go to a non-kosher establishment.

Raquette Lake Girls Club, in upstate New York, was my first experience of being in the country. The site was ravishing. A large blue lake, picture-card mountains, and clear summer skies left me breathless with enchantment. The work was not difficult; I set tables and brought out huge trays of platters and bowls of food, which were then passed around by the campers. After clearing off the tables, I was free to indulge in any and all camp activities, including swimming, crafts, and hiking—all new activities in ideal surroundings. Best of all, on many an evening we would sit around a campfire and sing. I soon learned the words and tunes to the songs I didn't already know, tripling my collection. For the first time in my life, I felt the heady pleasure—however short-lived—of being accepted into a new and unfamiliar community.

CHAPTER III

Trying My Wings

AFTER MY FATHER'S DEATH, I continued to attend Washington Irving High School, the all-girls' school that my father had chosen for me because of its art curriculum. I went to school still angry at the sudden deprivation not only of my father and the special relationship we had but also of my future career. Despite that sad beginning, I remember Washington Irving with great affection. We had drawing classes, painting classes, and life classes in addition to regular high school subjects. For life class we each had to contribute ten cents to pay for the model, and a brown paper shade was taped over the door's glass window so non-art students couldn't peek. The models were all middle-aged or older, both male and female, and most of them looked like the homeless people we see on the streets today. I remember one old female model washing her feet in the sink before getting up on the platform to pose.

The hour-long subway ride home kept me from hanging out with friends after class except on occasion. The only school friend I was able to make was a girl named Geraldine Adams. She was taller, older by two years, and very sophisticated, I thought, because she had a boyfriend whom she slept with! She bossed me around and I submitted willingly, grateful to have a friend. I longed for friends, for relationships of any kind, and I welcomed a connection with anyone, even someone who dominated me and told me how to act and what to do.

Geraldine had thick, short black hair on a head that was a little small for her Henry Moore-esque body. Her father worked on Broadway, which I found glamorous even though I think he was a ticket-taker. Her knowledge of the theater made her enchanting in my eyes. Unlike me, she was always properly dressed and groomed. She even had manicured nails. I still had a beautiful antelope coat, piped in brown leather at the edges, which my father had made for me, but I didn't have a single pair of stockings without rips or mended holes. When my old handsome clothes wore out, there was no money to replace them. I began to sew, buying inexpensive materials and paper patterns, learning by trial and quite a few errors how to make a decent-looking blouse and a simple dress. I knew how to hand roll the edges of a blouse ruffle so that it looked good, but the insides of the garments left much to be desired, due to my impatience.

Geraldine's mother sold ladies dresses from the uptown apartment where they lived. Against my better judgment, Geraldine seduced me into buying a dress that cost fourteen dollars. It was black with a small pink print and a ruffled edge at the neck and hem. She assured me that I could pay for it in tiny increments and that she would never press me for payment. Of course, the time came when I was unable to make the payments and this became an embarrassing millstone around my neck. The dress, which had seemed so pretty when new, lost its charm for me as Geraldine began to demand payment on my debt. After what seemed like a long, long time, it was finally paid, but the anticipated pleasure of having a new party dress had been spoiled by worry about when I would be able to make the next payment.

Probably spurred by this disaster and the need for even a little pocket money, I got a Saturday job in a local Bensonhurst dress shop as a saleslady. Saturday was the biggest shopping day of the week, and my job was to help ladies of all sizes and shapes, mostly large, try on dresses and, of course, persuade them to buy. I learned more than a college course's worth of psychology on that job, as well as how difficult it was to earn a dollar. I was paid two dollars for a twelve-hour workday.

As my wardrobe became worn and then shabby, for any special occasion I would borrow something from Rosalind's or Julie's closet. At first they tried good-naturedly to share with me. Rosalind, on a salesclerk's salary, was supposed to look not only tidy but also chic for work. Julie had become a gorgeous showgirl; she spent a good deal of her much larger salary on clothing as she began to date well-known theater people like Earl Carroll and Vincent Minelli. Still living at home, she became proud and possessive of her elegant new wardrobe, bought with her own money. She was now worried about my spotting or spoiling her things and instructed me not to borrow without her permission, which was frequently denied.

Our lives began to take different directions. When the insurance money ran out, the question of who was to pay for what became a growing concern. Our sisterly goodwill began to disintegrate under stress and strain, and our life was interrupted by quarrels, tears, and misunderstandings. Tempers became shorter, and a new and unpleasant atmosphere took hold. The pervasive feeling was something like "every man for himself."

I had my first date with a boy named Arnold Serwer whom I met at one of Rosalind's prenuptial gatherings. Considered too young to really participate in the party, he had discovered me in a corner and we talked. He would come to the house and we would go for a walk or just sit and talk. I was pleased and excited that he had come to see me, and not Julie or Rosalind. He was not good looking, but he was sweet; he wore glasses and wrote me long love letters with witty nonsense verse, which I shamelessly read aloud to my classmates. He invited me to go to Coney Island. Finding nothing suitable for such an important occasion in my own closet, I went to Julie's and borrowed an alluring short shiny red leather jacket. Julie wasn't home, so I couldn't ask her permission, and I was certain I would return before she came home after showtime, at midnight, and she would never have to know about the borrowing.

Just as Arnold and I were leaving the house, Julie returned home unexpectedly, took one look at me, and *in front of Arnold* said in her best theatrically commanding voice, "You have some nerve taking my jacket without permission. Go right upstairs and take it off." Dying of embarrassment and bitterness at Julie's shaming me in front of my first real date, I did as she ordered and changed into an old jacket of my own. To my astonishment, sweet-natured Arnold wasn't the least bit troubled by the scene, and we were soon off to the pleasures of Luna Park, eating cotton candy and trying our skills at the shooting galleries.

At Luna Park the scenic railway had terrifying uphill routes and especially steep downhill swoops that were so swift they took your breath away and everybody screamed and clung to each other. There were also slides made of varnished wood, wide so that several people could slide down at a time. It reminded me of a time when I was about eleven when I got on a slide with a group of children and my dress slid up as I went down. By the time I reached the bottom and picked myself up, I experienced a painful burning sensation in the area of my bottom. Too embarrassed to say anything, I waited until I got home to examine my back in the mirror and discovered that I had an enormous friction burn that was oozing and ugly. I don't remember reporting my wound but put peroxide on it and waited for it to heal.

Arnold continued to be my friend, and I grew out of my adolescent need to read his letters aloud to my classmates. I had been so proud that someone was writing me such interesting letters that I had to show off, but as I came to know him his admiration more than replaced my momentary pleasure from the exaggerated responses of my classmates.

ONE day Geraldine announced that there were to be tryouts for a school play, Sheridan's *The Rivals*. "Why don't you come along," she said. "You might get a servant's part." I trailed along to the auditions, and lo and behold a miracle occurred: I was given a lead part—young Jack Absolute, the hero. Geraldine was cast as Sir Lucius O'Trigger, a secondary figure.

The Rivals changed my life, most significantly in that I was able to make new friends for the first time and escape from the thralldom of being Geraldine's willing slave. Mrs. Malaprop was wonderfully played by my classmate Viola, daughter of a famous Yiddish actor, Jacob Adler, who was part of the large acting clan that included Stella and Luther Adler. Viola and I became friends, and several times she took me to her home in Greenwich Village, where I was introduced to her family, who seemed to be "on stage" at all times. Compared to the silent gloom of my home, hers seemed amazingly rich, colorful, and lively. Suddenly I had other friends, too: Louise Vetter, the lovely blond heroine of *The Rivals*, and Bettina Butler, whose straight brown hair was always fashionably cut. Bettina came from a wealthy and sophisticated family and wrote for the school publication, the *Sketch Book*. Of course, they all seemed well-to-do in comparison with me, for whom losing gym shoes and being unable to earn the $3.50 to replace them was a tragedy.

The production called for a fencing match in one scene between Jack Absolute and Sir Lucius O'Trigger. A fencing master, Mr. Ferro, was called in to give us instruction. It turned out that I was talented as a fencer, being slender and spry, and I learned very quickly what was needed. My instructor's son, Albert Ferro, began to take me to fencing matches. I don't remember exactly how it happened, but I found myself in the *salle d'armes* of a handsome Milanese fencing master, Mr. Antonio Greco, who after a tryout offered to teach me for nothing. (I couldn't have afforded lessons.) Mr. Greco fenced Italian style, as opposed to the more common French style. The difference was in the wrist: The French fencing foil was managed with a loose and flexible wrist while the Italian style relied on a rigid wrist with the foil strapped to the arm by a leather wristlet, which produced greater strength both in thrusting and parrying. He taught me well and I became an excellent fencer, and shortly before or after graduation I found myself fencing in the national championships at the Philadelphia Athletic Club in Rittenhouse Square. I remember in my first bout getting three touches on Marian Lloyd, the U.S. champion. I lost the bout, of course, but because I touched the champion three times my fencing master was assured that he had been right about my talent, and he was pleased with me. Following the matches there was a dance, for which I bought my first long evening dress, black velvet, reduced three times at B. Altman's. I felt beautiful and almost confident for the first time in my life.

One day Mr. Greco and I happened to be alone in the *salle* doing the daily exercise of one-step-forward-and-lunge repeated in quick succession until exhaustion intervenes. At the end of the routine number of lunges, say fifteen, Mr. Greco would say "just one more." With an enormous effort I would comply, whereupon he would repeat, "just one more." The aim of the exercise was, of course, to increase endurance since in a competition the more bouts you won the longer you had to fence. In a winning streak, when all feeling had left your arm and wrist, the ability to continue automatically was paramount. Endurance rather than skill often crowned the winner. During this particular exercise, Mr. Greco had repeated the cruel phrase "just one more" about five times. I made a Herculean effort to comply but felt near death. When at last it was over, Mr. Greco moved toward me, removed his mask, and embraced me, taking me completely by surprise. He proceeded to tell me how wonderful I was and that he loved me and wanted to marry me.

I liked Mr. Greco but never even reached the stage of calling him Antonio. His confession of love left me uncomfortable and ambivalent since I couldn't return his feelings. Because I commuted long hours to an all-girls' high school, I had had little time or opportunity to meet boys my own age, except for Arnold. I was naïve and inexperienced, and I felt confused and frightened by Mr. Greco's advances. I didn't know exactly what my own feelings were and had no practice in talking about them. That he was at least twice my age seemed wrong to me and, though I may not have understood why, may have had incestuous overtones for me.

I suppose I might have found another fencing teacher, but the chances of finding one who would teach me for nothing were very slim. Our lessons continued in a carefully controlled ambience even after I graduated from Washington Irving. I would fence early and then go to work. Finally I got a job that made fencing lessons impossible, and our relationship ended with something like relief as well as sadness on my part. That marked the end of my fencing career, but I maintained a lifelong interest and appreciation of a sport that used mind and body simultaneously.

THE most important development to come from the play was my relationship with an English teacher named Ruth Galey, who made our costumes.

Ruth Galey was a pretty, animated woman, fair-skinned and dark-haired, not tall, slightly overweight, in her middle- or late-forties when we first met. She talked continuously as she fitted me with young Jack Absolute's fine white woolen britches—about the play, about the author Oliver Goldsmith, about eighteenth-century history and music. Lively in body and speech, she was a graduate of Barnard and the first truly cultivated person I had ever known. Her husband, tall, handsome, terribly dignified and distant, was a graduate of Harvard College and Law School and a partner in the prestigious admiralty law firm of Burlingham, Veeder, Clark & Hupper. They lived on Jones Street in Greenwich Village in a small but lovely eighteenth-century house filled with antiques.

Mrs. Galey became interested in me and, having no children of her own, more or less adopted me. She began by letting me carry her packages home and running errands for her after school. She lent me books. Having grown up in a house devoid of books except for those for school and prayer, I found this to be the most meaningful of all her many acts of generosity. With each book came her enthusiasm for it and the certainty not only that I would love it too but also that it contained enlightenment capable of permanently broadening my horizons. She taught me that the reading of books was a supreme pleasure and one that had to be cultivated if one aspired to be a proper, cultured person. "Proper" was a recurring word in her vocabulary—proper manners, proper dress, proper job.

The idea of reading books for pleasure was new to me. I had read school assignments dutifully, reported on them in class, written about them for homework. I cannot recall experiencing much pleasure in any activity except music until high school. Mrs. Galey introduced me to every kind of writing, including Proust and Galsworthy, Jane Austen and Shakespeare, the poetry of A.E. Housman and Edna St. Vincent Millay. "For God's sake, read a book," she would say as she handed me a volume of Dickens from her complete set. After I had read it, we would talk about it. One at a time she introduced me to most of the classic authors and urged me to keep up with new books, too.

Her pleasant voice and perfect diction fascinated me, and I tried to imitate them and loved her correcting my slang and imperfect grammar.

Music and theater contributed to Ruth Galey's good life. I inherited her unused tickets to the New York Philharmonic and heard Toscanini, and Town Hall concerts, where Artur Schnabel played Beethoven and Schubert and I heard my first string quartets. Following *The Rivals*, while I was still in high school, she organized a theater party and took half a dozen of us to our first "real" play on Broadway. We had the wondrous luck to have it be Leslie Howard and Margalo Gilmore in *Berkeley Square*. I was hooked from that moment onward. The first musical I ever saw, sitting way up in the second balcony, was Gertrude Lawrence in *Oh, Kay*. Ruth Galey had given me the money (fifty cents, I think) to buy the ticket. To this day I melt when I hear the words "There's a somebody I'm longing to see, I hope that he, Turns out to be, Someone who'll watch over me," and I remember vividly that great presence, alone on the stage with a white spotlight, singing that wonderful Gershwin song.

One day Mrs. Galey took me to lunch at Longchamps on Fifth Avenue, my first expensive-restaurant experience. She urged me to have cold lobster, which I had never eaten before. I knew it was supposed to be very special, and I was secretly disappointed by its bland taste. She improved my table manners and taught me how to use the now-obsolete finger bowl. She taught me that Woolworth pearls and earrings with a very plain black dress were preferable to colorful, fussy clothes, which she termed "gypsy." She gave me little presents and encouraged me to sew simple, good-looking blouses and dresses. I looked to her for guidance, and she enjoyed being in charge and directing me.

I endowed Ruth Galey with goddess-like qualities. She was, to me, noble, erudite, and cultivated. She had been abroad often, and I loved to hear her tell of her European travels. She had a remarkable collection of antique American, English, and French pewter, and she loved to tell me the provenance, purpose, and value of each piece. The pewter was tastefully displayed on the top shelf of the high bookshelves that filled her apartment. The hall had floor-to-ceiling shelves that held the dark blue old Staffordshire china that she also collected.

I have only one slightly disappointing memory of Ruth during this time. I was a smoker, having found it a wonderfully useful affectation in the first exchanges with a new male friend. Having some "stage business" like taking a cigarette and lighting it, or having it lit gave me time to think up an answer to a puzzling question or one I was reluctant to answer. Ruth wanted me to stop smoking, and to spur me on she promised me a pair of beautiful French covered wine decanters as a reward. The thought of *owning* a pair of those wide-hipped, narrow-topped jugs with their hinged covers was an electric spur. I stopped smoking, but the jugs were not forthcoming. I shyly mentioned the promise but discovered from her abrupt change of subject that she was unable to part with the tankards. It was my first serious disappointment with her. But if you love someone, you accept their flaws and keep your grievances to yourself.

During school days I often stopped by Jones Street before traveling home to Bensonhurst on the subway. After graduation, when I was working, I continued the habit. My sisters felt that Ruth was alienating me from them. But I was already alienated, and they were deeply immersed in their own lives, concerned with their own survival, when I met her. She came along during a time of deprivation, fear, and loneliness. I thought they might be envious. Ruth Galey was lively and merry, and she enjoyed food and drink, books, art and music, clothes, and socializing. She loved to teach and knew how. I loved to learn, sopping up all knowledge, as I had in that all-too-brief year when my father recognized my talents and began to teach me. I was starved for attention, curious to know and learn about everything, and she became the fountainhead of all knowledge, taste, and ambition for me. She taught me that most problems had solutions and that there was another life out there, crowded with fascinating people and beautiful things, an expanding universe about which I desired to learn more. I became her willing disciple, shifting easily from Geraldine to a larger, more all-encompassing, and far more interesting role model. My initial school-girl crush deepened into love, respect, and admiration.

Ruth Galey became my "good mother," the one we search for if we feel we don't have one. My own mother had not been a bad mother, but even before Poppa died she didn't seem to have the energy to give me the love and attention I needed. After my father died, she ceased being a mother at all. I had loved her dearly, but when I felt she was unable to love me back, when she became closed up inside herself, I told myself that I didn't feel anything for her. I was wrong, of course, like the four-year-old child who says "I don't care" as the tears stream down his cheeks.

As every teenager does in the process of growing up, I longed to leave home, to put behind me that house in Bensonhurst. Ruth Galey suggested that I move instead to the attic, where Aunt Rose had been and where I could live as if on my own. It was an *idée géniale*. She helped me find an ivy wallpaper, and I papered the sloping ceiling and walls and painted the floor pale green. (The sticky paint took forever to dry; perhaps in my precipitous way I hadn't stirred it sufficiently.) I bought a little gas heater that glowed like a fireplace and announced to my sisters that no one could come up without an invitation. Nobody wanted to, so that was never a problem. But I could cook up there and invite someone to dinner and feel grown up and emancipated. I begged and borrowed furniture. My one big purchase, again with Ruth Galey's help, was an old mahogany chest of three drawers, very plain and beautiful, from a secondhand dealer; it cost eighteen dollars—then a huge sum.

Having my own attic calmed me down and gave me an exhilarated feeling of liberation. My parents had slept in the front master bedroom on the second floor of our house, Julie and Rosalind shared a smaller room facing the backyard, and Myron and I slept in the smallest room, adjoining theirs. Now at long last I had a room of my very own, with a bookshelf holding my small, precious hoard of books. Once more I dared to think cheerfully about the future. Newfound hope and ambition spurred me on to dream large dreams again.

CHAPTER IV

Romany Marie's and Bucky Fuller

*I*N 1930, I WAS INTRODUCED (probably by a classmate) to Romany Marie's restaurant, on Eighth Street between Fifth and Sixth Avenues. A gathering place for artists, writers, journalists, actors, dancers, and singers, it drew people who were interested in or connected with the arts. Some of its customers were famous, like black-haired, dour Eugene O'Neill and the beautiful young poet Edna St. Vincent Millay. Best-selling novelist Fannie Hurst, who always wore black relieved by a fresh or jeweled calla lily, her trademark, would arrive accompanied by the tall, white-haired arctic explorer Vilhjal-mur Stefansson. Some of the habitués of Romany Marie's became famous later on, like painters Stuart Davis, Alexander Brook, Mark Tobey, and Arshile Gorky. Sculptors like plump William Zorach and thin, handsome Isamu Noguchi came too, as did composer Edgar Varese, professor-writer Will Durant, and modern dancers Martha Graham, Helen Tamiris, and Paula and Kohana, who were sisters and went by only their first names. Many frequenters were aspiring and unknown, and some, like me, were students.

Marie herself was a Romanian gypsy with a warm bass voice; she was married to Marchand, a multilingual, mustachioed gentleman who worked at Ellis Island as an interpreter. Marie loved people and enjoyed introducing them to each other. The place was more like a club than a restaurant. Some of her customers were "regulars," who came almost every night, while others would drop in every once in a while for a meal or a cup of the strong Turkish coffee. For fifty cents you could get a large bowl of *tschorba*, a rich meatball soup, served with generous portions of delicious black bread and butter. When I had the money, earned from my sales job on Saturdays, from hand-coloring Christmas cards, or from any other odd jobs I could get, I would often stop there after school and have my supper before taking the subway home. Because of Prohibition, no liquor was served, but you could order a cup of coffee and stay all evening. Conversation was the thing.

Entering Marie's from the street, you went through a narrow passage containing a coatroom that opened abruptly onto a two-story-high, windowless, large oblong space lit mainly by candles, enough to see people's faces clearly but in a soft, forgiving light. The tables were scrubbed old wood, with many wounds but worn smooth and polished by many elbows. Banquettes lined the wall space and extra tables occupied both ends of the room. An open space in the center provided a space for performers and, occasionally, for dancing, if a musician was present. The old grand piano was kept tuned.

Customers supplied the entertainment. Marie behaved as though the restaurant were her living room and the customers her guests. She would invite a musician to play the piano, a poet to read one of his poems, a dancer to perform, a singer to sing. Without fuss or self-consciousness, most would oblige.

Bobby Edwards, the village troubadour, who edited a small magazine called *Greenwich Village Quill*, made and sold "futuristic ukuleles." He composed and often sang his own songs, accompanying himself on one of his cigar-box instruments. I remember one, "The Belle of Hubert's Cafeteria:"

> She's the belle of Hubert's Cafe-te-teria,
> Down in Sheridan Square,
> Where the nuts and the bums with their sex hysteria
> Patiently give her the air.

She hasn't a home,
No place of her own.
She domiciles anywhere,
And her name should you ask it
Is Lizzie Mossbasket,
The Peril of Sheridan Square.
This village queen, Lizzie, I mean,
Walked into Hubert's to feed.
She hoped to mash some boy with cash,
To pay for the food that she et.
But it seems she had little success,
For the poor thing is sitting there yet.

CHORUS

She's the belle of Hubert's Cafe-te-teria, etc.

Colorfully-costumed Romanian gypsies would come by from time to time, families of them, including children, singing and dancing and passing the tambourines for donations. Flamenco guitarists and jazz musicians would show up late, after their uptown performances.

At first I was wide-eyed with wonder at being in the presence of so many accomplished persons, most of whom were friendly and often engaged me in conversation without being condescending to a young, still-wet-behind-the-ears art student. It was exciting simply to listen to what was being said and to feast my eyes on these new and interesting faces from so many different backgrounds and cultures. My ears were tuned to the depth and quality of their conversation and their music, whether gypsy guitar, classical, or jazz. I took in their complex hairdos, diction, mannerisms, and costumes. When the talk among the artists turned to discussions of who was doing what and who was or was not a good painter, every cell in my brain was activated, recording what they said and deciding whether I agreed or not. I seldom spoke since I knew little about modern art, but I was as usual eager to learn everything new that I could. I gained many a clue about which exhibitions should be visited and who had a show opening when and where. As often as I could, I would go to the nearby Whitney Museum, which was then downtown, in the Village, on Eighth Street, too. I slowly developed my own taste and opinions about art, and in time got over my initial shyness about joining the conversations, but I never lost the gratitude I felt to Marie for offering the haven of what seemed to me a family of artists of every description. The time I spent there was golden, and more than sixty years later it glows again as I recall it—the colorful evenings with fascinating, gifted people whom I eventually came to see in three-dimensions—as humans, some good, some flawed, some not kind, but all interesting.

It was here I found myself first singing folk songs a cappella to a friendly audience: "Molly Malone," "On Top of Old Smokey," "Sweet and Low"—songs I had learned in school, from my sisters, my mother, neighbors, and at camp. I had a parrot-like ability to imitate anything spoken or sung and was very quick at learning a new song. Without thinking about it, I had always "collected" them. A small, box-like, wind-up portable Victrola that someone had discarded ended up in my attic room. I had borrowed and bought a very few precious records, including one of Lucien Boyer singing "Parle Moi d'Autre Chose," which I learned perfectly without knowing what the words meant, and another of Marlene Dietrich singing, in English as well as German, "Johnny, When Will Your Birthday Be?"

I was seventeen and still in high school when Romany Marie introduced me to Buckminster Fuller, one of the restaurant's regulars. Bucky, as everyone called him, was short and stocky, his crewcut prematurely grey. He wore thick-lensed eyeglasses, and I soon learned that he had been born with eyes crossed and unfocused, and that until he was four years old and fitted with glasses he couldn't see anything clearly. He had designed the interior of the restaurant, and in lieu of pay Marie had offered him free meals. He was ebullient, animated, articulate, and effervescent in manner. His speech was distinctive; his accent was old Boston and Harvard, and his fast flow of talk was larded with words he coined himself, plus a scattering of words like *entropy* and *synergy*. He appeared taller than he actually was. At thirty-five, he had not yet acquired the charisma that characterized his later years, but it was latent. Perhaps because of his early childhood blindness, he gave me the impression of someone newly landed on the planet and delighted with everything he saw.

Bucky's forebears went back to revolutionary times and included journalist and feminist Margaret Fuller, of whom he was particularly proud. He had been twice expelled from Harvard, joined the Navy during World War I, gone into business unsuccessfully, and was, when I met him, an architect, editing a magazine called *Shelter*. My first memories of him are of sitting in a group while he held forth with his high-speed delivery. As time passed, I noticed that whenever we both were present he would be sitting next to me and beginning a dialogue rather than a group conversation. Then he invited me to one of his talks at some such place as the New School.

Bucky one night offered to drive me home to Bensonhurst in his Ford. An hour's drive with this interesting older man was easily preferable to a subway ride alone. The drive to Bensonhurst became a habit. Afterwards, he would drive all the way back to the Village to stay with this friend or that, wherever he could light. I couldn't imagine why he was willing to make the double trip until it dawned on me that he was attracted to me and wanted to develop what he called a "friendship." I was flattered and excited. During this period Bucky presented me with a poem, of which I remember the opening lines: "Come little Ford, tell me the worst, Have you ever been to Bensonhurst?" Because Bucky was twice my age I didn't think of him as a boyfriend. He was someone I could learn from, a teacher. I was hungry to learn but also naïve. Going to an all-girls school I had missed the experience that co-education provided in mild flirting, verbal fencing, and judging persons of the opposite sex.

Bucky percolated within me new ways of thinking. He thought on a global plane, putting forward logical-sounding solutions to world problems like hunger, transportation, housing, population growth, and industrial waste. He wanted to replace Euclid with his new theory of mathematics. His original ideas came to him with the speed and dazzle of fireworks. Dazzled by his vocabulary, I eagerly pressed him to explain the words I didn't know, and I found myself listening, enthralled, to his astonishing ideas for reinventing the world and benefiting humanity. He wanted to recycle all the raw materials we used, making them cheaper, more plentiful, and available to all. One of his coined words was "dymaxion," combining dynamic and maximum. He applied the term to his revolutionary design for a circular, prefabricated house suspended from a central mast; it would be mass produced, would cost fifteen hundred dollars, and could be erected in a day. He designed a one-piece bathroom that could be stamped out of a single sheet of metal, like an automobile body, and then hooked up for a fraction of the cost of an ordinary one. When he made a prototype, the American Radiator Company bought the design but predictably scrapped the idea.

He frequently lectured on his Dymaxion House, and I often helped put the model together. Once I went with him and his writer friend Christopher Morley to Lippincott's to discuss the publication of his first book, *Nine Chains to the Moon*. Chris, like Bucky, could produce instant verse, and finding a tune that fit we came away from the meeting singing, "When you've got such a lot of nice people in one spot, what we do is say thank you, Joe Lippincott."

As our amicable relationship developed, a certain flirtatious quality was added. Soon thereafter I learned to my shock that he was married. He had never told me and it had never occurred to me to ask the question. His wife, Anne, was a daughter of the architect Maurice Hewlett, who lived with his large family, including Anne, in Hewlett, Long Island, in an historic eighteenth-century house. Bucky drove me out to meet them on the weekends often. There was a cheery, club-like atmosphere in the high-ceilinged old house where visitors came and went easily and often. The Hewletts had no servants, and everybody participated in cooking, serving, and cleaning up after meals.

Anne's siblings included a set of female twins with turned-up noses and adenoidal speech. Anne shared this family trait and, wearing no makeup, looked "old" to a teenager like me. Carmie, the oldest Hewlett, had an angry-looking, disfiguring skin disease, which he scratched at continuously. Roger, the youngest Hewlett, was a tall, handsome, gangling student in his last year at Harvard. Everybody greeted me in the friendliest way; I gathered it was customary for Bucky to turn up on weekends with one or more friends. During one visit Roger took me aside and to my embarrassment said that he had fallen in love with me, and proposed, amending his offer to say we couldn't be married until after graduation. Astonished and flattered, I gently managed to extricate myself, confessing that I did not share his feelings; indeed, mine were otherwise engaged.

Being an expert con man, Bucky explained smoothly that Anne didn't like sex and encouraged his having other girls. Later in life I discovered that "my wife doesn't like sex" was a typical opening line of married men interested in extra-curricular sex. This was the first time I heard it and it didn't have the weight it later acquired. Greenwich Village in the thirties encompassed many kinds of relationships. Trying to appear more sophisticated than I was, I somehow naïvely accepted the strange fact that we could be friends even though he had a wife.

Once a year in January, before the depths of the Depression, New York's architects and bohemians, along with a large sprinkling of socialites, held the festive Beaux Arts Costume Ball at the Hotel Astor. The theme in 1931, the World of the Future, was a natural for Bucky, who designed a costume for me. The top, made of sheet aluminum lined with cork, resembled armor with two pointy breastplates. Bare skin showed between the breastplates and the short skirt, which consisted of a bright silk underslip covered by alternating chains of silver and gold, like a hula skirt, which swung out when I danced.

It was the first ball I had ever attended, and at it I was introduced to the architects of New York's most famous skyscrapers. I remember the man who designed the Chrysler Building, William Van Alen, wearing a headdress that replicated the top of his building.

A prize was awarded for best costume. I have no memory of that part of the evening, but Alden Hatch describes it in his 1974 book, *Buckminster Fuller, At Home in the Universe*. Apparently, twelve of the best costumes were paraded before the judges and slowly narrowed down to two—mine and the winner's. Hatch thought the prize should have gone to the costume Bucky designed. But since he describes me as "a dashing blonde" and my hair was dark brown, and calls me "Mrs. Evelyn Baird," a name I didn't acquire until years later, and describes my "luxuriant bosom" though I wear an average 34B bra, his two-page description of the evening is suspect; I don't know whether he or Bucky was responsible for it—they probably both were.

Before the ball Bucky took me to his mother's house, where his sister Rozzy also lived, to show off my super-modern costume. Rozzy, whom I had met before, was as usual warm and cordial, but his mother, a formidable white-haired dowager, at our first and only meeting gave me a freezing reception that I have never forgotten. In my extreme discomfort, I searched for reasons for her behavior. What had I done wrong? Since I wasn't *sleeping* with Bucky, I naïvely assumed that I wasn't doing anything wrong by spending so much time with him. But her Boston Brahmin coldness forced me to think of how our situation looked to others. I began to worry. Like most geniuses, Bucky was somewhat deficient in empathy and had difficulty understanding my feelings of unease. He could rarely see when he was at fault.

Bucky and I were now seeing each other irregularly but often, and he began to introduce me to his other friends. One, who shared many of his ideas and ideals, was the sculptor Isamu Noguchi. Isamu was the son of a famous Japanese scholar and a Scottish mother.

Slender in frame and gentle in manner, he was to my eye extraordinarily handsome—a beautiful, gifted hybrid. Once when the three of us were meeting at Isamu's studio, Bucky was late and Isamu went back to work. He said he needed a model for feet. Would I pose? I removed my shoes and stockings and took the pose willingly. Later, when Isamu became famous, I remembered with pride that I had posed for the great artist, whose work I have always passionately admired.

Through Bucky I met several men from Old New York "Society," though none as interesting intellectually as Bucky. Ruth Galey had taught me the basics of table and social manners so that I was confident in that ambiance, but there was too much drinking and sexual "playing around" to suit my taste. I was far more attracted to the company of artists and writers, and more comfortable in the bohemian, alcohol-free atmosphere of Romany Marie's.

When money was scarce, we ate at Romany Marie's, but when a windfall arrived occasionally Bucky could be extravagant and we would dine at the Lafayette or the Brevoort Hotel or meet with some of his Park Avenue friends. Bucky seemed to be either poor, relying on friends for a place to stay the night, or suddenly rich for a short period. There were no in-betweens.

As our interest and affection for each other grew, we became a couple in the sense that wherever we went it was known that I was his girl. During this time I graduated from high school and began to look for a full-time job.

Then we discovered we had fallen in love! It was my first time, and in my love-deprived state every good feeling I encountered seemed multiplied by a thousand. The profound happiness I experienced had been unimaginable before. Our chaste goodbye kisses grew into long passionate encounters. He would drive me home to Bensonhurst, and while everybody in my big house was asleep we would neck. Bucky urged me to go "the limit," but this was not to be contemplated. I was innocent in both the experience and the knowledge of sex, but, in those days of inferior birth control, I knew having an illegitimate baby carried a lifelong stigma and disgrace.

However, our sexual attraction grew more intense and frustrating. When Bucky finally acquired a place of his own, a tiny penthouse atop the then-new industrial Lehigh-Starrett Warehouse Building on West Twenty-sixth Street in Manhattan, I finally gave in to his promises of divorce and we began to sleep together. Bucky was an experienced and tender lover, and I was gloriously happy.

In the beginning, loving Bucky was such a grand, enlightening, exhilarating experience, feeding my voracious intellectual hunger as well as my hunger for love, and plumping up my low self-esteem. Bucky was affectionate. He called me "darlin'." He praised my looks and spirit and eagerness to learn "everything." He delighted in teaching me. He adored my responsiveness. But I also had an old familiar feeling of frustration, one I had had as a young child, when I was trying unsuccessfully to catch up with what my older sisters knew.

One Christmas Bucky gave me a copy of Margaret Kennedy's novel *The Constant Nymph* with this inscription:

"Christmas, 1931. In our little penthouse, L.S. [Lehigh-Starrett] Bldg, N.Y.C.
To the dearest nymph my life shall experience—
may the world never injure her laughing heart or break
the spontaneous inclusion of every beautiful thing.
Evelyn
It is some years since I read this book, but I
remember that though I was immature it bespoke in my
mind that some day Evy* would happen to me.
Whatever devious course this may lead us through
I know that Evy is eternally my love and unity itself."
BF

---

* That was Bucky's spelling. I spell it with two vv's, but it is often misspelled. Some write Evie, others Evey. Stef called me Evelyn, as in John Evelyn, with a British pronunciation. John Nef asked me what my family called me, so he called me Evvie. Bil Baird called me Ev, with the "e" as in every. I answer to all.

Alas, it was Bucky himself who took up the "devious course" and injured my "laughing heart." That summer of 1931, Bucky was scheduled to take his boat up to the Fuller-family summerhouse on Bear Island in Maine. He said for propriety's sake I had better not write to him but that he would write me regularly. With anxiety on my part, we said a painful goodbye with avowals and promises of many kinds.

Not a single letter or word arrived from Bucky during the hardest, most bitter summer of my life. During this time Rosalind became engaged to Maxwell Feller and was completely absorbed in wedding plans. Julie was on the road in Earl Carroll's *Vanities*. They were aware that I knew Bucky but never dreamed that I was having an intimate relationship with him. Since in those days we were taught that you remained a virgin until marriage, I didn't feel I could talk to them about my problems with Bucky without shocking them irrevocably. I couldn't tell Ruth—I knew she would never accept the mores of my new bohemian circle of friends, who thought nothing of going out with a married man. I suffered greatly and alone during the two long months when silence, distance, and cold reality told me that Bucky would not divorce his wife and that we could never have a legitimate relationship.

It was hard for me to accept the unfeeling cruelty that permitted this man I so loved to have a marvelous summer while I waited in anxious sadness for each day's delivery of mail. As the days passed without a letter, my hopes slowly faded and were replaced by deep anger. It was not until he had left Maine and was homeward bound that I finally received a cheerful, newsy letter, the tone of which indicated he had no notion that I had been suffering. He was fully expecting to pick up where we had left off, with no apology. I couldn't get over it.

Rage! At him, then at myself for being so mistaken. How could he profess to love me and hurt me so? I was overcome by a terrible sense of loss. Like my father, love, too, suddenly died. The wondrous rapture of it was wiped out for all time. I had never consciously hated anyone before, but I now hated Bucky.

That hackneyed old excuse "she had no mother to guide her" was certainly true in my case. No one had ever told me that men often say things they don't mean, make promises they don't keep, may be sincere at one moment and insincere the next. That they may consciously or unconsciously let you believe things that they would like to be true but aren't. I had no person in whom I could confide my feelings, no one to caution me to go very slowly into a sexual relationship. No one to warn me about the ugly duplicity that inevitably results from loving someone who is married to someone else. Although I tried desperately to appear sophisticated, suddenly I felt like a character in a cheap novel—the trusting, naïve girl who falls for the smooth, worldly man-about-town.

During the stormy scene that followed, Bucky pleaded and promised, unable to understand why I was so hurt and angry and why I would not see him anymore. This obtuseness confirmed my conviction that he was incapable of empathizing with me. Hopelessly, I tried to bandage my emotional wounds, but the pain did not stop, not for an agonizingly long time. In the end it was an educational, bitter episode. I felt as though I had been "had," and of course I had been. I vowed then that I would never again have anything to do with a married man.

After our break up I didn't see Bucky for awhile, but in our small Greenwich Village world our paths often crossed, and eventually we became friends again. Sometimes I would not see him for years at a time. Then he would turn up and we would pick up our acquaintance again. Bucky was never able to acknowledge, or indeed even talk about, what I felt was his selfish, egotistical, insensitive behavior. Still, with time my anger disappeared and my pleasure in his company returned. We stayed friends for the rest of his life.

CHAPTER V

Life with Bil Baird

O NE OF THE FANCIER VILLAGE GATHERING SPOTS was a club called the Meeting Place, over Lee Chumley's restaurant on Bedford Street, where tall, handsome, white-haired Max Eastman, the writer, might be found on a given evening presiding over hot debates about the Soviet Union and communism. An informal place where people would wander from table to table meeting old friends and being introduced to new ones, the club also had a small dance floor that was usually neglected by the talkers.

I cannot remember who brought me to the Meeting Place in 1932, a year after the end of my relationship with Bucky. That memory was displaced by the more momentous occurrence of my being introduced to an attractive young man in his late twenties, a puppeteer, named Bil (with one "l") Baird.

Bil asked me to dance, and some kind of instant magic rapport shot through the cells of both our bodies. We danced together perfectly. He made me laugh in an innocent, childlike way. Laughter and humor had been so rare in most of my life that Bil's happy, funny personality was deliciously intoxicating. And we had talents in common. He made marionettes for a living, and in high school I had made marionettes. He could sing and I could sing, and when we sang together the whole was larger than the parts. Our voices blended beautifully. Neither of us could get over our surprise or our delight in each other. The end of my relationship with Bucky had left me sad and dispirited. I was ready for laughter.

With his blue eyes and curly blond hair, Bil was very handsome, and he came with a long catalogue of talents. He could draw, paint, carve, and carpenter; play the guitar, accordion, and piano by ear; speak foreign languages without an accent; and create puppet characters as easily as he could breathe. He was the perfect playmate, the greatest entertainer.

I was looking for a job when we met. Bil was working for Tony Sarg, the artist-illustrator who had popularized marionettes in the United States, and arranged an interview for me. I was hired. Tony Sarg was a cheerful, middle-aged, pear-shaped gentleman with a ruddy complexion and a lively managing manner. He had come to New York in 1915 from England and retained his British accent. In addition to producing touring marionette shows, he designed the Macy's Thanksgiving Day Parade.*

In a huge unheated warehouse about six of us worked in jeans and sweatshirts to construct the floats for the parade. Wooden armatures were covered with chicken wire, which in turn were covered with pieces of scrim (unbleached muslin) that had been dipped in a glue soup. When the scrim dried, paint was sprayed on in appropriate colors. Bil was in charge. If anyone did something extra that was wonderful or came up with an idea that saved work or time, Bil would get the spray gun and, using a stencil, spray a medal on that person's sweatshirt. On Thanksgiving Day during the parade we were on duty in different capacities. The most desirable job, which I had only once, was to ride the helium ambulance that would race through the parade at great speed to plump up any balloons that were beginning to droop.

Under Bil's tutelage I also learned to operate marionettes professionally, starting out as an all-around helper, then graduating to small

---

* Tony Sarg was also an active member of the Society of Illustrators and would enlist all the company to provide entertainment for its famous annual show and party, where I was thrilled to meet James Montgomery Flagg, Arthur William Brown, Lejaren Hiller (the photographer), and other celebrities.

parts and eventually to having a marionette of my own. Was my delight in this new world the result of my childish desire for a doll being satisfied at long last?

The world of marionettes offers space for every dream or fantasy one has ever had. Punch-and-Judy shows are so appealing to children because the characters act out their own feelings of aggression. Violence in this ritualized form is permissible without punishment. The children scream with delight, fear, relief, and encouragement. We see that kind of behavior in adults at boxing matches, when otherwise sane men stand on their feet and shout *kill him, finish him*. The marionette theater offers everything that live theater offers, with the added dimension that the audience does not expect realism and willingly enters a world of make-believe, where fairytales and magic reside, the impossible becomes possible, and miracles occur regularly. *Alice in Wonderland*, the musical, which Tony Sarg and Bil produced in 1933, was a perfect marionette vehicle. The illusions of shrinking and growing, falling through space, and crawling through tunnels were easily and well managed on the marionette stage. Alice was played by lovely Elsie Dvorak, an excellent actress who was able to project the ridiculous and the touching, the partial comprehension and the misunderstandings that are constantly present in the mind of a child, and sometimes in adults as well.

When Bil left Tony Sarg's employ sometime in the early 1930s, branching out for himself, I went with him. He set up his own workshop and began to build his own company. Most of the small group were both marionette makers and puppeteers. We brought our lunches to work and ate together, and while we worked we sang or listened to classical music. It felt like a happy family, a new experience for me. On the road, the company was more like a family than ever. We stayed at the same hotels, ate together, and, in rare moments of free time, played together.

One of the great gifts that Bil gave me was the ability to use and care for tools. I knew paint and brushes, but Bil taught me to use the power tools in the shop. I learned to respect them and make them work for me, and I lost any fear of them I might have had. I learned how to turn wood on a lathe, to use a band and a jig saw, and to operate a power drill. I fell in love with the Italian wood rasps that we used to shape wood and plastic wood for the puppets. Bil taught me how to sharpen wood gouges and knives, to the enjoy the feel of a well-made tool, and to take pleasure in using it correctly.*

Since I could sew, I was often assigned to make the costumes for the marionettes, a task which proved more difficult than I thought it would be—making a *miniature* man's dinner jacket with collar and lapels, for instance, was challenging. But with patience and a few misses I soon learned and became creative about translating big to little and guessing how to achieve the needed appearance. The little group was versatile and adept, and we switched roles easily and often. Painter, carver, plaster caster, sewer, stringer, operator—whatever was required at the moment each of us would willingly supply. The theatrical and handicraft skills I learned at Washington Irving were all improved and perfected through daily use.†

I WAS still living in Bensonhurst when I began working for Bil, and the subway ride home alone began to seem endless if it was late

---

* While Bil taught me to use tools, many years later my younger brother, Myron, who became an inventor, taught me how to take something apart carefully and in a certain order so that when it was cleaned or fixed it could be put back together properly. I have taken pleasure and pride ever since in fixing things.

† The making of a marionette head, for instance, was a fairly complex operation: First we would make a Plastline model. Then we would construct a plaster cast, in two, three, or even four parts, if the model was complicated. When the plaster was dry and we had removed the brass shims that separated the sections of plaster, we would grease the inside of the plaster cast with Vaseline to keep the plastic wood that was to form the head from sticking to the plaster. Then we would press a layer of plastic wood, a quarter to half an inch thick, into the cast, pushing it into every crevice and then smoothing it into a firm shell. We would match the pieces of the plaster cast and insert a finger inside, through the neck hole, to smooth the inner seams. Then we would bind all the pieces of the cast together firmly with string and dump it into a pail of water in order to shrink the plastic wood evenly as it "dried," or hardened. The following day we would remove the cast from the water, with the plastic wood solidified, remove the outer cast, and hang the head on a dowel to dry thoroughly. Then we would sand it and, if necessary, accentuate the features with carving tools. An undercoat of paint would follow, then an overcoat, with eyes, lids, brows, lips, and cheeks appropriately colored. Hair could be made of nylon string, knitting wool, silk, horsehair, sponge rubber, steel wool, or even pot cleaners. We would glue on the wig and trim it, and the head would then be ready to attach to the body.

at night. Bil and I were dating, but he had a roommate, an artist named Nat Carson, who worked in the theater, and privacy was hard to come by. When we found we were in love, we began to sleep together, carefully using birth control, but I would have to get up and go home afterwards, alone, before Nat came home from work. This routine became more and more difficult until I finally protested and declared "no more sex." In bohemian Greenwich Village during the thirties, many couples lived together without being married, but that was too "advanced" for me. Bil and I continued to work together and spend time together, but the strain was beginning to tell on both of us.

The subject of marriage arose. Nat advised Bil against what he considered a rash act, but Bil finally decided that it was the right thing to do. We became engaged by Bil very solemnly and formally pinning me with his black enamel, seed-pearl-surrounded Sigma Chi fraternity pin. Since Bil was already twenty-eight years old (I was nineteen), I thought it a poor substitute for an engagement ring, but I was in love and wanted to be married.

Because he was Episcopalian and I was a lapsed agnostic Jew, we decided to get married at City Hall. In the fall of 1932, we obtained the necessary license, and I managed to round up my sister Rosalind to represent my family on the expected day. But Denny Holden, a friend of Bil's, thought a City Hall wedding was too grim a way to celebrate the occasion and suggested that despite our gathered readiness we cancel that date and let him arrange something more memorable. So a day or two late, on the September 18, William Britton Baird was married to Evelyn Schwartz at St. John's Church on West Eleventh Street in the Village, near Denny's grand lower Fifth Avenue apartment.

I was miffed and hurt that Rosalind was not there. With the change of date, she said couldn't take *another* day off from work; neither Ruth Galey nor any member of my family was present. That was not unusual. Our lives had become very separate and attenuated. When I graduated from high school and made a speech on behalf of all the art

students, no member of my family was there to see me, and when all
the other girls were embraced and congratulated by their family members after the graduation ceremonies, I was alone. No member of my
family saw my triumph in *The Rivals* or my subsequent performance
as Romeo in *Romeo and Juliet*. I longed for someone from home to witness my wedding, but it was typical that no one did. My high school
friend Louise Vetter, who had played the heroine in both *The Rivals* and
Romeo and Juliet, served as my witness. Denny, whose proper name was
H. Hamilton Holden, was Bil's. Denny and his wife gave us a cele-
bratory dinner at their house, just the four of us, and we went back
to work the next day.

We moved into a tiny walk-up apartment in the Village, with one
room, a kitchenette, and a bath. I tried to fix the place up by sewing
glazed chintz curtains and a bed cover. Bil had made a chair out of a
barrel and was enormously proud of it. I hated it because it was unfinished and didn't look like normal furniture to me. I was grateful, however, that his carpentry skills managed a long table, and we improvised
lamps and hunted secondhand furniture stores for the rest.

I learned how to cook in earnest. We had very little money, and
what we did have came in irregular spurts. Bil was almost pathologically frugal: When we went out to eat, he would order the cheapest
thing on the menu, and if we went out with others, he would always
manage to be in the men's room when the check came around. To my
intense embarrassment, he did not like to pick up the check or even
to pay his share if he didn't have to.

I worked, of course, all the time, sometimes without pay, and when
we were lucky and had a paying job, I would get a salary. I always put
what I earned into our joint account, but Bil made the decisions about
how it should be spent, and I was not always in agreement with those
decisions. He could spend a huge sum, like a thousand dollars, for a new
accordion, but he would still make me uncomfortable asking for anything for my personal needs. One of the bitter times I remember
occurred when we had just finished a job and I asked him for some

money to buy a winter coat, which I lacked. He suggested that I do without. "Put on an extra sweater under your spring coat—you'll manage." "But it's *my* money I'm asking for, what I *earned*. Am I not entitled to spend some of it on myself?" He argued me out of it, and I became very reluctant to ask him for any money at all. It was too painful.

Not long after we were married, Bil decided we should make a trip to Mason City, Iowa, his hometown, to show me off to his mother. Never having been west of Chicago, I looked forward to the trip and to meeting his mother and the people he grew up with. His mother was a darling, but Bil told me that she was a religious Episcopalian and was very worried that I had never been baptized. Since I was an agnostic and it didn't make any difference to me what faith I was against, I told him that if it would make his mother happy I would gladly be baptized. So I studied some words, met with a charming minister, became an Episcopalian, and made Bil's mother rest easy. I soon forgot the incident, which turned out later to be important.

During our visit with his family, Bil's mother gave a party in our honor. I didn't own an evening dress and asked Bil for money to buy one. As usual he found seven reasons for not giving me any. Close to tears, I confessed to Mrs. Baird that I didn't have an appropriate dress to wear to her party. She gave me the money, and at a local dress shop with little selection I found a long white silk dress. It really required an underslip, which I didn't have, and I was not about to ask either Mrs. Baird or Bil for more money to buy one. So I wore it and suffered as only an insecure Jewish girl, especially one newly baptized as an Episcopalian, could in a crowd of WASPs, most of whom had never met a Jew. I was sure that they could see the outline of my legs through the translucent silk and spent the evening desperately trying to remember to keep my legs together.

IN 1932, the year I married Bil, we were doing a marionette performance at the New York Automobile Show. I was not feeling well, but we all had a strong "the show must go on" mentality, so I continued working. By the end of our week long engagement, I was in great pain and had to lie down between shows on the marionette bridge that the puppeteers stood on to perform. I had always had terrible cramps when menstruating, and I assumed that was what my difficulty was. Ruth Galey came to see the last performance, and when she visited backstage she was shocked by my appearance. By then I was running a fever and having difficulty standing upright. Even though the company was packing up to leave for Detroit for our next engagement the following day, she insisted that I come home with her. I agreed gratefully, promising to rejoin the company as soon as I could.

At home with Ruth on Jones Street, I knew something was extraordinarily wrong with me. I was relieved when she called her own doctor and he was able to come that night. Just a few minutes after his arrival, he and I were in a taxi on our way to St. Joseph's Hospital in the Bronx. He thought I had a burst fallopian tube from an ectopic pregnancy, but during the emergency operation it was discovered that I had been working for two days with a ruptured appendix. Peritonitis was advanced and gangrene had set in. I was told that my appendix was abnormal and had been wound around an ovary, which explained the horrid pain I had always had during my period.[*]

Coming out of the anaesthetic, I found myself in a private room with bare white walls except for a far too realistic image of Jesus crucified on the cross. The bloody and suffering Jesus was exactly placed so that it was visible to a prone patient. It might be a comforting sight for a believing Roman Catholic, but for a doped-up nice Jewish girl from Bensonhurst it was a surreal, terrifying presence. As my head gradually cleared, I realized I was in a Catholic hospital. The nurses who came and went were nuns in brown habits with

---

[*] Curiously, I was not the only Schwartz child who suffered a ruptured appendix—all four of us eventually did. When she was sixteen, my oldest sister, Rosalind, had an appendix attack and begged my concerned mother not to call the doctor because she was having her period. Mother reluctantly complied, but the postponement almost cost Rosalind her life. Poppa informed us solemnly that she had ruptured her appendix and was fighting for her life. For several days we tiptoed around the house as though she were ill at home instead of far away. We were all sad and muted until finally word came that she would recover.

beautiful white headdresses. They were unfailingly kind and gentle, with the single exception of a short, pert sister with a super-cheerful manner and a macabre sense of humor. She told me with a chuckle that a man had died in the night and, since they were very short of space, they would be moving his body into my room for the time being. I didn't know whether to believe her or not, but she certainly succeeded in frightening me. As days past and no corpse appeared, it became clear that this was her idea of a bizarre joke. By then, I was no longer doped up and the fear had disappeared, replaced by pain and loneliness.

In the days before sulfa drugs or penicillin, appendicitis was often fatal, and a *ruptured* appendix was almost always fatal. The surgeon told me that my peritonitis was so advanced that I had "stunk up" the operating room. He made several extra incisions to try to drain the pus as quickly as possible, which was all that could be done for me. He told Ruth Galey and my family that I would probably die. I was thin and healthy, and all that fencing had left my body in fine physical trim, but nevertheless my recovery was long and painful. Ruth's intervention had certainly saved my life. I didn't know that I was expected to die, of course, so my greatest worries as I lay there were who was replacing me in the company tour and why I hadn't heard from Bil.

Visits from my sisters and friends were few during my month long hospital stay. Ruth would have come, but her claustrophobia prevented her from using the subway. Most of my friends lived in the Village, and my family was still in Bensonhurst, two hours from the Bronx by subway. One day, to my utter surprise, a friend from Romany Marie's, Vilhjalmur Stefansson, arrived, bringing a copy of *The Adventures of Sherlock Holmes*, by his friend Sir Arthur Conan Doyle. I was too weak to hold the book up in my hand, and Stef (he was always called Stef, Vilhjalmur, Icelandic for William, being impossible for most people to pronounce) did an amazing thing: Before my eyes he tore the hardcover book apart, so I could read it a chapter at a time without having to bear the weight of the whole volume.

It seemed to me an extravagant act of kindness that belonged to a lost chivalric age.*

I never rejoined the show—my stay in the hospital was longer than the tour. At first I tried to excuse Bil's lack of communication by imagining how busy he was, having to train someone to replace me, but it soon became clear that his behavior really did indicate a lack of concern for me. My hurt and anger joined a collection of lesser grievances, and I realized that he, like Bucky, was a self-absorbed and selfish man, however gifted. In the silence during my long convalescence, I felt utterly alone.

When the tour ended, Bil was not willing to hear of how close to dying I had been and changed the subject when I tried to talk about it. Perhaps it frightened him, for he was always concerned about looking and staying "young"—death was a subject never to be discussed. What followed is a blank, too painful to remember.†

My hospital stay was a milestone in my life. The enforced leisure gave me time to think about my past life, take stock of the present, and consider the future.

I WAS still in love with Bil and once I was in his sunny presence again I was caught up in the pleasure of our work together and our singing together, but there was now an undercurrent of unease in our relationship that hadn't been there before.

---

* I was deeply impressed and even more puzzled by this famous great man's visit. Why had he come all the way up to the Bronx to visit me? I knew he liked me, but I also knew he was busy with lecture tours, writing books, and directing a large research staff at the Stefansson Library. Many years later he told me why. As a graduate student at Harvard he had roomed with a young Icelander named Valdi Thorvaldson, who was a chess genius. He would play six simultaneous games while doing his homework, with Stef calling out the moves. One day Valdi felt ill and went to the College infirmary, where he joined a long line of waiting students. The doctor, who was a friend, pulled him out of the line, examined him hastily, gave him some medicine, and sent him on his way. But Valdi had a ruptured appendix, and by the time it was discovered it was too late, and he died. Hearing about my burst appendix, Stef thought I too was going to die and felt it was important to pay me a farewell call, something he had not been able to do for Valdi. His visit was as much homage to Valdi as kindness to me.

† Twenty-five years later, at Dartmouth, I ran into Wally Roach, who had been a member of our little company on that tour. He told me that Bil had not wanted to know how sick I was and didn't think it was necessary to be at my bedside. Wally, who thought I was dying, was outraged.

The Chicago World's Fair of 1933–34 opened a new era for Bil and me. Bil had his first large-scale marionette show, which was performed on a specially-built outdoor stage at the A & P Pavilion. We lived in makeshift arrangements—a bed in the corner of Bil's artist friend Eddie Millman's studio on the Near North Side. It was a very hot summer, but we were in an exciting new city; the Art Institute with its magnificent collection of Impressionist paintings beckoned; we were young; I was healthy once again; and we were doing work we loved.

The hit of the fair, which ran for two summers, was Sally Rand and her ostrich-feather fan dance. Maneuvering her fans skillfully, she hid her nakedness until the very last moment, when she would drop her fans for a few seconds, followed by a blackout. The following year we were hired by the Borden Company to work at the Swift Bridge, which spanned an artificial lake bordered by an amphitheater where the Chicago Symphony played. We had a marionette of Elsie, the Borden cow, which did a very funny imitation of Sally Rand's fan dance.

The temperature in our unventilated marionette theater was at least ten degrees above the outdoor temperature, which was in the high 90s. One night after our work was done and the fairgrounds were closed, we all went swimming in the raw in the lake. We were caught by the fairground police, and Rufus Rose gallantly swam off and distracted the cops to give me time to get out of the water unobserved.

One of our more interesting assignments was a stint at Radio City Music Hall. Bil had made a huge, twenty-foot-long snake marionette, which we manipulated to accompany a live snake-charmer dancer. Bil operated the head and I the tail. Our marionette bridge (the platform that we stood on) was only eighteen inches wide, with a front rail to lean against but no safety rail in back, and we were working fifty feet above the stage floor. During rehearsals Leonidoff, the director, shouted up instructions to us, often calling out "more *tail* Mrs. Baird, more *tail.*" Bil and I laughed so hard we endangered our lives.

Bil was so creative and successful in thinking up and executing marionette shows that we began to prosper. Many of our friends were in the theater. Bil knew Morris Carnovsky and Phoebe Brand, who were members of the Group Theater, and we saw them in their great success, *Awake and Sing*. We met young Orson Welles, who was doing Shakespeare, and puppeteers like Rufus Rose, who worked with our company and later formed his own famous marionette troup. As a couple, Bil and I were sought after socially, applauded, and flattered. Bil was a perfect entertainer, the life of any party, playing his guitar and singing a wonderful variety of folk songs. He taught me hundreds of songs, and when we sang together we were a hit. We were asked out a great deal, and Bil always brought his guitar. If we were asked for a weekend in the country, Bil could organize and call a square dance and play the accordion to accompany the dancing. He could also hold a room spellbound with a single marionette, walking it around the room, without any dialogue, making the marionette climb up on someone's knee or look under a woman's dress or pat her leg. As long as he had an audience, he was so inventive and funny—it was magic.

L IVING and working so closely with Bil, I soon discovered that he *needed* to perform. He craved the attention, the spotlight, and the applause. Sometimes when we would go to a party he would keep waiting to be called on, unwilling to go home until he had performed, often way after midnight, forgetting that we had to be up by a certain hour to be at the shop, and that we were losing sleep. I, too, loved to perform, as long as it was pleasurable and fun, but I didn't *need* it the way he did, and eventually I came to resent the time we spent at parties when we should have been home sleeping or living our lives. Slyly appealing to his notoriously frugal side, I pointed out that he was being exploited, giving free entertainment to his hosts, sometimes for people he hardly knew. But he couldn't see it that way.

Despite the headiness of our life, to my surprise I began to long for a quiet evening at home, a chance to read a good book and to discuss it with someone—non-hectic time to think and grow. I had a reflective, serious side that Bill did not seem to want to know or share. He was always "on stage" but oddly not present in our marriage. He seemed incapable of looking me straight in the eye or talking seriously about anything, especially about our future. He didn't want to have children—he didn't want the responsibility for another person—and that was a bitter disappointment to me. He himself had never completely grown up, which was why he was so appealing, to children and adults alike, as a puppeteer. My earlier sense of unease was growing and I worried about our future together. I had the strange feeling that I was growing up and that Bil didn't want to or couldn't. The only role ahead that I could visualize was as Bil's satellite, continually playing and always subject to his word and decision.

We were both relatively inexperienced sexually, and that may have been an important part of our trouble. We would become wildly passionate having sex, but once Bil was satisfied he would go to sleep, leaving me excited, non-orgasmic, and sleepless. I found myself being "tired" when I should have been eager for sex. My old defense system of getting my feelings hurt and retreating didn't serve me well in our marriage. When Bil insisted that I defer to him in matters of money, work, and play, I did so to avoid the confrontations in which my views, however reasonable, never prevailed. He always "won," and I would brood. My underlying low self-esteem made me reluctant to fight for my rights. The few times I dared to, Bil would promise me anything to change the subject, but nothing ever came of his promises. Somehow my needs were never met, but all his seemed to be.

About two years into the marriage I was consumed with developing ideas of my own, discovering and trying out new talents. By this time I was an excellent puppeteer and puppet maker, handy and knowledgeable in the workshop. I could also sing on pitch publicly, without embarrassment or accompaniment, and knew a thousand or more songs. I learned new things quickly. I could speak distinctly and be heard in the back rows of any auditorium or theater. Suddenly, I was aware of myself and my blossoming ego. I knew I could support myself, however modestly, and was eager to try. I also knew by then that many men found me attractive, and while I never thought of myself as beautiful I knew that my looks were presentable and that "in the dusk with the light behind me" I could pass for good looking. With all the intensity of the late-blooming, rebellious adolescent that I still was, I decided to leave Bil. Some ferment within me told me that I could make a better life for myself.

Ruth Galey was pleased with my decision. My marriage had brought serious friction into our relationship for the first time. She had never completely approved of Bil and perhaps she was glad to once more be my only emotional support. She had wanted me to develop in her own image, to have a more conventional and proper life; in marrying Bil I had chosen a free, unconventional, bohemian life, which I had always been drawn to and which she scorned. She behaved a little like a mother-in-law with Bil and had little success in influencing his ideas or decisions. He, in turn, enjoyed flouting convention. She was helpful when we were setting up housekeeping—too helpful, from Bil's point of view. As our marriage deteriorated, he unfairly blamed her for that, too, but then Bil, the boy who never grew up, was ever unable to take responsibility for anything that went awry. The real problem in my relationship with Ruth was that while I was deeply grateful for everything she had done for me, she wanted to retain her influence over me, and I wanted to be free and autonomous.

My family as usual was unconcerned. Rosalind had married Max Feller, a labor relations expert, in 1932 and was busy with her new life and the first of her three children. Julie, the family beauty, was in show business, often on tour, and we lived in different worlds and saw little of each other. Bil's friends remained Bil's friends, and none offered comfort or understanding. As a showpiece, Bil was perfect. If I was leaving him, there had to be something the matter with me. They stayed friendly but cool.

When I finally found the courage to leave, in 1936, Bil sent word through a friend that he wasn't worried—he was sure I would come back when I got hungry. Bil was never consciously mean or cruel, but that message eradicated any doubt I might have had about my decision.

In 1983, when Bil was writing his autobiography, he wrote to me about our first encounter: "And the back of my head keeps tapping me back to a time when I first went up to The Meeting Place over Chumley's and your excitement walked—or rather ran in my direction. The picture is just as firm in my head as though it's happening now. There must be something more powerful than we understand when the magnets are right. How fortunate that I have this to keep."

More than sixty years had passed since that meeting. His vivid recollection, which he felt compelled to write and tell me about, confirmed my feeling that something extraordinary *had* taken place at our first meeting. Our marriage had lasted just over three years, although we didn't divorce for six or seven years after we separated. But with a little time my disappointment and anger faded, while my appreciation of Bil's genius remained; we were able to be friends again, and occasionally corresponded. In 1983, when he began to write his autobiography, his letters became more numerous. He sent along duplicate pictures and liked to recall the "good times" we had shared.

When Bil learned that I had become a psychotherapist, he wrote: "Please send me lots of two cents plain psychotherapy for my right knee which don't walk so good any more." And then: "Ev, ma cherie et naissance de beaucoup des memoires, two cents plain is beginning to work but I think I gotta give it a little more time before I apply for the five cents special. Keeping the brain focused on the sore spots gets sidetracked on account of the total amount of priceless junk that creates so much of total recall of yesteryear. Remember how much radio we turned down because we wouldn't sing nothin but Capullito d'Alleli and Quereme Mucho and all that Spanish stuff? The old love hangs on in many memories—all good!"

In another letter, he talks about attending one of Bucky Fuller's birthday parties.* "Were in touch with Bucky's Birthday party in Philly

---

* I had introduced Bil to Bucky Fuller, and they became and stayed friends after the divorce.

last year. We did a shadow play of his life (funny) at the National Arts Club when they gave him a medal. He don't dare wear all of his medals at once for fear of falling over frontwards."

One year when John Nef and I were vacationing in Greece, I sent Bil a postcard of a nude sculpture of a Greek god. His next letter said, "I have been a long time answering your beautiful Greek postcard. What a flattering thing you done to me. I'm not so nekkid publicly as I once was. I yam still a skinny person. I sure wisht you'd come and see me some time—I can be home at the above address any time you indicate. Come for a visit. I got no wife!" He had been married four times by then.

Sometime in the '80s I did go to see Bil when I was in New York, and we had an hour together. He had changed little. The laugh lines running from nose to mouth were deeper, and his blond hair was a little thinner but had surprisingly little gray in it. We examined each other carefully. We had both aged well. After exchanging news, and before the hour was up, he became self-conscious and began to play the piano so he wouldn't have to talk. But we were both glad to touch base and remember the good times. Being happily married, I felt sorry that he was alone. We embraced and I left.

Bil died on March 18, 1987, of bone cancer. His *New York Times* obituary ran across the entire page, three columns of text and a three-column-wide picture with some of his *Wizard of Oz* puppets. I went to the memorial service at the Community Church in New York and met his brother George, whom I hadn't seen for fifty years. I also met Laura and Peter, the two children that he and his second wife Cora had adopted. Cora, who was also his partner in the marionette world, was married to him for thirty years, until her death. Bil had become famous in the movie and television world and had produced many beloved children's shows at the Bil Baird Theater on Barrow Street. His work combined sculpture, dance, music, painting, and the theater, and all of his gifts had been fully utilized.

CHAPTER VI

Making My Way Alone

WHEN I LEFT BIL IN 1936, I had no money and needed a job to support myself. Through Russell Patterson, a well-known illustrator, I learned that the Earl Carroll Theater at Broadway and Fiftieth Street was going to be converted into a theater restaurant called the French Casino. Sol Hurok, the famous impresario, was importing a huge Folies Bergère type of spectacle with an all-French cast to open it. On what had been the mezzanine floor, "the longest bar in the world" would be erected, and a marionette show designed by Russell would entertain the barflies. There was a job open for a Puppeteer/Mistress of Ceremonies, but she had to be French or French-speaking. I was neither but I wanted and needed that job. The day I heard about it, I went to a Maurice Chevalier movie, listened very carefully, sat through the movie twice, and emerged from the theater with a newly memorized persona. Speaking "wiz a Fransh ac-sant," I applied for the job and to my delight and astonishment got it.

The marionette theater was at one end of a space that covered the entire width of the theater. Just below the miniature stage were two black grand pianos. Ruth Cleary, a stunning blue-eyed, black-haired beauty who was Russell Patterson's girl and later his wife, and an equally handsome blond, both chosen for their looks as well as their musical ability, graced the pianos. They played the specially composed

musical accompaniment for the marionette show and filled the inter-
ludes between shows by playing popular songs. In addition to being
Mistress of Ceremonies and operating the marionettes, I also sang
French songs, most of which I had learned from Bil, but some from
Lucien Boyer records. I also sang American songs with a French
accent. Russell Patterson and the entire company knew, of course, that
I wasn't French. We all thought it was a good show-biz joke.

I was called Fifi, a name that reminded me of a French poodle,
and I had to sing a song whose lyric, believe it or not, ran "Allo, Fifi
/ A fella's lucky if he / Can holler 'allo Fifi' / And have Fifi say 'allo.'"
This deathless song had the advantage of being memorizable after a
single hearing, so that hordes of well-oiled folk could join me in
singing the second verse.

Puppeteers always wear trousers at work. When you have to climb
ladders and work in small crowded quarters backstage, dresses are a
hazard. My Fifi pants were like men's evening trousers—black wool
with satin stripes down the outside legs—but instead of ending at
the waist they rose about five inches higher, hugging my body as tightly
as my own skin across my then very flat tummy. Above, I wore a white
satin shirt with full sleeves and a Pierrot ruffle at the neck. The costume was made by Brooks, the famous theatrical costumer, which
made me feel professional. I was on Broadway! And, indeed, Fifi
became a well-known Broadway character.

Every once in a while a French-speaking person would come up to
me and start talking in French. I was ready with a response: "Mesieur,
you must to excuse me, I am such short time in zis country zat I have
promis' my muzzer to speak only ze Anglish, so as to learn ze most
while I am 'ere." Most believed me; those that didn't were kind and
kept my secret. My masquerade lasted for more than a year and a
half.

At that time my sister Julia had taken the stage name of Julie Jenner
and had appeared as a dancer in the Ziegfield Follies, Earl Carroll's
Vanities, and a Beatrice Lillie show called *Life Begins at 8:40*. She was a

friend of Louis Sobol, who wrote a daily Broadway gossip column in *The New York Mirror*. One day she confided to Louis that not only was Fifi not a French girl, she was her sister. Louis wrote an amusing column in which he told about the marvelous French girl named Fifi, who had become so well-known on Broadway with her little song at the French Casino marionette theater. After a laudatory description, he blew my cover: "Only Fifi isn't French, she is Julie Jenner's sister and was born in Brooklyn." (Like many a columnist, he got my birthplace wrong.) Since everybody in show business read Sobol's column, I expected to be fired at any moment, but after a week or two his column was forgotten, I wasn't fired, and my life as Fifi went on. All this confirmed what P.T. Barnum knew—the public likes to be fooled.

After leaving Bil, I had moved to the old Prince George Hotel, which was respectable but gloomy, and lived in a minuscule room taken by the month. The French Casino job paid a then-handsome salary of $150 a week and lasted long enough for me to accumulate a little surplus. Eventually, I found a tiny apartment in an old house on St. Luke's Place in the Village. It was three flights up, at the back of the house, and it looked down on a garden. It had a fireplace, wide-board floors that took a polish, and a large bathroom made from an old hall bedroom, with room for a piano—a small upright that a friend wanted to store. When I needed to cook, two boards went over the bathtub, and with a two-burner hot plate I could feed myself inexpensively. It was the first place that I had all to myself, and it was beautiful. I had kept some of the things from my Brooklyn attic, and Ruth Galey gave me a pair of old French candlesticks and loaned me a gilt-framed print to put over the fireplace.* It was cozy and pleasing, and it satisfied my female nesting urge. I loved it.

During my French Casino days I met a great many movie people and .was offered screen tests galore, almost all with strings of one kind or

---

* I had left my marriage with very few possessions of my own. When I was setting up housekeeping in the new apartment, I asked Bil if I could take some of the household materials from our old place. I wanted sheets and towels and a few plates and some silverware. Bil raised objections to each request, which reminded me of how hard it was for him to part with anything. I was angry because I had certainly paid for half of the things in our apartment.

another attached, like sleeping with the man who was offering the test. Republic Pictures in those days made grade-C movies and a lot of westerns. They offered me a test without strings and I accepted. From Julie, who was still living at the Bensonhurst house with my mother and little brother, Myron, I borrowed an evening dress that was exactly wrong for me, but I had no choice—I didn't own an evening dress. No one told me what to do. Among other gems, I sang the "Allo Fifi" song. I was asked to do a more extensive test for a particular film project to be directed by John Auer. This time I was given a makeup man named Eddie Sens, part of a famous makeup family. (His father had been in charge of makeup at the Metropolitan Opera, and his sons, including Eddie, had become famous in Hollywood.) Because it was the heyday of Joan Crawford, the most chic look was to have no eyebrows at all, only a thin pencilled line. To my horror, Eddie Sens tweezed out every one of the hairs in my naturally thick eyebrows and pencilled in a hair-thin line above where they had been, giving me a perpetually surprised look. I didn't recognize myself. Then he gave my long curly hair a very elaborate hairdo, shampooing it and then setting it with some kind of gel. Suddenly it was time to shoot, and my hair hadn't dried completely. It was combed out too soon and looked like a fright wig. I was so upset by the way they had made me look that I had trouble concentrating on my lines, and that was the last I heard about my potential role in the movie. My eyebrows grew back and were never tweezed again. One unexpected result of this test was a proposal of marriage from the director, who had to return to Hollywood and asked me to go with him. Needless to say, I declined.

Once the job at the French Casino ended, I began to look around again for work. Because I had always sung with Bil, singing alone presented a new challenge for me. I didn't have an accompanist and couldn't afford to hire one. So, adapting to necessity, something I learned early, I became an a capella singer. Without accompaniment I would sing folk songs, in several languages I couldn't speak. Fortunately, while I didn't have perfect pitch, I did have relative pitch and a good ear, and was able to end a song in the same key in which I started. One of my jobs was singing in a night club called Tony's on Fifty-second Street, across the street from the Onyx, where Billie Holiday was singing. Good jazz was the mainstay of many of the clubs on that street, and my experience there provided me with an introduction to what became a permanent source of pleasure.

Tony's was a simple restaurant where you could dine on good Italian food, but its main attraction was its entertainment, usually a female singer. My predecessor was an old professional who had an expert piano player and could afford special arrangements made to suit her voice. By comparison, I felt very much like an amateur—I didn't have a big or trained voice. But at least it was a "true" voice. I sang short French songs like "Aluette," "En Passant par la Lorraine," and "Valentine"; English music-hall songs like "The Old Kent Road"; and folk songs like "Uncle Tom Cobbly," with its chorus consisting of villagers' names, and "Molly Malone," with its echoing ghostly chorus of "Cockels and Mussels." I knew a few temperance songs, which always brought a laugh: "Father has signed the pledge and we are happy, bright and gay." I also sang "The Man on the Flying Trapeze" and other Victorian songs, like "Oh, Fred, tell them to stop, that was the cry of Maria, but the more she said 'Whoa,' they said let her go, and the swing went a little bit higher." I had two World War I standbys, including this one:

> What are ya gonna do for Uncle Sammy,
> What are ya gonna do to help the boys,
> If you're gonna stay at home,
> While they're fighting o'er the foam,
> The least that you can do is buy a Liberty Bond or two,
> And if you're gonna be a sympathetic miser,
> Just the kind that only lends a lot of noise,
> Then you're just as good as if you loved the Kaiser,
> So whatta are you gonna do for Uncle Sam.

The second war song was "Joan of Arc," a sentimental song, a heart breaker, which I spoofed by accompanying the lines "Can't you hear the cries of Normandy / Can't you see the drooping fleur de lys" with a gesture using my two curved arms as petals of the drooping flower and slowly lowering them. To my relief, surprise, and delight the audiences were pleased with my performances. I was certainly different from the average nightclub singer, and I had a few admirers, including the poet William Rose Benet, who came in more than once to hear me.

I had another singing job at a Hoboken bar and restaurant where there was an in-house piano player and a male singer of romantic ballads. Here I sang the popular songs of the day, like "You're the cream in my coffee." When the place closed at three o'clock in the morning, I would take the Hudson Tube from New Jersey back to Manhattan. In those days it didn't occur to me that it might be dangerous traveling alone at that hour, because it wasn't. No one ever frightened or molested me.

SOME years after our affair ended, Bucky charmed his way back into my life and became a good friend again. His great friend in the mid-thirties was Christopher Morley, a rotund, merry, middle-aged writer whose novel *Kitty Foyle* had been a bestseller and was made into a movie. Chris was feeling good about the world and was unexpectedly rich. After I left Bil, the two men would call often and take me to dinner or lunch. Like many other writers, Chris was a good friend of Frances Steloff, who owned the famous Gotham Book Mart on Forty-seventh Street. When once more I needed a job, Chris introduced me, and I was hired as a clerk. I made eighteen dollars a week, paid twenty-five dollars a month rent for my tiny St. Luke's Place apartment, and had money enough left over to entertain occasionally with English muffins and tea on a Sunday afternoon.

The Gotham Book Mart was a marvel. Located in the heart of the theater district, it was much more than just a bookstore; it was a gathering place for writers, poets, editors, actors, and stage designers, especially the avant-garde. Writers stopped in to see how their books were selling, to meet each other and talk, as well as to buy books. The Gotham hosted the James Joyce Society, held poetry readings, and gave publication parties for new books. In good weather the backyard would be opened up, bookstalls just like those on the left bank of the Seine would be set up, and a few privileged writers, like Chris Morley and Bucky Fuller, were permitted to eat their lunches there in the garden.

Frances Steloff, a small, prematurely white-haired, sharp-tongued, fiercely energetic woman, had started the shop at a different location, back in 1920. Among her many talents was knowing what was going to be a good seller. She would buy up remaindered books, holding them sometimes for years, later to sell them as scarce or rare items. She also stocked books that some thought pornographic, such as Aubrey Beardsley's illustrated books, Pierre Louys's *Songs of Bilitis*, and the like. With the assistance of Kay Steele—brainy, Southern, and second in command—the Gotham did a huge business in out-of-print, hard-to-find books. Besides theater, ballet, and art books, it also offered dozens of little magazines, published here and abroad, many with short lives, which became collector's items. Miss Steloff had excellent and wide-ranging taste.

Chris was only one of the many authors who loved the Gotham Book Mart. Among the regular habitués I remember were Edmund Wilson, Padraic Colum, James Laughlin, and William Rose Benet. If she thought the customers were important, Miss Steloff would wait on them herself, and if not, I was permitted to serve them. The best part of working at the Gotham was that Miss Steloff let me, even encouraged me, to take books home to read, one at a time, which was how I was introduced to Kafka, Joyce, and Gertrude Stein. I loved the bookstore, the writers who peopled it, and Kay Steele. I hated Miss Steloff, who I thought was mean to the help and smooth as silk to the customers, especially the famous ones.

Difficulty with Miss Steloff arose when Bucky and Chris would arrive at the bookshop to take me out to lunch. We were a jocular threesome, and Miss Steloff became jealous. Apparently they had formerly taken *her* out to lunch, and now she was furious and took it out on me. Each morning she would launch into her list of criticisms of me, 90 percent of them unfair; the barrage would go on and on, and I was not permitted to interrupt to defend myself, so I almost always ended up in tears. That was the signal for her to stop and comfort me and offer a glass of carrot juice (she was a vegetarian). It began to seem as if the comforting part were the final goal of what I now see was a genuinely hysterical performance. Each day I promised myself that this day I would not cry, but it was weeks before I was sufficiently in charge of myself to stay dry-eyed.*

Christopher Morley, wonderfully erudite in all things literary, began to give me books. The first one, a little volume presented to me in 1937, was a valentine; he had cut a window out of the end paper, taped it back in place on one side so that it could open and close like a door, and drawn a red heart containing the words "S. Valentine" on the outside. Inside the paper-door window he had written, "Not for a bevy, but just for Evvy, not for a shelf, but for herself." He loved to make up jingles. St. Valentine's Day of 1938 brought another note containing a large red heart within which was written, "Evvie dear my hand has been sore / I couldn't cut Valentines like before / But just the same without any phlegm / Is a big big hug from your CM" Not physiological but spiritual—see Dictionary." He later gave me a Rockwell Kent–illustrated Shakespeare and several of his own books, all of which still live on my bookshelves after more than fifty-five years.

Chris sometimes took me out to lunch without Bucky; on those occasions we would go to Christ Cella's restaurant, where I became the

* Although at the time I thought of Frances Steloff as a tough taskmaster, looking back I see that she was a remarkable, enterprising woman who passionately loved books and the people who made them. Thanks to the opportunity I had to work in that exceptional place, I reached a level of literary sophistication I might never have achieved on my own. She lived to a high old age, over a hundred, and remained active and vigorous almost to the end.

only woman member of the Three Hours for Lunch Club, composed of mostly writers who met there regularly. He told me he thought he had fallen a little in love with me. But in the aftermath of Bucky, I had acquired an ironclad rule about married men. I forgave myself the mistake I had made with him because I realized that I had learned something from it, but I had no intention of making the same mistake with Chris. So we remained good friends.

Chris would often stop in at the bookstore with an out-of-town author to whom he was showing the sights. After one such visit, with the writer Hulbert Footner, he wrote the following in his weekly essay, called "The Bowling Green," for the *Saturday Review of Literature* (December 4, 1937):

> Tell her, said my wise friend (I don't think he guesses that I realize his wisdom; often I pretend to disregard his best sayings, not to embarrass him), tell her she always seems to be on tiptoe. Tell her that from me, so she'll know I recognized her quality. This was of one he had but chancily met, but he saw (O canny watchman of vaulted moods and emotional safe deposits) that uplifted eager salute to the oncoming and uncalculated: the mind that runs to the sill to meet the glamour and the grace. He was aware of the full clear eye that says a thousand converse before slow speech—yet not so slow, neither—negotiates its dullard scholarship. In short, the quality that takes the instant by the forward top, improves the moment as it flies. (These, I suppose, are aftermath of Bartlett.*)

I've always loved how this passage captures exactly my eagerness and delight. I not only *seemed* to be on tiptoe, I was—open to everything in view and reaching for more. Stimulated by the Gotham ambience, it seemed to me that I had grown taller suddenly, like

---

* Chris had recently finished editing a new version of *Bartlett's Quotations*.

Alice in Wonderland. I was reveling in my new life and enchanted with my discoveries. Thanks to Frances Steloff, the new books, the new people, I could feel an adrenaline rush and loved it. That someone met *chancily* could be sensitive and smart enough to discover my inner being was remarkable.

CHAPTER VII

Unexplored Territory
at the Stefansson Library

ONE DAY WHILE I WAS WORKING at the Gotham Book Mart, I discovered that Vilhjalmur Stefansson, the arctic explorer who came to see me in the hospital, lived just around the corner from my St. Luke's Place flat, at 67 Morton Street. We began to bump into each other fairly often on the street, and occasionally he would ask me to dine at Romany Marie's, where we had first met, or a neighboring Italian restaurant on Barrow Street. During one of these get-togethers, Stefansson asked what I was doing with my life. I told him that I was looking for a job that would use my artistic skills. He had an idea about how I might find such a job.

An Icelandic pavilion was planned for the New York World's Fair of 1939. Stef's parents were Icelandic, and he spoke the language fluently. The government of Iceland had asked for his help with the fair exhibits; he was also writing a book for Doubleday—*Iceland, The First American Republic*—that would be published in time for the opening. David Gaither, whom we both knew, was in charge of the exhibits, and Stef thought he might have a place for me in his workshop. I didn't realize at the time that Stef was planning to offer me a job in the Stefansson Library once the fair was over. During an early dinner meeting I found myself telling him enthusiastically about how much

I was enjoying William Stearns Davis's *Life on a Medieval Barony* because it was packed with just the kind of detailed information that made the era come alive for me. Stef owned that it was one of his favorite books but that he had never thought I was interested in that sort of thing. Our relationship moved into another phase after that meeting. We met more often and talked about books we were reading. We entertained and admired each other.

David Gaither did have an opening for me. In order to qualify, I had to join the Painters, Paper Hangers & Scenic Designers Union. I did so and was soon making models of the hills and dales and the ponies and sheep of Iceland and picking up a good deal of information about its culture, too.

When the fair opened, Stef thoughtfully invited me to be his guest for the festivities at the Iceland Pavilion, and I met many Icelanders for the first time. The fair's public relations department had arranged celebrity parties to attract notice and people, and Stef invited me to come along to many of these events as well. I remember meeting the conductor of the Boston Pops Orchestra, maestro Arthur Fiedler; Sir Hubert Wilkins, another explorer; and Dr. A. A. Brill, the psychiatrist who first translated Sigmund Freud's writings into English.[*]

When the Iceland Pavillion was complete, Stef offered me the job of librarian and researcher at the Stefansson Library. I was surprised by the offer and told him that I had always been artistically inclined and didn't even know how to type. He suggested I go, at his expense, to typing school. He assured me that my curiosity and enthusiasm

---

[*] Later, Stef told me an amusing story about Dr. Brill. Although they had never met, Dr. Brill had telephoned him saying he felt he had made a momentous discovery and needed Stef to help him confirm it. He invited Stef to dinner and, intrigued, Stef accepted. It wasn't until after dinner, when Brill had lit a cigar, that he finally consented to talk about his discovery. While reading books about Greenland, especially about the Inuit and their dog teams, he had found descriptions of a mental illness common to dogs and men, and he wanted to know whether Stef had encountered the same illness among the western Inuit and their dogs. Brill believed that if he could prove that the same illness attacked both men and dogs, this knowledge might lead to a valuable breakthrough in understanding mental illness generally. Stef asked him the name of the illness. Brill said it was called *piblukto*. Stef, one of the very few explorers to master the incredibly difficult Inuit language, then smiled and said, "Dr. Brill, I don't think this is a medical problem; it's a linguistic one." "Why?" asked Brill. "Because," replied Stef, "*piblukto* is an Inuit word that simply means 'there is something wrong with him.'"

would make me a good researcher and librarian. The wise man was right on both counts. After two weeks at a typing school, my skills still wobbly, I turned up at the Stefansson Library on Morton Street.

As the newest member of the staff of ten, I was assigned the most menial chores. But looking around at the huge library that occupied several apartments, meeting Olive Wilcox, Stef's charming chief of staff, and feeling the happy ambience of people doing work they obviously enjoyed, I was enchanted from my first day. I even found myself enjoying taking the mail and the books to the post office, doing the dirtiest library-shifting job, indeed doing whatever was needed. I was just so glad to be a part of this new and exciting world.

Staff lunches were an institution at the Stefansson Library. Designed primarily to save time, they also gave staff members an opportunity to meet and interrogate various scientists from many disciplines—people who used the library both before and after their expeditions to the polar regions. As the newest member of the staff, I was automatically elected to cook. One of my most vivid memories of the staff lunches was my first disaster. I had the canny idea of making a huge lamb stew that would last for a week, getting tastier each day. So I found the largest pot in the kitchen and took most of an afternoon to make it. When I found that the pot wouldn't go into the refrigerator, I left it on the stove overnight. The next day I proudly served the stew, which was received with a most polite frozen silence. As soon as I tasted it, I realized what had happened. I had left the stew pot over the pilot light, which had provided sufficient warmth to make a happy fermentation in the stew but not enough to cook it through. The whole mess had turned sour, and in great shame I dashed down to the nearest delicatessen to buy cold cuts and potato salad.

That was the worst thing that ever happened at lunch. But there were plenty of good times as well, such as when Owen and Eleanore Lattimore came to tell us what they had found on their most recent trip to Mongolia, or Sir Hubert Wilkins modestly told about some hair-raising recent flight in the Antarctic, or Eloise McCaskill informed us that she had found the fifty-ninth variant spelling of the Elizabethan explorer Sir Martin Frobisher's name. A Royal Canadian mounted policeman named Larsen described making the first complete Northwest Passage in a small boat, and an anthropologist named Ethel John Lindgren reported on her experiment to raise reindeer in a remote northern part of England. I was openmouthed with wonder.

Stef was president of the Explorers Club, then at 10 West Seventy-second Street, facing Central Park; that building's enormous rooms displayed portraits of the club's most famous members, along with huge elephant tusks, expedition flags, arctic sledges, and maps and globes showing the treks of various explorations. The club included a library and large meeting rooms to which members could bring their wives and friends for public lectures. In those days, before U-2 planes and space flights had photographed the entire planet, the world map still had many white spots, indicating that no man had ever set foot in those areas. From Tierra del Fuego to the North, South, and magnetic Poles, members were busily filling in the blank spots. The Stefansson Library seemed to me like an annex of the Explorers Club. A gathering place for scholars doing wide-ranging work, the library always had a lively stream of people passing through it, including anthropologist Ruth Benedict, Arctic journalist Ruth Gruber (who traveled to Siberia), anthropologists just back from Tibet, oceanographers going to Alaska, an engineer interested in what the Russians were doing in permafrost research, and specialists of all sorts—in Medieval Latin, the history of Rome's taxation of the Republic of Greenland in the year 1000, the aurora borealis, Kodiak bears, and many other areas.

Scientists and explorers often would visit the library to prepare for an expedition by looking up all the previously known information they needed, then afterward would come back to share their discoveries with us. Thus, long before results were published, we knew what was happening in our territory. Anthropologists wanting to compare notes

with Stef; engineers needing to know about permafrost; historians track-
ing expeditions, ancient and new; scientists of every description from
Alaska, arctic Canada, Iceland, Greenland, Lapland, and, rarely, from
Russia and Siberia—they all came to use the library, compare notes, discover who else was working on their subject and where.

It was Stef's desire to corner the market for Arctic and Antarctic
information. If he didn't have the answer to a polar question, he
knew where to find it—among his network of friends, through fellow Explorers Club members, or in his huge library. He received catalogs from more than four hundred book dealers throughout the
world. He would take a suitcase full of them on his lecture tours and
mark them during his long train journeys. He haunted the secondhand bookstores of whatever city he happened to be in and bought
whatever looked interesting. He would mark the book catalogs with
notations: buy, buy if we don't have, buy even if we do. He knew
the rarity and value of polar books, often better than the dealers
themselves did, and was a terrific horse trader in the book world,
using either one of the twenty-seven books he had written or a rare
duplicate he owned that another collector lacked. In one case he
took his lecture fee in duplicate and discarded books at the Macy
Whaling Museum in Nantucket. and returned with some of the
greatest treasures in the library. The bundles of books would pile up
faster than they could be catalogued. Some wouldn't be opened for
a year or even five years. In 1951, when we moved the 70,000-item
library to Dartmouth, we found a few that were twenty-five years old
and had never been opened.

One of my jobs was to try to keep up with the steady stream of
new books arriving daily in the library. I learned how to catalog them
using a homemade system of cross-referencing that reflected Stef's
special interests, like "permanently frozen subsoil" (the word permafrost had not yet been coined) or "elimination of salt from sea ice
by freezing." Soon after I came to work, Stef said a surprising thing
to me: "When you find something that is interesting to you, please feel

free to stop and read. You will be educating yourself and making your-self more valuable to us." Reading on company time seemed to me a generous gift, and I took complete advantage of it.

Even as objects, the books were a fascination. Having grown up in a house with very few books, I found joy in the mere sight of the multicolored backs of the library's thousands of volumes, variously sized, some covered in cloth, some in leather, and a few in velum, each promising the narrative of an exploration to a far place. The maps and the atlases, especially the dazzling antique ones with the beautiful hand-colored plates, stirred in me a desire to learn every place name in this new territory.

At first, much of my time was spent copying marked materials out of books and periodicals for the researchers or for Stef. One day he came to my desk and said, "Please get me all the material you can find on the botfly."* I was thrilled at the prospect of doing my first piece of real "research." I went through dozens of books and pam-phlets and compiled three or four pages on the subject and handed them in, worried that they might be handed back to me for a dozen different reasons. Stef accepted the pages with no comment beyond a polite thank you, which to my mind was the highest praise.

Stef would design with cunning a problem calculated simultane-ously to excite my imagination and to take me one step further into Arctic lore. He constantly asked provocative questions that made me determined to discover the answers for myself. He would hand me a book and say, "I haven't time to read this. Please read it and write a two- or three-page summary of what it contains, how knowledgeable the author is, and how important you think the book is." I received great pleasure from the request because it showed that I was beginning to accumulate some know-how and that he was trusting my judg-ment. Much later, when I directed the Arctic Seminar at Dartmouth, I

---

*The botfly is an insect that attacks and burrows through the skin of reindeer and lays its eggs underneath. When the eggs hatch, the larvae burrow their way out through the skin to escape, thereby making open sores in the rein-deer's skin and ruining it from a commercial standpoint.

recalled the technique and made use of it, although I was unaware of it being a technique when it was first used on me.

Each encounter with an Arctic phenomenon—from the aurora borealis to permafrost, from the engineering principles involved in Inuit snow-house building to the differences between glacier ice and sea ice—had a revelatory quality. The polar world was completely foreign to me, but I made it my own. I fell in love with the idea of learning everything about everything, and Stef, with his encyclopedic storehouse of knowledge, was a rich source of wisdom during this intellectual awakening.

Many years later, in my afterward to Stef's autobiography, I wrote the following:

> Stef discovered my 'intellect' such as it is, and it would have been difficult to decide which of us had more fun as he led me farther and deeper into his world of books and learning, always graciously making me feel that I had something to contribute as well as take. He was a gifted teacher, and I had been deprived. His need to teach and my need first to learn and then to give pleasure to myself by pleasing him became inseparable. I still catch my breath remembering the steady, cumulative unfolding of intellectual discovery.

This new, unexplored world of the intellect, which I had seen only glimpses of before, with Ruth Galey and Bucky Fuller, now became my own everyday territory.

CHAPTER VIII

The Beginning of a Beautiful Relationship

I LOVED MY JOB, AND AS THE NEWEST MEMBER of the
staff, with the most chores, I often found myself happily working overtime, until six or seven in the evening. Stef had no hobbies
and took no vacations. He loved his work and preferred doing it to
anything else the world offered. It often happened that if both of us
were working late and neither of us had plans, we would go out to
dinner, usually at an Italian restaurant on Barrow Street, and sometimes even return to the office afterwards to work some more. Over
dinner we would talk first about work and then about each other, and
found we got along smoothly. This habit soon extended into the weekends as well, and both of us found contentment in working together
and being in each other's company.

On the evening of March 5, 1934, I was dining alone at Romany
Marie's when I heard the news that Bucky's shiny black, three-wheeled
Dymaxion car had been in a bad accident. I had ridden the blunt-nosed,
whale-like automobile in the days when Bucky and I were close. It was
the prototype for a car that he had hoped would eventually be manu-
factured in quantity. Riding in it at the time of the accident en route to
the Chicago airport was the Master of Sempill, Colonel William
Frances Forbes Sempill, the English entrepreneur who was planning
the commercial production of the car. The accident killed the well-

known professional driver and badly injured Sempill, ending his interest in Dymaxion car production. Stefansson, who was at Marie's that night, too, had been responsible for introducing Sempill to Bucky and, remembering that Bucky and I had been close, sat down next to me to commiserate. He offered to walk me home, and as we approached his place at 67 Morton Street he asked me in because he wanted to give me a book he had written, the first of many I was later to receive, called *The Standardization of Error*. He had appended to the title these words, in black ink: "a coherent and basic system of philosophy, is nevertheless submitted with diffidence to Evelyn by her friend Stef." The little gift first awakened my interest in Stef as a compassionate person.

Romany Marie's rented out its upstairs area for private parties. Stef often gave what I think of as Explorers Club parties there. Here I met Lowell Thomas, the world traveler and news commentator; Sir Hubert Wilkins (whom I first met at the World's Fair), a pioneer polar aviator who sported a black Van Dyke beard and had been on Stef's third Expedition to the Canadian Arctic; and Joseph Spinden, the great Maya Indian expert who was a curator at the Brooklyn Museum (and who married Isamu Noguchi's sister Ilis). I especially remember the dinner for Matthew Henson, the black explorer who had accompanied Admiral Robert Peary on his journey to discover the North Pole in 1909.[*]

Growing up in an unnaturally quiet household, deprived of good conversation, I was thrilled with Stef's way of talking, which had a

---

[*] Matt, modest and gentle in manner, was a veteran of fifteen years with Peary. He was expert in handling sledges and sled dogs, and Peary considered him the equal of any Inuit in Arctic coping techniques. Peary had written in an early book that "no man worth his salt would ride on the sled." But by the time of his final Greenland journey he had lost nine of his toes to frostbite, and he rode much of the way. Peary and his family always referred to Matt condescendingly as the admiral's "body servant," and Peary once wrote of him that he was an excellent, gifted arctic traveler but that he had not "as a racial inheritance, the daring of" the white members of the expedition. It is hard for some of us to remember how extensive the racial prejudice of the time was. There was some criticism in the press of Peary for having taken only Inuits and a Negro with him to the Pole. Some believed, cynically but possibly accurately, he wanted to be the only white man to have stood at that mythical spot. Stef fought against much opposition to make Matt a member of the Explorers Club and finally succeeded. Long after his death, in the years after the Civil Rights movement, Matt was rediscovered and recognized as a black hero who had not received his rightful share of fame. Books were written about him as co-discoverer of the North Pole, and in 1988 his body was moved

natural grace and form that delighted my ear. Listening to him conversing with a fellow scientist or writer was like listening to a Bach two-part invention. The turn of phrase, the witty reference, the scrap of peculiarly apt poetry produced a harmony that was literally music to my ears. I listened, enchanted, and wanted more and more. Stef introduced me to new words, new names, new books, unimagined joys of poetry, an explosion of new possibilities.

He also had a way of listening with respectful attention that encouraged me to state my view, however naïve it might be, about a subject. While Ruth Galey had played the teacher role and I the pupil, Stef had the gift of treating me and indeed everyone he encountered as an equal. I knew perfectly well I wasn't his equal, but that he found what I had to say worthwhile was not only flattering, it was ego-nourishing.

Stef began what I now see as a courtship by giving me, outside of office hours, one after another of the two-dozen books he had written, in chronological order, each one signed and dated ceremoniously. He would invite me to dinner, not at Romany Marie's, but at one of the excellent Italian restaurants that abounded in the Village, where we could be alone. On the first such occasion he ordered a bottle of Liebsfraumilch and explained what the name meant. It was the first time I had learned the name of a fine wine, let alone tasted one, and I was charmed. The white wine, a whole bottle of it instead of the more familiar single glass (which during Prohibition was often served in a coffee cup with a saucer), helped us both climb over the hurdle of workplace formality, and we became more open and confiding with each other. In time our formal goodnight kiss grew into more purposeful embraces, which were entirely agreeable and startled me into thinking of this fascinating older man as someone more than a friend. But no—he was sixty years old and I was twenty-six. Was I out of my mind? I put off thinking about it too seriously and decided to postpone any decision-making.

I was not consciously aware that my blossoming affection for this man was connected to my feelings for my father, after he "discovered" me at age twelve. Here was another mentor who recognized, encouraged, and cared for me. But this time there was the added intensity of a growing physical attraction.

Stef was tall—five feet eleven inches—and Scandinavian-fair-skinned; his bright blue eyes had the farseeing look of a sailor. His hair, once blond, was now the whitest white, thick and worn a bit long for those days. His long-fingered, beautiful hands were used sparingly but expressively, especially when lecturing. His clear, medium-pitched voice was generally soft but could fill a hall effortlessly, having been trained by much speech-making in the days before microphones. His mien was typically serious but could change strikingly when a boyish smile lit up his countenance. He often appeared shy in a group because he had no small talk, but when a subject interested him he would become animated and might take command of the conversation. He walked with a rolling gait as though he had spent years aboard ship and, whatever the weather or season, always marched outdoors without a hat or an overcoat. He had a wonderful sense of humor, but since irony was his style he was sometimes misunderstood.

Stef had never married. He told me on one of our dates that he had had a sixteen-year relationship with novelist Fannie Hurst, which had ended long before we began to see each other. I remember once that she called at the office and he told Olive Wilcox to say he was not in. He told me that she was married but lived separately from her concert-pianist husband. When she asked her husband for a divorce in order to marry Stef, the husband agreed on the condition that she pay him a million dollars—an impossibly large sum in those days, so Fannie stayed married. Her affair with Stef had been conducted with the greatest secrecy; he told me that their letters contained code words that read respectably but had secret meanings.

Despite his reputation as a perennial bachelor, Stef began to ask me out fairly regularly, to Explorers Club celebrations and then to dinners given by his friends. Some of these people, like the Eustace Seligmans and Mrs. Kermit Roosevelt, had grand houses filled with art and antiques. Others, like Edward and Susie Weyer,* who became lifelong friends, had places that were simpler and cozier.

While away on his lecture tours, which he did for several months out the year, Stef asked me to write him often and regularly, not only about what was going on at the polar information factory (a.k.a. the Stefansson Library), but also what was happening politically and with any of his friends in the news. Uncertain about my writing abilities, I nervously asked if my first efforts were alright. Below is his reply:

> Your second letter is best yet for reasons you will guess correctly three times out of the first three tries. You say you have felt self-conscious, but you don't show it—certainly you are far from that in the second letter, but I don't notice it in the other.
>
> How are you doing? You are doing very well indeed.
>
> What do I want to hear? The things that interest you.

We grew closer with time, and in 1940 we became lovers. Despite the age difference, it was with Stef that I had the first good (indeed the best and always satisfying) sex. He was accomplished as well as patient, and we soon found the rhythm that gave me the first orgasms of my life and guaranteed that I would have one every time. I had not anticipated this new kind of pleasure on top of what I was already receiving in the way of intellectual pleasure. It cemented our good relationship into what seemed to me a miraculous one.

Now when Stef went off on his lecture tours, we wrote to each other every day, sometimes twice a day.

On May 14, 1940, from Knoxville, Tennessee, he wrote:

> DD [Dear Darling]
> Your thrilling letter was here awaiting me. It has in it every kind of thrill. There are memories of (is it?) nine years that have

---

* Ed was an anthropologist who had lived with South American Indians and was the editor of *Natural History* magazine. Susie wrote short stories.

been climbing higher peak after higher peak the last six or more months with the highest, most beautiful, Saturday. Tonight both memories and imagination center around 14 St. Luke's [my address]. Some time when both of us are intoxicated, with the wine we know, I may be able to express a tenth of what I feel.

You'll write me early Wednesday morning, I know. That letter will not reach me till evening, by airmail—may not reach me at all at the Hotel Ralston, (Columbus, Georgia) so make it cryptic, that only you and I may understand it.

On May 15, the next day, he wrote:

DD

I forced myself to open last of all waiting letters and messages the telegram which I thrillingly knew was yours and would tell of the success of your experiment. And, of course, it did!

First I could not for a long time write anything. Then I could not write any telegram that was not hopelessly inadequate. First it was a very long one that I tore up. Thereafter, I tore up several short ones and had to get a new bundle of telegraph forms. Finally I sent ten words that say, if you read them correctly, that I cannot now delay for anything and must reach New York to dine with you Friday. That is not wholly—perhaps not even mainly—because I am thirsty to drink in your report. It is mainly because I love you. And I love you since receiving your telegram more than I ever did before, which is saying a good deal. In short, you are the most human, lovable person I have ever known—you are proving to be everything I instinctively loved and everything I subconsciously dreamed.

If only I could talk to you now instead of writing, perhaps I could say at least a small part of what I feel and mean. Perhaps I can Friday! (with your help).

BB [Best Beloved]

Over sixty years after the event, I am unable to remember the nature of the "experiment" described in my letter that kindled such a loving response. My own unexpectedly passionate feelings for Stef have always remained fresh and clear. What I had forgotten over time and what shocked me so pleasantly as I reread his letter was that the intensity of his feelings more than matched mine.

Being together had become a necessity for both of us. At last we dared to talk about marriage. Stef asked for a two-year engagement or trial before the ceremony. Having made one mistake with Bil, I was not in a hurry to make another. I agreed. We talked about children, but it became plain that he was not enthusiastic about the idea. He dwelt on the dangers for me, such as the possibility of producing Downs' Syndrome babies, as our friends the Weyers had—identical twins, both victims of an extra chromosome. I realized that he may have felt too old to have children. Or perhaps he wanted to be sure of having my entire attention. In any case, I was so in love that I agreed to no children, though it was a sad loss since I would have loved to have had his child.

After a year we were both certain that we wanted to spend the rest of our lives together and decided not to waste any more time waiting. We were sure of our love when we decided to marry, but I was unprepared for the accelerating strength of our attachment, the breathless anticipation of each meeting after a separation, and his increasing pleasure and pride in me as I began to develop with his help writing and speech-making skills. He loved my letters as much as I did his. Deeply impressed by his growing love and passion, I was immeasurably strengthened by the knowledge that *I* was the cause of them.

After we decided to marry, I began searching for an apartment and had the good fortune to find a suitable one at 5 St. Luke's Place, next door to where Mayor Jimmy Walker had lived and just down the street from my one-room apartment. It was a floor-through in a beautiful old house with a garden at the back. I decorated it inexpensively with framed, huge old maps in the hall and some small, lovely, colorful

Oriental rugs from a local auction house. I made curtains for the sunny windows and covers for the daybeds. Fireplaces in the front and back rooms added warmth and color. In this place I taught Stef to dawdle over Sunday breakfast reading the papers, with a fire in the fireplace. He learned to relax, but he never really learned to play, except verbally.

We planned to be married in April 1941 at the home of Stef's friend Gretchen Switzer, a professor at Columbia, who lent us her house at Santeetlah, North Carolina, where we were also to spend a week's honeymoon. Because of our different schedules, we arranged to meet there separately, I arriving a day earlier than Stef. On my way south I opened the morning newspaper and read that the United States was occupying Greenland because the Nazis had conquered Denmark, its mother country. To forestall their taking over Greenland—too close to our own shores for our defensive comfort—our armed forces had taken this important strategic step. My first thought was that *he* wouldn't be able to make it to our wedding. The army or the navy or some government department would demand his presence, and our carefully laid plans would be shattered. But come he did, on schedule, and my eyes were blurred with tears of relief and happiness as I spotted his conspicuous white head in the crowd getting off the train. We were married outdoors in a simple ceremony. A week of blissful solitude followed in our handsome borrowed home, far from New York, Washington, the European war news, and inquiring reporters.

Being married provided me with a sense of security I had never felt before, no doubt partially the result of our deeply pleasurable sex life. The gaiety that comes only from being in love with a remarkably satisfactory partner left me smiling and happy. I might have married Stef even if we had no sex life. But to receive this new and lasting gift, in addition to everything else he brought me, made me think of Ethel Merman singing the last line of "I Got Rhythm"—"Who could ask for anything more? Who could ask for anything more!"

CHAPTER IX

A Brief History of Viljalmur Stefansson

W HAT KIND OF PERSON WAS THIS MAN I had just married? I knew he was one of the foremost explorers of his time and that unlike most men of action he was also a man of thought who had made his mark as a scientist, geographer, writer, bibliographer, and lecturer. When I first went to work for him, however, I knew little about his actual work and accomplishments. I began to read systematically through his books and daily learned how many and how wide his interests were.

Vilhjalmur Stefansson was born in 1879 of Icelandic parents in a Manitoba town called Arnes, which no longer exists. His father and mother had fled the disaster and poverty that overtook Iceland toward the end of the nineteenth century following a series of volcanic eruptions. Disaster followed the Icelandic immigrants with the flooding of the shores of Lake Winnipeg when Stef was two. Once more his parents fled, moving south into what was then the Territory of Dakota (later divided into the states of North and South Dakota). Two of his siblings died of malnutrition. Stef grew up miles from his nearest neighbor in a log cabin with a sod floor in an atmosphere of plain living and high thinking, speaking only Icelandic.

He had been taught to read and write in Icelandic (or Old Norse) when he was about five years old by an itinerant tutor who moved from one frontier Dakota homestead to the next, staying long enough to teach the children to read. He practiced reading from the family Bible, standing with the book open on the table before him. Before he was six, he had read the entire Bible to his mother as she went about her household chores, correcting him and explaining what the words meant.

Stef once estimated that his entire early formal schooling amounted to eleven months spread out over a period of five years. He would walk eight miles to school in one direction from his frontier cabin home, and when that short term ended he would walk six miles in another direction to add two more weeks to his schooling. It was in those remote rural schoolhouses that he learned English.

In 1898, when he was nineteen, he boarded a railway train for the first time in his life to study at the University of North Dakota at Grand Forks. His educational goals were only vaguely formed, but he did have the notion of studying poetry, not surprising for a young man brought up in the tradition of the Icelandic sagas. Somewhere along the way, however, he decided to change his major, after reading in *Scribner's* magazine a poem by William Vaughan Moody called "Gloucester Moors." He concluded that it was alright for someone who was dead to write a poem he could not equal, but when a living poet, about his own age did, he had better look for a different career. Thus he shifted his dreams of glory from poetry to anthropology.

Another important milestone occurred in Stef's junior year at the university when he heard one of his professors remark that it was a pity that so many immigrants Anglicized or Frenchified their names and thereby lost evidence of their heritage. That struck close to home and caused Stef to decide to change the "imitation Canadian-Scottish name," William Stephenson, he had had since birth and "formally resurrect" his Icelandic name. His family had always called him Vilhjalmur, or Villie; his classmates, Bill. From this point, he was known as Stef.

It was also about this time that he was expelled from the university. The official reason was that he had been absent for three weeks without sufficient excuse. (He had taken the place of a Grand Forks high school principal who had taken suddenly ill and received his salary, an unexpected boon to a poor student.) The real reason for the expulsion, however, was that the students were getting out of hand and Stef was thought to be behind the worst of their obstreperous mischief.

In those days expulsion deprived a student of all credits, and the universities maintained an effective blacklisting system. A North Dakota lawyer Stef consulted advised him to enter another university as a freshman with permission to take immediate examinations for advanced standing, in order to bypass the blacklist. Stef looked into universities that would be amenable and that would ask no probing questions about how he had acquired his knowledge. Of the six he considered, the University of Iowa was the nearest and relatively inexpensive, and it offered more courses that he thought he could pass easily. Iowa assured him that if he passed with a grade of C or better he would have permission to take the next-higher examination. Entering in the fall of 1902 as a freshman, he was a sophomore by Thanksgiving. He got his degree the following June, three days before his former classmates graduated from North Dakota. Two days later he was a student at Harvard Summer School.

STEF arrived in Harvard Yard hoping to acquire a graduate fellowship in anthropology. He was unsuccessful but was offered one in the divinity school instead. He accepted on condition that he might study comparative religions as a branch of folklore. After a profitable year studying with Harvard greats like Ephraim Emerton, George Foot Moore, and William Wallace Fenn, he was awarded the Phoebe Hearst Fellowship in anthropology and transferred from Divinity Avenue to the Peabody Museum.

In 1905, under the auspices of the museum, Stef made his first expedition to his ancestral homeland of Iceland, with a dozen fellow Harvard men. He and Jack Hastings, a young man of means, formed the anthropological section of the expedition and excavated an eleventh-century graveyard that was being eroded by the sea. They were particularly struck by the discovery that none of the eighty-six skulls they measured had any tooth decay. Noting that the diet of those early Icelanders contained no sugar or carbohydrates, Stef developed a lifelong interest in the relationship between diet and tooth decay.

Later that year, Stef became a teaching fellow and the department of anthropology's authority on the polar regions. In April of 1906 he was preparing to go to Africa when a telegram arrived offering to pay his round trip expenses to Chicago to discuss taking a job with a polar expedition. Ernest de Koven Leffingwell, a geologist with a year's Arctic field experience, offered him the job of ethnologist on the Anglo-American Polar Expedition. Professor Frederick Ward Putnam, head of the Peabody Museum, advised Stef to take the job but to go overland and meet the expedition ship at Herschel Island in northwest Canada, since he could do little ethnology aboard ship.

With the backing of two universities, Harvard and Toronto, Stef left Cambridge for the Mackenzie River Delta. Arriving at Herschel Island, he found six whaling ships in the harbor but no sign of his expedition ship, the *Duchess of Bedford*. While he waited, Stef struck up an acquaintance with Roald Amundsen, whose sloop, *Gjoa*, had just completed the first Northwest Passage by sea. Stef took advantage of Amundsen's hospitality and conversation to learn everything he could from the experienced explorer. When Amundsen left and the last of the whalers departed, the island was cut off from the rest of the world until the following year. Through necessity Stef now became the guest of the hospitable local Inuit and began his decades-long study of their language and ways. They taught him how to dress and hunt and live off the land. He later learned that the *Duchess of Bedford* had been caught in the ice, sprung a leak, and eventually sunk. No one aboard had died, but the event put a temporary end to Stefansson's plan of visiting Victoria Island, where it was rumored that Inuit who resembled white men lived.

STEFF returned to New York and immediately began planning his next expedition. He received a letter from an Iowa classmate, Rudolph Martin Anderson, who had heard of Stef's plans and wanted to go with him. Anderson was Phi Beta Kappa, an all-American athlete with a Ph.D. in ornithology; he was knowledgeable about geology and botany as well. With the backing of New York's American Museum of Natural History and the Canadian Geological Survey, the two men met in Toronto and started north in May 1908, following the route Stef had taken two years earlier.

Anderson was to concentrate on the collection of birds and mammals, but the chief object of the expedition was anthropological: Stef was to seek out the Inuit peoples he had heard were living in the Coronation Gulf/Victoria Island-area of the Canadian Arctic, a culture still unknown to social scientists. Having learned the previous year from the Herschel Island Inuit how to survive and travel comfortably in the Far North, he was eager to experiment with making the expedition self-sufficient. Under Inuit tutelage, Stef had become an excellent Arctic hunter, and that experience influenced his whole philosophy of how exploration should be conducted. If one could live off the land, that would preclude the need for a base camp, which meant that one could travel extensively and for long periods. He knew the Arctic always provided caribou, seals, bears, or salmon, if you knew how to find them and hunt effectively. By providing a diet of fresh meat, a hunter could avoid getting scurvy, the vitamin C deficiency that was the bane of polar exploration.

Early in the four-year expedition, Stef found the Inuit for whom he was searching. As he later wrote, "Here were not remains of the Stone Age, but the Stone Age itself, men and women, very human, entirely friendly, who welcomed us to their home and bade me stay." Unlike the Inuit that were already familiar to anthropologists and explorers, some of these men had beards, some of which were blond and others even red. Stef named these people the Copper Eskimos after their use of native copper for implements. In his speculation about the origin of these European-looking people, he considered the possibility that the Inuit may have intermarried with the Scandinavian Greenlanders who had disappeared from Greenland in the fifteenth or sixteenth century, when the Black Plague cut off their European communication. Another possibility was that some of the members of Sir John Franklin's lost expedition of 1847, which had set out in search of a Northwest Passage might have survived and intermarried with Inuit.

In late August 1912, coming south from Nome at the close of the four-year expedition, Stef was met by a well-known reporter named John J. Underwood, who covered Alaskan matters for the *Seattle Daily Times*. On September 9, 1912, he picked up a copy of that newspaper to find himself famous, or rather notorious. The headline read, "American Explorer Discovers Lost Tribe of White Descendents of Lief Eriksson," and Underwood's story went as follows:

> Ranking next in importance from an ethnological standpoint to the discovery of the lost tribes of Israel is the discovery made by Prof. Vilhjalmur Stefansson of the American Museum of Natural History of a lost tribe of 1,000 white people, who are believed to be direct descendants of the followers of Leif Eriksson who came to Greenland from Iceland about the year 1000 and a few years later discovered the north coast of America. . . .
>
> The tribe of white people, which Stefansson declares are purely of Norwegian origin, never had seen other persons of their own color. Their number is about 1,000, and more than half of them have rusty-red hair, blue eyes, fair skin and two-colored eyebrows and beards. They live on both shores of Coronation Gulf, on the mainland of North America and Victoria Island, which formerly was known as Prince Edward Island.
>
> It was for these people that Roald Amundsen, discoverer of the South Pole, searched while making his celebrated trip through the Northwest Passage. Amundsen, it will be remembered, stated

that natives had told him of a race of white people living to the northward, but he was unable to find them. Amundsen sent an expedition along the shore of the island, but saw nothing of the tribe, nor did they see anything of him. . . .

Professor Stefansson accounts for their existence by the fact that in the year 982, Greenland was discovered and settled by 5,000 Icelandic Norsemen. One thousand of these people sailed from Norway and missed Greenland but landed on the coast of Newfoundland, where they established a colony, built fourteen churches, two monasteries, a nunnery and other structures, the ruins of which are still in existence. . . .

The Norsemen settled in two colonies, one on the north and one on the south side of Newfoundland. In the fourteenth century Eskimos came from the North and exterminated the people at the northern settlement.

Their record was complete till 1418, when the black plague scourged Europe, and for two centuries communication between Newfoundland and the old country was cut off. When communication was restored, the people of the second settlement were missing. Their graveyards, buildings and other adjuncts of their semicivilization were found, and the theory was formed that the people had drifted to a settlement further to the west, across the narrow straits that divided them from the Arctic archipelago, where they intermingled with Eskimos, whom they took along with them to the islands on which their descendants now live. . . .

The story was a hodgepodge of facts, half-truths, non-malicious fiction, and sheer nonsense. What Stef said to acquaintances aboard ship on the way to Seattle and to Underwood on shore was merely that he had found Inuit in and around Victoria Island, some of whom were quite unlike other Inuit in physiognomy and coloring, most of whom had never seen a white man or a rifle, and all of whom used Stone Age implements.

As an Icelander Stef knew from the sagas that in Labrador and Greenland from the eleventh to the fourteen centuries Scandinavians mixed with Inuit. Travelers as early as Nicholas Tunes in 1685 and as late as John Franklin in 1824 had reported the same blond traits among Inuit they had seen. Stef believed that while there was no reason to believe that the Inuit on Victoria Island were descended from Scandinavian colonists in Greenland, there was no reason historically or geographically to assume they were not.

Underwood's story caused a raging storm of telephone calls, telegrams, and letters from thousands of members of the American Museum of Natural History. The story was cabled around the world. Charlatan, liar, publicity seeker, and worse were some of the names Stef had to endure, along with the ridicule. Although he never used the words, the *New York Times* headlined their interview, "The Blond Eskimos." The media latched on to the novel term, which was repeated over and over again. Finally, the *New York Sun* offered him a fee if he would give them an exclusive story of any desired length, which they would syndicate to all their affiliates and make available elsewhere. After the *Sun* agreed to interview the American Museum and his other backers and to print their responses, Stef signed up. His story was printed exactly as written, occupying a full page, including maps supplied by the museum (September 15, 1912). It was his first opportunity to tell his side of the story in depth. He had hoped it would end the controversy, which was still continuing in 1961, the year before his death. Unresolved after forty-nine years of debate, it doubtless will continue as long as history books about arctic exploration are written. The damage that a single reporter with an inaccurate story can do is even more familiar today, when the media makes and breaks reputations regularly.

WHILE distressed by the suggestion that he might have fabricated his account, Stef was able to use the attendant publicity and his newfound celebrity to find sponsors for his next, even more ambitious expedition. His last Arctic expedition, from 1913 to 1918, was to be financed by the National Geographic Society, the American Museum of Natural History, and the Harvard Travelers Club. In seeking further funds to enable the expedition to purchase a ship, Stef approached the Prime Minister of Canada, Sir Robert Borden. Borden consulted his cabinet, and they decided that it was beneath the dignity of Canada to go into partnership with others to back the expedition and proposed that Canada finance the undertaking entirely. Thus the Canadian Arctic Expedition was born.

The plan for the expedition called for two divisions, a northern and a southern party. Stef was overall commander of both divisions and in charge of the northern division that was to explore the ice north of Alaska to search for new lands. Under Stef, Rudolph Anderson, his partner from the 1908 expedition, was in charge of the southern section and would do anthropological, archeological, geological, and zoological research in the vicinity of Coronation Gulf. Anderson had found fault with Stef's "living off the country" method of exploration and had been a source of worry to Stef and the Canadian government officials in charge of supplying the expedition because he opposed and contradicted Stef's orders. He had recently married, and his new wife was said to feel that he was being cheated of the recognition he deserved, with Stefansson getting all the publicity. Though he was urged to get rid of Anderson before the expedition left for the north, Stef, who always found it difficult to believe ill of his colleagues, thought matters would smooth themselves out in the field.

Then a tragedy befell the expedition. The *Karluk*, the largest of the three ships serving the expedition, was caught fast in the pack ice slowly drifting eastward, and Stef realized it would not be freed until spring. He also knew that the party would now need more food. True to his ideal of living off the country, he decided to go ashore with a small hunting party. Soon after leaving the ship, the party encountered one of the worst Arctic storms Stef had ever met. When it subsided, the *Karluk*'s masts, visible before, had disappeared. Supplies, scientific instruments, all of Stef's diaries and papers, and many of his best men were aboard, all carried off by storm, winds, and current. Devastated by the shock and loss, Stef notified Ottawa of the situation and courageously made plans to go on to the McKenzie Delta to get the southern section of the expedition going and then continue his own planned northward journey over the ice of Beaufort Sea.

When Stef reached Anderson and told him of his plans to continue despite the loss of the *Karluk*, Anderson said that with the loss of the ship, Stef was now a leader "without anything to lead" and had no right to any supplies or equipment from the southern party. Nor did he believe that Stef had any authority over him. Optimistic, Stef, still believing the personal difficulties could be overcome, issued orders to the southern men. Anderson acknowledged receipt of the orders but decided not to obey them. This was mutiny.

Despite the loss of the *Karluk* and Anderson's refusal to turn over the supplies he needed, Stef carried out his original plan to go farther north than any ship had ever penetrated and to live by hunting. The final exploration party consisted of six dogs, one sled, and three new recruits, all Scandinavians: Ole Andreason, Storker Storkerson, and Stef. The party set off northward across the ice in March 1914. They found the polar sea was not lifeless as predicted.

The party was equipped with two rifles, 305 rounds of ammunition, and a machine to take soundings to determine the edge of the Continental Shelf and the approach of new land. Demonstrating the validity of his method of Arctic travel, he and his men reached Banks Island, where they wintered, meeting up with the northern expedition's auxiliary schooner, the *Mary Sachs*. Because Stef had been presumed dead, none of his requests for sounding wire and other equipment had been met. The captain and crew were surprised to see him alive. The expedition broke important new ground. In his discovery of four hitherto unknown islands—Borden, Brock, Lougheed, and Meighen—Stef added 100,000 square miles of new territory to the known world. He mapped the unknown sections of Banks and Prince Patrick Islands. He proved explorers could make long journeys in the Arctic unencumbered by a base camp or a mass of supplies. And he had collected a good deal of valuable ethnological information about the Inuit.

Anderson did creditable work leading the southern section of the expedition, but his hostility toward Stef deepened rather than diminished with time. In talk and print he attacked Stef and called him a charlatan. He described Stef's best-selling book about the expedition, *The Friendly Arctic*, as "a species of Arctic fiction couched in excellent literary style" and spent the rest of his life trying without success to undermine Stef's credibility. In my view he used much of his energies in anger and hatred instead of in productive work.

Having acquired new territory for their investment, the Canadian government was satisfied with the results of the Canadian Arctic Expedition. Several geographical societies of the world agreed by conferring their gold medals on Stef. He went on to write twenty-seven books and hundreds of articles, collected the best polar library of his time, and became the country's greatest authority on the polar regions, earning medals, honorary degrees, and other honors.

CHAPTER X

A Man of Many Talents

*A*MONG THE TRADITIONS carried from their ancient home by Icelanders is a passion for literary things. Every evening when the chores were done, someone would read or tell a story. Most Icelanders knew huge sections of the sagas by heart, and poetry played an important role in Icelandic life. One popular parlor game involved each person improvising a four-line poem, something like a limerick, called a *rimur*. If you couldn't improvise one on the spot, you might recite an old one. Long before he understood its meanings, Stef's ear was tuned to the cadences of poetry.

Like many Icelanders, Stef wanted to be a poet. As a young man, he knew what seemed to me thousands of poems and had written many himself. The experience of reading Moody's "Gloucester Moors" thoroughly discouraged him, however, and he destroyed the poems he had written. But he never lost his taste and his ear for a good poem, as well as for amusing doggerel. He once wrote that "the explorer is the poet of deeds," finding in his chosen profession a way to express his love for the art of poetry.

Stef had taken an India paper edition of Richard Harris Barham's *The Ingoldsby Legends* to the Arctic.* He read them so often that he knew

---

* Indian paper editions were printed on almost tissue-thin paper and were much lighter and smaller than ordinary volumes.

many of the verses he loved by heart. At appropriate moments he would happily recite them, including this one, my favorite:

> The Lady Jane was tall and slim, the Lady Jane was fair,
> Sir Thomas her Lord was stout of limb, his breath was short and
>   his eye was dim,
> And she was uncommonly fond of him and they were a loving
>   pair.

One of my prized possessions is the copy of that book he gave me before we were married.

His friend Margaret Culkin Banning, a popular novelist and short story writer of the 1920s and 30s, gave him a short poem that appealed to his political sympathies and employed his favorite form of humor, irony:

> The golf links are so near the mill
> that almost every day
> The working children can look out
> and see the men at play.

Another poet friend, Ridgely Torrance, who also lived on Morton Street, was a tall, handsome, white-haired, elderly gentleman with almost transparent skin and a diffident manner. He told Stef that once when he was very ill, indeed delirious, he had a revelation that he had at last composed the greatest poem that had ever been written. Desperately, he thought to himself, "I *must* remember this." Using every ounce of strength left in his fevered body, he repeated the poem over and over again until he had memorized it. Recovered from his illness, he was miraculously able to recall the treasured lines:

> It's white to be snow
> And its cold to be ice

It's windy to blow
And it's nice to be nice.

One of the verses that Stef used to delight audiences with was by a newspaper columnist named B.L.T. (Bert Lester Townsend). He recited it so often that I too learned it by heart:

Behold the mighty dinosaur
Famous in prehistoric lore
Not only for its weight and length
But for its intellectual strength.
As you perceive by these remains
The creature had two sets of brains.
One in his head, the usual place
The other at his spinal base.
Thus he could reason a priori as well as a posteriori.
No problem bothered him a bit
He made both head and tail of it
And if in error he was caught
He had a saving afterthought.
And could think without congestion
Upon both sides of every question.
Oh, gaze upon this model beast
Defunct, ten million years at least!

Once, in Chicago, with me in the audience, Stef was addressing a convention of about two-thousand food editors. He took as his subject the primitive food tastes of the Inuit. He told them that in an all-meat diet, which he had shared for many years with the Inuit, the fat and bone marrow are particularly delicious and necessary for good health in the absence of carbohydrates and vegetables. The fat behind the eyes of an animal, he said, is considered the most delectable. Even in those days, before cholesterol had become a household word, this

was a little much for the food editors. Stef, always attuned to his audience, began to bolster his argument by telling of Elizabethan times,
when meat was a most valued luxury food and the fat in particular was
highly prized. Suddenly, I heard him call down to me from his platform, without warning, "Evelyn, sing the 'Boar's Head Carol' for
them." Never having sung the carol *a capella* and terrified I would forget
the words, I was faced with the unseemly choice of arguing in public
with my husband or singing the song. I chose the latter, emphasizing
what Stef wanted them to hear.

> The boar's head in hand bear I,
> Bedecked with bays and rosemary;
> And I pray you, my masters, be merry,
> > Quot estis in convivio: [So many are in the feast:]
> > Caput apri defero,
> > Reddens laudes Domino. [The boar's head
> > I bring, giving praise to God.]
> The boar's head, as I understand,
> Is the rarest dish in all the land
> When thus bedecked with a gay garland,
> > Let us servire cantico: [Let us serve with a song:]
> > Caput apri defero,
> > Reddens laudes Domino.
> Our steward hath provided this
> In honor of the King of bliss
>
> Which on this day to be served is,
> > In Reginensi atrio: [In the Queen's hall:]
> > Caput apri defero,
> > Reddens laudes Domino.

We both loved the Boar's Head Carol, but for different reasons—
I, because it was very old and had a macaronic text (that is, part

Latin and part English), and Stef, because it praised the *head* of the animal.

S TEF carried on an enormous correspondence with people all over the world. If he had a question or a problem to solve, he would write a letter, make ten carbon copies, and send a copy to anyone in the appropriate field who might know the answer. He had the mind of an archivist and was always writing memos and notes; he saved every scrap of paper that had writing on it. He carried his money in a white business-size envelope and used the outside of the envelope for making notes. A friend, the literary agent Elizabeth Marbury, noticing this, sent him a Mark Cross wallet one Christmas. He put it in a bureau drawer and went back to using his envelopes. She noticed the white envelope again and, forgetting that she had already done so, sent him another wallet the next Christmas. This went on for years. The bureau drawer was full of wallets when I married Stef, but he was still using his envelope, which he would replace with a fresh one only when his notes had covered it. He never would discard his notes!

He had a belief that the world harbored too many false ideas and advocated the establishment of a University of Unlearning where one could learn to discard error and unlearn things that weren't true. His charming book, *The Standardization of Error*, has an ironic and witty meditation on this theme. This small book had nothing to do with exploration and was therefore unlike anything else he had written.

Here is a taste of it:

Having studied the bird of Africa, let us turn next to the ostrich of literature, philosophy, and morals. Instead of the confusion in the case of the ostrich of zoology we have clarity and precision. This is because the ostrich of literature exists by definition only. He is a bird that hides his head when frightened. You may too precipitately object that men would not accept universally this definition of the ostrich of literature if it did not fit also the zoological ostrich. The answer is that the definition has never received any support from zoologists, hunters, or owners of the domesticated birds, and yet it has been accepted universally throughout Europe since Pliny's time (about 50 B.C.). It has survived all attacks from science and from the bigoted common sense of those who did not recognize its true nature. Like the definition of a four-sided square or a good Christian, it has survived because it is useful. Can you imagine any real attribute more instructive than the head-burying of the ostrich-by-definition? As a text for moralists, as an epithet that politicians use for their opponents, as a figure of speech generally, what could serve as well? Our literature is richer, our vocabulary more picturesque through this beneficent bird of hypothesis. He has many inherent advantages that no real bird could have. Since his habits are defined we need not waste time studying him first hand, nor in trying to adjudicate at second hand between books about him that disagree. Since he never existed as a beast, he is in no danger of the extinction that is said to threaten the lion and swan. . . . The ostrich by definition is, therefore, not only less trouble to deal with than a real bird; he is actually more useful and instructive than any real bird or beast. When we consider how often he has been used in sermon and precept we must admit that this model creature has contributed substantially, not only to the entertainment and instruction of nations, but also to the morality and general goodness of the world.

IN addition to his literary and scholarly interests and abilities, Stef was a gifted speaker. In the 1920s he visited Australia on a lecture tour, at the invitation of the government. While speaking at Melbourne's largest auditorium, he noticed an imposing woman in the front row who seemed to be in agreement with everything he was saying, nodding her head in approval at appropriate intervals. To his delight, after the lecture someone brought her backstage and introduced her. It was Dame

Nellie Melba, the world-famous opera singer. She greeted him enthusiastically, saying, "I know something about you, young man. You had a
wonderful voice teacher—your voice is *perfectly* placed." With disappointment Stef realized it was not his ideas she approved of but only his
voice placement. No doubt he had learned over many years of lecturing,
through trial and error, how to "place" his voice, but he had certainly
never had a voice teacher in his life.

Stef had been an accomplished debater from college days and was
an experienced speaker. On the old Chautauqua circuits and later with
the agent Colston Leigh arranging his lectures, he sometimes spent
half the year on the lecture circuit. In the days before television this
was a big business. He was gifted as a speaker, never used notes, and
seldom knew what he was going to say until he started, often taking as
a subject something that had been in the daily newspaper to begin.

Stef liked to start his platform talk with a provocative statement
that would galvanize his audience's attention. One such opening line
was "An adventure is a sign of incompetence." He would then elaborate that a good expedition leader should be able to anticipate everything that might go wrong and prepare for it. An "adventure" was
something for which one was unprepared and which should not happen on a well-organized expedition.

I once heard him give a talk to about five hundred spellbound children at the University of Chicago's Laboratory Schools about how the
Inuits hunt seals in wintertime through the ice. For twenty minutes
he described in minute and precise detail the tension of the hunt,
how once caught the line of the seal was wrapped around the hunter's
waist, how the breathing hole was enlarged with a snow knife, how
the seal was drawn up and out of the water, and how, finally, the animal landed on the ice, at which point the children gave a roar of
approval as great as football fans make upon the winning touchdown.

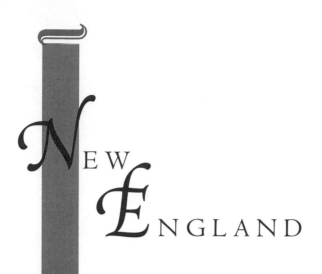

NEW ENGLAND

CHAPTER XI

Dearing Farm

*I*N 1940, WHEN STEF AND I DECIDED TO MARRY, he told me he had once had heatstroke and needed to avoid the hot New York summers. Olive Wilcox, his longtime assistant, and her husband Jack had found a summer home in Gaysville, Vermont, and Stef suggested that I go farm hunting in that area. At the time I was making an index for his current book, *Ultima Thule.* So I took the galleys and a portable typewriter to an inn in Bethel, Vermont, and sandwiched looking at farms between typing.

Surprisingly, I soon found a charming old farmhouse with attached barns six miles west of Bethel, at the head of Camp Brook, on the divide between two branches of the White River. It had a wonderful, forty-foot-long covered porch facing a wooded mountain that turned glorious colors in the autumn. The property's 210 acres included 40 acres of wildflower meadow surrounding the hilltop house, a beautiful sugar bush of ancient towering maple trees, and deep woods. Two brothers, Benny and Edgar Dearing, had owned the farm and used it to raise hops for beer making. They left behind a mountain of patent medicine bottles and various kinds of tonics, all of them containing alcohol, in the hop house. (The brothers were, of course, teetotalers.)

During our first summer on the farm we camped out while deciding what we would need to do to make the place habitable. It was apparent that we would need help to make the kind of summer home we had in mind, and Stef remembered Karsten Anderson, or Charlie, as everybody called him. A Dane who had been on Stef's third Arctic expedition, Charlie was now an orange-grove farmer in Florida. He had also been the "control" in a year-long all-meat diet experiment that Stef had orchestrated and also participated in to prove to a group of "Who's Who" skeptical doctors that a person could be perfectly healthy on such a diet, as the Inuit were.* Stef and Charlie had gotten along so well together both in the Arctic and during the nutrition study that Stef thought he would be ideal to help with the work at Dearing Farm. Charlie agreed to stay and work with us during the summer, the orange grove's off-season.

His face was tanned to mahogany and lined by Arctic winds and Florida suns. Energetic and cheerful, he loved to reminisce about the old days in the Arctic and had a rich hoard of adventure stories. He would punctuate each new scene he described with a sucking noise he made with his very white, loose upper denture. A jack-of-all-trades—gardener, carpenter, painter—he did whatever was needed. He cleared out an ancient overgrown garden, revealing a beautiful old stone wall, with hosts of surviving peonies and other perennials, yellow and red raspberry bushes, and current bushes. He planted a vegetable garden that provided lettuce, radishes, carrots, beets, and corn—oh, the fresh corn! He planted a Concord grapevine to augment the plentiful wild grapes and mountain ash trees to shade the huge lawn, and he made a wildflower garden for me at the north side of the house.

We hired a Finnish woman from the village to paint and paper, and

---

* In 1928 Stef and Charlie had entered the Dietetic Ward of Bellevue Hospital to give "modern science" a chance to observe human subjects for twelve months on an all-meat diet. Under the direction of Dr. Clarence W. Lieb, the committee included Dr. Raymond Pearl of Johns Hopkins University as chairman, Dr. Clark Wissler of the American Museum of Natural History, physical anthropologist Ernest A. Hooton of Harvard, Dr. Eugene F. DuBois and Graham Lusk of the Russell Sage Institute of Pathology, and other notables. The two men were subjected to every imaginable physiological test. In the first months of the experiment everything they ate was measured and weighed, as were their excretions.

Stef did a great deal of lecturing at that time and was on his honor to observe the rules of the study: no carbohydrates or vegetables, just meat and water. Charlie stayed at Bellevue throughout the year. The medical savants thought the men would get scurvy and die from various predictable diseases, but Stef was as usual vindicated. Both were healthier at the end of the year than they had been at the beginning. Dozens of articles in medical journals were written by the doctors overseeing the study, and many textbooks had to be revised as a result of their findings.

we replaced the huge round sitting-room stove with a Vermont-made soapstone Franklin stove, whose doors could open. Wonderfully efficient (the soapstone could hold and radiate heat long after the fire was out), it became our little fireplace. The farm had an ancient Delco system of batteries that provided a pale electric light in the single bulb fixtures in each room. By the time it stopped working, there were rumors that rural electrification was on the way. Until then, we used kerosene lamps, which provided a soft and lovely light. The Delco system was never strong enough to supply current for machines, so we had a huge, modern-looking refrigerator that used kerosene for fuel in the summer kitchen.

The huge farm kitchen had windows on two opposite sides, each looking out at a superb view, one close-up and the other far away. Having been used to gas stoves with their immediate heat, I had to learn to utilize the lower steady heat of the ancient wood-burning stove and how to feed the fire to broil and bake. There was almost always some soup simmering on the stove or beans baking in the oven, providing welcome heat on cool fall nights. (In the hottest weather, we used a kerosene stove.) The stove also had a tank that provided hot water. Our spring was piped directly into an open-topped, tin-lined copper tank in the kitchen, from which we could ladle delicious, ice-cold, fresh, sweet water. Before we had a refrigerator, the tank also served to keep submerged butter and milk fresh and cold.

We simplified the household chores to a minimum. Everybody made his own bed. We ate at the walnut kitchen table, which had a linseed oil finish that could be wiped clean with a damp cloth. We used paper napkins. Everyone wore blue jeans. I made stews that lasted for many meals (taking care to refrigerate them, remembering my office lunch disaster). I used every housekeeping shortcut I could think of, such as making a concentrated tea essence from a pound of leaves, draining them off, and then using the concentrate to make tea with just the addition of hot water, which meant cleaning the pot once a week instead of at each meal. Occasionally I would find a local high school girl to help with the cleaning and washing up. After electricity arrived, we installed a dishwasher and an electric stove in the summer kitchen, though we kept the old wood stove for warmth. Stef was not mechanically minded, so I became the electrician, plumber, and fixer when things stopped working. Since we were six miles from Bethel, our nearest town, I always tried to fix what went wrong because it was expensive to have a plumber come all the way out to us.

Neither Stef nor I could drive, so I went to school and learned. Afterwards, we bought a Ford and every late spring loaded it to the limit with books, papers, and various necessities. When Stef was lecturing at Harvard, we would go to S. S. Pierce, the Boston-based gourmet food company, and order cases of fancy foods, scrapple, and canned tree-ripened peaches for the farm. We spent every summer there, arriving in June or July and staying longer and longer each year, once as late as November. Dearing Farm eventually became known as the Stefansson place.

We both loved the farm. The simplicity of country life suited us. Stef appreciated the cool summer days (in the spring he would say, "there is a threat of summer in the air") and the even cooler nights. Once the area was electrified, we installed in the main farmhouse a huge attic fan, which we used to swoop up the cool night air so we could close the windows during the day if it was hot; through this method we were able to keep the farmhouse comfortable during even the hottest August days. Having been a city child, I was enchanted with being a farm wife. I loved the color and smell of new-mown hay and picking fruit from both the ancient apple trees and our newly planted trees. In the fields we found wild onions and strawberries, and I would gather up armfuls of Queen Anne's Lace, goldenrod, and other wild flowers to make stunning bouquets. I went to country auctions and purchased white ironstone china for the table and old red tablecloths to use for parties.

But we both also worked at writing and often had one or more secretaries living with us. We made a study for Stef out of the old horse barn by cutting a large picture window in the outer wall. When lined with floor-to-ceiling shelves the horse stalls made excellent library bays. Duplicates from the Morton Street library soon filled the shelves, as did exploration classics and works by our favorite authors. We shipped up bulky runs of old periodicals like the *Atlantic Monthly*, *Scribner's*, *Century*, and *Harper's*, making welcome room for the nonstop flow of new books arriving at Morton Street. With the addition of dictionaries, encyclopedias, and other reference works, we had a working library, allowing Stef to continue his writing in an informal and comfortable setting.*

As we spent more and more time in Vermont, we began to involve ourselves in local affairs. Stef would talk to the Rotary Club; I gave talks on Alaska and the Artic at the high school and began to sing in the Congregational choir, which consisted mostly of high school girls who were shy about singing out on the first notes of the hymns or anthems. It was my main function to attack the first notes, after which they would join in. Like a Judas goat, I thought. Little did they know I was born a Jew, baptized an Episcopalian, and living as an agnostic!

We made friends with the Town Clerk, Robert Bundy, a charming Vermonter badly crippled by arthritis, and his wife Grace, who was a lawyer and became ours. The Bundys were knowledgeable about every aspect of local life and were willing to share their knowledge with us, whether it concerned where to purchase a soapstone stove, the significance of town elections, or the best Vermont newspapers, carpenters, painters, and plumbers. They educated us and were generous with their time. We were eager to learn everything we could about the local mores from them, and they found us interesting.

Marshall and Gladys Dimock summered in Bethel and eventually lived there year-round, when he retired from his history professorship

---

* In addition to our horse-barn library, Dartmouth College's Baker Library was less than an hour's drive away, and once we had electricity we could get the Canadian news broadcasts and excellent BBC programs on our radio. Stef was a news nut, and of course during the war we listened to the news, good and bad, religiously.

at the University of Chicago. Gladys came from a large local family. They provided intellectual nourishment, and since they had been summering in Vermont for some years we were able to benefit from their experience, too.

Dorothy Thompson, the foreign correspondent, journalist, writer, and radio personality, summered at Twin Farms in Barnard, Vermont, about eight miles from us, and became a central figure in our social life. Dorothy wrote for the *New York Herald-Tribune* a thrice-weekly column, "On the Record," that began in 1936 and continued for twenty-two years. She was said to have between 8 and 10 million readers and next to Eleanor Roosevelt to be the most influential woman in the United States. She also wrote a monthly article for the *Ladies Home Journal* and was a magnificent public speaker, often speaking on the radio. She surrounded herself with a group of brainy people—political, academic, and artistic, most of them celebrities.*

With the impending and then the actual war, as our troops moved into Alaska, the polar regions were much-discussed in the news. The tapping of oil resources in the Arctic, the building of the Alaska Highway, the war with Japan in the Aleutian Islands, aviation problems in the North—were all subjects about which Stef's opinions were solicited. Dorothy discovered us, and we soon fell into her lively circle and were invited for dinners, discussions, and parties.

Blond, blue-eyed, once beautiful, and still good looking, albeit *zoftig*, she usually dominated any social occasion at her home†; she

---

* Dorothy's fame began in 1934 when, on the personal order of Hitler, she was expelled from Berlin. Overnight she became a heroine and celebrity. Thirteen years earlier, she had arrived in Vienna as a young journalist with a good knowledge of German, which she perfected, and began interviewing famous people for the *Philadelphia Public Ledger*. After her expulsion, she became the leading foreign correspondent on Eastern European affairs, especially those relating to Germany and Austria. The *Saturday Evening Post* would send her on special assignments, NBC signed her up for a series of radio broadcasts, and throughout the war she broadcast often. She was entertaining as well as informative.

† Dorothy's stormy marriage with Sinclair Lewis was over by the time we met. Their young son Michael summered with Dorothy in Vermont. Neglected by both his famous parents, he was, not surprisingly, a difficult child. His father ignored him, and his mother alternately turned him over to servants or smothered him with love and instructions. One summer I remember she insisted on teaching him Latin, which he really didn't care to know. Michael was expelled from many schools and finally went to the Royal Academy of Dramatic Arts in London, where he learned to become a pretty good actor.

permitted a certain number of questions and exchanges at the beginning of the evening, but by the end, having consumed considerable alcohol, she was a one-woman show. She would pick Stef's brain on some subject on which he was an authority, and later in the week we would read what he had told her in her column, although she seldom acknowledged her source. Stef never cared—he had more than enough fame for his needs—but I was sometimes resentful. This lack of generosity together with her habit of ignoring the wives of her coterie of admiring male celebrities caused me to feel a mild dislike for her, mixed with genuine admiration for her brilliance and courage.

James Vincent Sheean, known to all his friends as Jimmy, had met Dorothy in Berlin in 1926, and both recognized an affinity that was to last for life. Handsome, erudite, gifted in music and languages, he and Dorothy had bonded intellectually in a kind of brother-sister relationship.

Jimmy was married to beautiful Diana, daughter of the famous English actor Sir Johnston Forbes-Robertson and niece of Maxine Elliott. They lived in the smaller of Dorothy's Twin Farms' houses, and we became friends. Diana and I would commiserate with each other about how Dorothy loved to hold forth of an evening and provoke interesting discussions but absolutely ignored the wives of the men with whom she surrounded herself. Diana suffered especially because Jimmy and Dorothy had a fierce kind of verbal love affair. Thanks to proximity, they would be invited to dinner evening after evening. Jimmy and Dorothy both loved to drink and would reminisce and talk shop, forgetting Diana was there.*

Every July 9 Dorothy had a huge birthday party, to which many famous people were invited from far away, along with locals like us.

---

* Not until the summer of 1997 did I make a discovery that clarified much of Jimmy's uneven behavior. Browsing through the biography section of Hatchards's bookstore in London, I was examining a book about Duncan Grant. In the early section, which described Grant's life before he was living with Vanessa Bell, my eye lit on Jimmy's name, and I learned that he and Duncan had been engaged in a passionate homosexual love affair. Back in the 1940s, I had known little about homosexual matters and never suspected what might have been the cause of Jimmy's aberrant behavior, his failings as a husband and father, and his heavy drinking.

On these occasions, it was not unusual to meet the likes of John Gunther, Harold Ross, Clare Booth Luce, or Jan Masaryk. Yehudi Menuhin and Nathan Milstein might be playing chamber music or her friend Ania Dorfman the piano. Whoever was in the news was there.

In 1943 Dorothy married for the third time. Maxim Kopf, a Czech refugee painter, was over six feet tall, handsome, and lusty. He spoke "seven languages badly," was full of good humor, and had a naturalness that was engaging. Maxim wanted to paint a portrait of Stef, so we visited for an extended weekend and had a chance to see Dorothy in her non-public mode — relaxed, feminine, and not determined to be the oracle.

We also had visitors from time to time. We gave jolly parties on the long covered porch when our friends Max and Joan Dunbar came for a weekend. Max was a distinguished professor of marine biology at McGill University in Montreal and had done most of his field work in the Arctic. He had a most beautiful tenor voice, played the guitar, and knew a thousand songs, including innumerable Scottish border ballads. We exchanged folk songs. When the Dunbars visited, Dorothy Thompson and Maxim would come over from Barnard, Douglas Burden (a fellow Explorers Club member who had made expeditions to southeast Asia) from Charlotte, and John Teal (who under Stef's direction was domesticating Arctic musk oxen) from Huntington Center. Olive Wilcox and her husband were just a few miles away in Gaysville.

Our farm was an oasis of renewal, serenity, and simplicity—the perfect counterpoint to the hectic New York life we lived in winter. We had found a haven that met our needs and became a source of annual renewal for more than two decades.

CHAPTER XII

Becoming an Arctic Expert

*T*HE STEFANSSON LIBRARY POLAR-INFORMATION factory had a practice of interviewing polar people when they came to New York, with a shorthand secretary recording the interview, which was transcribed and integrated with our other research materials. Another source was Stef's correspondence with an extensive network of persons with special polar knowledge. One of the latter group was a young artist named Fred Machetanz. He had a trader uncle who lived in the remote northern Alaskan village of Unalakleet, and Fred often visited him for long periods. Fred had published two charming children's books about the Arctic for Charles Scribner's Sons and was planning a third about Alaska when he was called up by the navy for active service in World War II. He had produced some of the most beautiful photographs I had ever seen of Alaskan Inuit life, and he asked Stef to write a text for them.

"I'm too busy with war work," said Stef, "but Evelyn here is ready to do a book. She can do it." That was how I found myself lunching with Alice Dalgliesh, Fred's editor at Scribner's. Knowing that the name Stefansson on an Arctic book would command attention, she assured me that I *could* do a book that would fit beautifully into their World Background Series. I kept repeating, "I don't know if I can write a *book*, I've never written a *book*." I had no intellectual background, no genius for words, and I had come into my work through marriage rather than training. I had difficulty picturing myself in the company of the writers I had come to know. Of the professional women working at the library, most had advanced degrees or were working toward them. One or two—perhaps uncomfortable with my place in Stef's life—made it plain to me that anyone without at least a bachelor's degree was to be pitied.

Perhaps even more importantly, I had never *been* to Alaska! How could I dare to write a book about a place I had never seen? But Stef said I could do it, and he was no fool. I reminded myself that I was an accomplished, accurate researcher who had prepared geographical, historical, and political reports, at least in first drafts, that the finest polar library in the western hemisphere if not the world was close at hand, and that Stef was there to censor or edit anything outrageous I might write from ignorance. Finally, I protested to Alice Dalgliesh, "I don't have any writing *style*. I only know how to write simple declarative sentences." Said Alice, "*That's* a style."

So I signed the contract.

I did the necessary research in New York at our library, and that summer when we migrated to the Vermont farm I wrote and polished the text. In the fall, when Stef was leaving for his annual lecture tour, I tucked the manuscript in his luggage and said, "Remember, if it's not any good we don't have to publish it. I don't want to disgrace the name of Stefansson. Please mark it up and make any corrections as needed." He promised to read it and let me know what he thought of it. When none of his letters mentioned it, my fears were aroused. When he returned, he still didn't mention it. I thought he clearly couldn't find a kind word to say about it. Unpacking his bag, I found the manuscript, and there wasn't a mark on it. My worst fears seemed to be confirmed.

Finally I could stand it no longer. "Did you read my manuscript?" I blurted out. "Oh, yes, I did," he replied. "Well, what did you think of it?" said I. "Oh," he said, "it's so good I didn't mark it up; you can send it in as is. I have a few minor suggestions about the chapter on the

Eskimos, but we can talk about that." My heart soared a thousand feet in the air. I had written a book and Stef thought it good enough to publish. I felt as he must have when he was the first human being to set foot on a previously undiscovered island. I was so grateful to him, for he had helped and encouraged me and believed in me.

Published in 1943, *Here Is Alaska* surprised both Scribner's and me by selling so well. Our troops were moving into Alaska at the time, and there was great interest and little knowledge of what the country was like. Most of the popular books written about the Arctic were filled with halftruths and myths. The reviews stressed the accuracy of my book, which may have accounted for its being bought by Carnegie libraries throughout the country, as well as by high schools for supplementary reading. Fred Machetanz's rich black-and-white photographs were reproduced exquisitely by gravure.

Written for teenagers and uninformed adults, the book sold in the adult as well as children's sections of bookstores. It won Honorable Mention in the *Herald Tribune*'s Sunday magazine book review. It was reviewed quite widely and well and eventually sold more than 100,000 copies, running into four printings and staying in print for more than forty years.

I now found myself going on book tours arranged by Scribner's, meeting other authors, making speeches, and being interviewed and photographed for the newspapers. My past theatrical experience was helpful—I wasn't frightened being in the spotlight or making a speech. Stef seemed unsurprised but proud. I felt he had invented me as a writer.

With the royalties, I splurged on a small Mason & Hamlin upright piano (the finest made in the 1920s and '30s), half a dozen pairs of nylons, and several new Bach records, and then I was at a loss, never having had that much money of my own before. So I paid off the mortgage on our Bethel farm and put the rest into the household fund—a big mistake. Where Bil had been pathologically stingy, Stef was prodigal. If a friend was broke, Stef would think nothing of giving him the rent money to help out. He bought books freely and thought I was very bourgeois if I worried about paying bills on time. He said that in England if you paid your bills too promptly you were thought to be hard up. Stef behaved like a Rockefeller but without Mr. R.'s reserve of funds.

Alice Dalgliesh at Scribner's was naturally delighted by the success of *Alaska* and asked me to write another book. *Within the Circle* (1945), an account of six culturally diverse communities living north of the Arctic Circle, was the result, the second book I undertook without having set foot in any northern latitude. However, I was blessed by my associations and acquaintances. For example, my telling of the discovery at Point Hope, Alaska, where three young archeologists had found an amazing and huge ancient village whose artifacts looked Chinese, had credibility in part because I knew the trio of discoverers: Helge Larsen, a Danish anthropologist of the National Museum in Copenhagen, and Professors Froelich B. Rainey and Louis Giddings of the University of Alaska, the latter an expert in dendrochronology (the science of dating ancient wooden finds by their tree rings). Like most scientists working in the Arctic, they had come to the Stefansson Library before and after their startling discovery, and with their help I could write with authority about this fascinating archeological dig. I introduced each chapter with a short historical summary of the various countries, gleaned from sources as old as the Icelandic sagas, and tried to convey some of the excitement I myself had felt on discovering these strange, exotic, scenically beautiful places.

Because of wartime shortages of paper, *Within the Circle* was printed on inferior paper. Despite handsome maps by my cartographer friend Richard Edes Harrison, beautiful end papers by Margarite Burke White, another friend, and many interesting and rare photographs, it sold only moderately well, but it was my favorite.

The Alaska book was dedicated, not unnaturally, to Stef. I dedicated the second book to my sister Julie. She had decided to leave show business and join the Women's Auxiliary Air Force (the

WASPS). To qualify she had to have a private solo license and a minimum of thirty-five solo hours. She took flying lessons, learned navigation, and, despite being close to the upper age limit, made it. She became a test pilot, towed targets for army gunners, and taxied officers around the country, freeing male flyers for active duty. She was the smartest of the Schwartz sisters and tested above some of the men flyers; she accumulated 500 solo flying hours.

Julie had the kind of athletic skill that enabled her to be a fine skier almost as soon as she tried on her skis; she was also a good golfer, swimmer, and diver. She had wonderful command of her beautiful body. When she was in Earl Carroll's Vanities, she won the company's "best pair of legs" contest. In flying she felt she had found what she had been designed for. She tried to stay in the flying business after the war, but she was too far ahead of her time—no airline would hire a woman as a pilot. She married instead.

When Julie left show business to study flying, we began to see each other more often, and my respect for her grew. She wrote very good letters, which Stef also admired, and we became much closer than we had been in the early years. I was very proud of her.

Julie kept some of my letters. One, postmarked November 19, 1946, gives some notion of the new life I was leading:

King Edward Hotel, Toronto, Ontario.

Julie dear:

I'm enclosing a picture that appeared on page one of the *Toronto Star*. I'm wearing a fur parka that a photographer brought back from the Arctic for his young son and its a good thing the photo only shows my head for it fitted me like a straight jacket. I do think the picture is fine considering it is a flashlight shot and taken after a sleepless night on the Lehigh Valley R.R. which probably has the rockiest road bed in North America.

I wish you were here with me for you would enjoy the festivities, I know.

Stef and I send our warmest love to you and Stege [her husband].

> Your
> Evie

10:30 P.M. and waiting for tomorrow's papers to come out with my interviews, etc.

My brother, Myron, had an interesting time, too, during the war. He was a good skier and had enlisted in the ski troops, the army's Tenth Mountain Division. In 1943 he was training at Camp Hale, Colorado, in the heart of the Rocky Mountains, when Stef and I visited. Stef taught the officers how to build Inuit-style snow houses. On the day that we had scheduled a lunch meeting with Myron, we learned that he had been injured in a maneuver on the mountain, breaking an ankle and tearing ligaments, and was being operated on in the camp hospital. During his extensive recovery, it was discovered that he was an inventor. Before entering the army he had invented the first flash gun for the Minox camera, often called a spy camera because it was so small and easy to conceal. While still recovering from his accident, he was put to work making miniaturized equipment for our spies, who were being dropped behind enemy lines. The government had a policy of patenting inventions for the inventors in exchange for free use of the inventions during wartime. Myron took advantage of this rule, which enabled him to start his own successful business when the war was over. The army gave him a laboratory and presented him with a problem; when he had solved it, he would be brought another. Instead of being killed in Italy, as so many of his fellow ski troopers were, he spent the war in his laboratory.

Sadly, some members of my family did not fare as well during the war. In 1956, at the time of the unsuccessful Hungarian Revolution, a number of Hungarians managed to escape first to Vienna and then to the United States. My sister Rosalind's husband, Max Feller, had many government connections and was able to arrange for my cousin Vera Scheyer Lorant to come to the States. She brought terrible news. Every member of my mother's family had been deported to Auch- witz and killed by the Nazis. She was the sole survivor. Vera's father, my banker uncle Imre, was taken first, sent to prison, and then deported to Auschwitz. He left a note saying "Save my daughter, there is money and jewelry in the safe."

Vera was taken to a concentration camp and lined up with several other prisoners to be shot. Just then a group of wounded prisoners were brought in. Vera, who was a trained nurse, lied and said, "I'm a doctor." She was permitted to leave the line to tend to the wounded. The execution of the lined-up prisoners was carried out. Vera's life was spared, and she lived long enough in the camp to be liberated when the Russians arrived. She went back to the family house, which was in ruins. In the rubble of the bombed building she found a photograph of Rosalind's family, on the back of which was their address.

When Vera came to the States, she lived with Roz and Max until she was back on her feet and able to work. Max got her a job at the International Latex Corporation, where he was vice president, and she became an excellent administrator. Like so many refugees she was damaged emotionally. How does one "get over" the loss of mother, father, grandmother, grandfather, step-brother, uncles, and aunts, not to mention friends, all lost within a short space of time? The bleed- ing stops, scar tissue covers the wounds, but memories remain. The thought also arrived that had my mother not stayed behind in New York to marry my father, I, too, would have been burned in the ovens at Auschwitz, along with my Hungarian family.

NOT long after we were married, Stef suggested that it would be useful if I learned Russian. He himself knew all the other lan- guages that dealt with the Arctic. I began to study and found that I had a certain aptitude for languages. I spent the summers of 1944 and 1945 at Middlebury College in Vermont, which has a famous summer language program, at the newly established Russian school. The town of Middlebury was not too far from our Vermont farm, and during the second summer I went home for weekends. I soon learned to read, write, sing, and act in Russian. Before long I was translating Russian materials and even managed one small article that was published in the American Geographical Society's *Geographical Review*. I was able to catalog the new Russian materials arriving at the Stefansson library and converse with Ambassador Gromyko in his own language when we met at a United Nations reception. I loved the Russian language and enjoyed studying and reading Pushkin, Gogol, and especially Lermontov in the original.

One summer at the farm soon after we were married, *Life* magazine sent the photographer Margaret Bourke White to do a picture story of Stef. Her boyfriend at that time was Alexander Schneider, violinist with the Budapest String Quartet, who was Russian. While Margaret was photographing Stef, I tried out my new Middlebury Russian on Sascha, who told me what a wonderful cook he was. We became so absorbed in our conversation that the chicken paprikash I was preparing for lunch overcooked and to my great embarrassment was tough and barely edible. While we were eating, I confessed that we had never had time to have a wedding picture taken. Margaret volunteered and took several, all of them remarkable, and they remained our favorite photographs of all those taken during our marriage.

It was about this time that we went to a party given by Bill Laurence, a well-known *New York Times* science reporter. In a darkish corner I met a balding, short, middle-aged gentleman with what I detected was a Russian accent, to whom I had not been introduced. "Vi govorite po-russki?" I inquired? He did. I asked him in Russian what he did in real life. "I'm a violinist," he replied. "Really?" I continued. "Do you play in an orchestra or do solo work?" "Mostly solo." We talked for some time and finally as we were about to separate I asked him what his name was. "Misha Elman," he replied. I blushed and stammered, "Forgive me, Mr. Elman, I should have recognized you."

"Dots all right," he said, switching to English. "I'm veering my glesses." And he took them off with a flourish so I could recognize him.

I N 1949 the government of Iceland invited us to spend a "midsummer month" in their country as their guests. The country's president, Asgeir Asgeirsson, whom I had already met, was a friend of Stef's. It was a wonderful opportunity for me to see firsthand the homeland of Stef's people, the country that produced the fascinating sagas I had begun to read with much pleasure. My interest had been sparked when I had worked at the Iceland Pavilion of the World's Fair. Now on my way to becoming an Arctic expert, I was eager to accumulate as much firsthand knowledge as I could about all the northern countries.

Stef spoke perfect Icelandic and thought the trip would be more pleasurable for me if I learned some of the language. Having enjoyed studying Russian, I was not at all loath. We got a textbook, and Stef became my teacher in our evenings after work. Although in so many other ways he had always shown faith in my ability, when it came to teaching me his own native tongue, he was a hard and impatient taskmaster. He would say, "You have such a good ear, you shouldn't settle for anything less than perfection." What I heard from Stef was mostly criticism, and I didn't make much progress. Then an Icelander named Steingrimur Arason, an elderly, experienced teacher, visited New York, and Stef relinquished his role. Steingrimur thought I was gifted and praised me regularly, and of course I then made swift progress. I already knew how to read Icelandic. The language is largely phonetic, and every word is accented on the first syllable. After studying Russian, a language whose accents fall unpredictably and some of whose words change meaning when the wrong syllable is accented, I found speaking Icelandic was easy. I made enough progress to be able to greet people politely and correctly and even made a short speech at the state banquet. I also learned about thirty Icelandic folk songs, always fun for me, which stood me in great stead during our trip.

Because Stef was an admired hero of the Icelanders, we were welcomed by the entire country. In fact, Stef could have been its first president. In 1944 Iceland had declared itself an independent republic, separate from Denmark. In a nationwide poll on the question of who the first president should be, Stef was the winner. He had declined the honor, but he was known and loved throughout the country.

Experiencing Stef's native culture firsthand, I saw where some of his love of reading and language and song had come from. Iceland has more bookstores per capita than any other country in the world, and there has been *no* illiteracy since the invention of the printing press. It seemed to me that almost everybody wrote poetry, read poetry, recited poetry, and listened to poetry. I was struck that a population so small, under three hundred thousand, could support universities, art museums, an opera house, and handsome parliament buildings. What was also striking was that no one was very rich but neither was anyone very poor. All schooling and health services were free.

We saw more of Iceland than most Icelanders see in a lifetime. By ship, by automobile, and by air, we circled and crossed the island. When we traveled by bus, everyone sang, and thanks to my homework I was often able to join in. (The Icelanders, a handsome people with more Irish blood than most other Scandinavians,* love to sing and were surprised when I could sing a song's third or fourth verse that some of *them* didn't know.) The country's landscape is unusual and peculiarly beautiful, ranging from matte black lava fields, shadowless and surreal, to stunning geysers that erupt at regular intervals, active volcanoes, and glaciers, the latter two sometimes side by side. Iceland is not a truly Arctic country; it lies almost

---

* Their Viking ancestors used to raid the Irish coasts and take slaves. But slavery didn't pay in Iceland, and the slaves were freed and intermarried, so the country has many red- and black-haired, blue-eyed people with typical Irish coloring.

entirely south of the Circle and is bathed by the Gulf Stream, so it is never very hot or very cold—during some winters the ponds do not even freeze. It rains enough to make the grass as green as Ireland's. The capital city of Reykjavik has the clearest air of any city I have seen.*

Just before our trip, my brother, Myron, gave me a Leica camera and some new color film. Not knowing anything about color film,† I broke all the rules, but by chance I took some stunning pictures in the rain and shooting into the sun—a neophyte's impulses that surprisingly paid off. In fact, some of the images were good enough to be considered by *Life* magazine.

Eliot Elisofen, a *Life* photographer who was about to make a trip to the Canadian Arctic, came to us for briefing about cold weather conditions and saw my Iceland color pictures. He was impressed and took them to the *Life* picture editor, who said, alas, they had just done a story on Iceland and couldn't do another so soon. But having my photos considered gave me enough confidence so that thereafter I always traveled with both a black-and-white and a color camera around my neck and plenty of film and flashbulbs. Later I did sell *Life* a picture of the North Pole taken from the air, which appeared as a double-page spread in a book on the Poles, and this success gave me even more confidence in my photographic abilities.

T HEN, in 1953, the government of Denmark invited us to visit Greenland (which was at that time still a Danish possession), offering us a summer trip on the supply ship *Umanak*, which would stop at every settlement on the west coast. Several other VIP's would be aboard, including the Danish Prime Minister, Erik Eriksen, and the Bishop of Greenland. The voyage would give Stef an opportunity

* Their heat is provided by piped volcanic hot water—burning coal is unnecessary, so there is little air pollution.

† One of the many jobs I had taken after I left Bil Baird was as assistant to a photographer named Dudley Lee. He let me use his darkroom in the evenings, and I began to take and sell my own black-and-white photographs. I had resurrected that old skill with a view to providing myself with pictures for book illustrations and lectures.

to meet with Greenlanders and to compare Mackenzie River Inuit with the Greenland dialect. In preparation for the trip, I studied Danish with Elly Nemiah, the Danish wife of Dartmouth's classics professor Royal Nemiah. Danish was very easy compared to Icelandic; many of the root words are similar, and, probably thanks to my puppeteering experience of imitating animal sounds, I had no difficulty with the "glottal stop."* Once more I learned folk songs and could communicate with the many Danes and most of the natives we met.

We flew first to Copenhagen, my first view of that enchanting city, and met many of the numerous Greenland experts. Then we boarded the *Umanak* for the journey northward along Greenland's west coast. Greenland is treeless but grassy. Of all the lands north of the Arctic Circle, it is the most spectacularly beautiful. The western mountain ranges are cut by deep fjords, and at the head of each is the white, glowing, glittering edge of the Inland Ice.† First settled by Icelanders and later by Norwegians, it was established as a republic with a parliament when in the year 1000 it accepted Christianity. Archeologists have discovered and excavated many of its ancient stone buildings and churches, and we saw the stone remnants of the bishop's palace.†† To this day the outlines of the Norsemen's cultivated fields are visible. Thanks to ancient fertilization, the grass of the symmetrical fields is visibly thicker than the neighboring uncultivated areas. The Greenlanders, albeit largely Inuit, have a considerable mixture of Scandinavian blood, and we saw many blue-

---

* The Danish glottal stop has been compared to coughing, spitting, and choking by some. However, those familiar with Scotsmen and their brogue will recognize it. It consists of a sort of hiccup achieved by closing and opening the throat, and most words are punctuated by it.

† The largest of islands or smallest of continents, Greenland was named in A.D. 984 by its discoverer, Erik the Red. It covers almost 376,000 square miles, with 85 percent of its surface covered by an icecap more than a mile deep (second only to the Antarctic Ice Sheet in size), which lies between two steep mountain ranges lining its east and west coasts. Greenland is most like what the average person thinks of as an Arctic country. However, the 15 percent that is snow-free is an area larger than the whole of Great Britain.

†† Literary sources tell us that Greenland had sixteen churches and a cathedral, and tithes to Rome were paid with walrus and narwhal tusks and live polar bears, the latter highly prized and destined for kingly zoos.

eyed, light-haired people with the characteristic broad cheekbones of the Inuit.*

By 1953 I was at home again with cameras and took many color pictures for lecture slides and black-and-white shots for book illustrations. The cover of my third and last book (until now), *Here Is the Far North* (1957), featured a color picture I had taken of a Greenlander in his kayak against the background of a cluster of icebergs lying at the foot of a huge, grassy-edged mountain.

IN the 1950s Scandinavian Airlines had just inaugurated their pioneering great-circle Arctic flights, and I thought describing the one that left Los Angeles and flew via northern Canada across Greenland to Copenhagen would make a good introduction to my forthcoming book. Stef had been an early advocate of great-circle flights and written about them in both magazines and books. Inquiring about the possibility, I discovered that the airline was happy to fly me free and give me every assistance, especially since I was going to describe the experience in my book. I was optimistic and only a little nervous about the flight. Having faithfully and enthusiastically served my apprenticeship in learning everything I could about polar matters, braced with research and writing experience, tutored by Stef and the more experienced members of the Stefansson Library staff, I now felt secure and ready to fly on my own. The exuberant feeling was enhanced by the VIP treatment provided by SAS—orchid corsage, early boarding accompanied by photographers snapping pictures, and a warm, attentive welcome from smiling hostesses who knew my name and introduced me to the captain, who invited me to come forward after take-off.

In May of 1955, loaded with photographic equipment, I took off at midnight from the jewel-lighted Los Angeles Airport for Copenhagen,

---

* During the Black Plague in Europe, shipping to Greenland came to a halt. By the time it was restored in the eighteenth century, the Norsemen and their culture had disappeared, but the Greenlanders still retained some of their physical and cultural aspects.

via Winnipeg, and Sondre Strom Fjord in Greenland. Flying at 300 miles per hour, we skirted the southern shore of Hudson Bay and cut across northern Ungava to cross Hudson Strait and Frobisher Bay, landing at Sondre Strom Fjord seven hours and ten minutes later.

Two navigators had boarded the plane in Winnipeg, and for the rest of the flight they were both very busy charting our course. In those days, before computers and high-tech machinery did the work, navigators had to redo their fix every time they crossed a line of latitude, which in our case happened often as we flew into the high northerly areas. With permission from Captain Bronsted, I moved forward into the pilot's cabin to talk with the full crew. The stop in Greenland was at Sondrestrom Fjord, the Bluie West of the U.S. Army bases built in wartime, when we occupied Greenland. Long before the base came into view, through the earphones the captain had given me, I could hear the conversation between our pilot and the radar operator at BW8, who was giving him instructions for landing the plane. He gave our captain his position, instructions for altering it, directions for lowering altitude, information about what speed to approach the runway at, and when to touch the ground, to all of which the captain responded like an expert dancer following a partner's lead.

The temperature when we landed was 9 degrees below zero, dry and comfortable.

IN 1957, when it seemed that Alaska might become a state, Alice Dalgliesh asked me to revise *Here Is Alaska*. Ashamed at the prospect of doing a revised, statehood edition without ever having been to the book's namesake, I asked for and received an advance of $1,500 to enable me to travel to the place I already loved. Thanks to Raymond Peterson, a pioneer Alaskan flyer who was then head of a small but growing Alaskan airline, I acquired a pass that was honored on all other Alaskan airlines. Facilitated by Stef's friends and my research, I traveled extensively throughout the territory, interviewing the governor, studying and lecturing at the University of Alaska in Fairbanks, visiting Indian and Inuit villages, making notes and taking photo-graphs*, and absorbing everything I could. I traveled by bush plane, helicopter, private and commercial plane, and railroad from Anchor-age to Fairbanks.

I was now something of a minor expert on the Arctic. Travel had produced a change in my knowledge, which I liken to the difference between mono-aural and stereo recording. I was asked to join and lecture at the Society of Woman Geographers, an organization of female explorers who were excluded from the then male-only Explor-ers Club. More invitations to lecture arrived, and I began to charge fees for them. I wrote newspaper articles for the *Toronto Star*, co-authored a small publication for the Foreign Policy Association, and began to review polar books for the *New York Times Sunday Book Review*. At last I began to feel like a genuine professional. As my confidence soared, the last remnants of my childhood sense of inferiority ebbed away. I stopped apologizing for my lack of a college education and began to look around for new skills to conquer.

---

* I was pleased to be able to use fifteen of my own photographs, in addition to Fred's, for the statehood edition of *Here is Alaska*.

CHAPTER XIII

World War II and the Encyclopedia Artica

WITH THE DEVELOPMENT of longer-range airplanes, international flights to South America and Europe became more common, and transpolar flights, flying north and south rather than east and west, were envisioned. In 1932, Pan American Airways, a pioneer in international flight, hired Stef as Arctic consultant, a relationship which continued until 1945. He was charged with investigating new air routes and gathering the necessary information to establish airfields and operate in the far north. As a close friend of Orville Wright's, Stef had long been well-informed on aviation matters, and his added geographical knowledge made him an early advocate of great-circle arctic flights. He used to surprise people by stretching a piece of string across a globe, between Chicago and Moscow, and showing that the shortest distance between the cities was straight north, across the Polar Sea, not east or west. Stef worked closely with Charles Lindbergh, who was also working for Pan Am at the time, and Ann Morrow Lindbergh on their 1933 North Atlantic flight, which passed over Labrador, Greenland, and Iceland. (Stef admired Lindbergh's brain but not his politics.)

In 1935, several years before I began working for the library, Stef and his research organization were commissioned by the War Department to make a report on living and operating conditions in the Arctic.

Taking three years to do so, they provided a report of almost two million words. It was the first of many reports Stef and his staff were to write with increasing frequency for various government departments, as war clouds gathered in Europe and the country began to understand the strategic importance of the most northerly regions.

One of these reports, written for the War Department in 1940 and later published by The Macmillan Company as a trade edition (*The Arctic Manual*, 1944), is still the basic book for explorers and travelers camping out as well as for airmen, who keep it in case their planes go down in an Arctic wilderness. It contains everything useful Stef had learned in his ten winters and thirteen summers of field work and provides every kind of information needed to survive in the Arctic, including how to build an Inuit-type snow house for shelter, how to make a campfire, how to protect oneself from frostbite and treat it if it occurs, how to judge and test sea ice to make sure it is strong enough to walk on, how to handle sled dogs, how to hunt arctic animals successfully (as well as descriptions of the kinds of animals one might encounter), and much more. Half a century has passed since Stef dictated the book to Olive Wilcox in about ten days, but it is still the best volume of its kind.

In October 1941, the year we married, Colonel William ("Wild Bill") Donovan, head of the office of the Coordinator of Information,* began to confer with Stef about obtaining information of every kind concerning the northern regions. Stef had proposed establishing an Arctic studies center; Donovan asked Stef and his staff to set up such a center and sent his deputy David Bruce to work out the details. Stef was to furnish on request complete information—geographic, economic, political, social, and religious—about any country in the world north of a line drawn at approximately 60 North Latitude; he was also to make available to Donovan's office all research he might do independently or for others. After Donovan turned over

---

* The Office of the Coordinator of Information later became the Office of Strategic Services and still later the CIA.

Stef's reports to the War Department, we lost touch with what was done about them.

One of the first reports considered how to free the United States from dependence on Venezuelan, Texan, and Californian oil, since in wartime shipping from these sources might be cut off. Stef knew the land surrounding the polar sea was similar to Mediterranean lands and that it was rich in oil, some already discovered but almost all geologically extremely promising. With Donovan's approval he published an article in *Foreign Affairs* ("Routes to Alaska," July 1944) suggesting the best way of meeting Alaska's wartime need for oil. Two important problems—how to utilize the northern oil and where to build a road to Alaska—were carefully researched and presented. Stef's plan to utilize Canadian oil and supply it to wartime Alaska resulted in the Canol (for "Canadian Oil") project. Between 1942 and 1944, the U.S. Army built a 1600-mile oil pipeline with a refinery at Whitehorse, Yukon Territory. However, its execution differed widely from the original plan. Stef also voiced the need for an Alaskan Highway to deliver the oil and connect the territory with the lower forty-eight states. Both projects were carried out, but Stef thought the army had chosen the worst possible route for the Alcan Highway. He wrote that both projects were carried out "not only the hard way, but in my opinion, in the wrong way."

Responding to a wartime call is a thrilling experience, and everyone at the library felt gratified that we were needed. The U.S. Air Force, Quartermaster's Corps, Air Transport Command, Navy, and others turned to Stef for information and guidance concerning life in the Arctic. However, his views were seldom accepted as he presented them. The men in command—Generals Marshall, "Hap" Arnold, Doriot, Buckner, and others—like William Donovan understood and respected Stef's views, but difficulties arose when their underlings misunderstood or were ill-informed about northern phenomena. Time and again his reports were buried on somebody's desk, sometimes ignored, sabotaged by an underling, or "improved" by someone without Arctic experience. Arctic phenomena like permafrost, the behavior of materials (especially metals under extremely low temperatures), bio-fog produced by men and animals at low temperatures, and whiteout conditions were so bizarre to the ignorant that they sometimes "corrected" Stef's instructions, with disastrous results.

For example, in his meetings with the Quartermaster General, Stef gave instructions about the design of an overcoat, based on Inuit design, which the Quartermaster Corps then tried to "improve" by adding a zipper or buttons. In extreme cold, zippers cease to work and a man might be unable to close his garment and freeze to death. If the zipper were metal, as they all were in those days, it would function as a conductor and drain normal body heat. Buttons are difficult to handle with very cold hands and impossible with mittens. An Inuit coat, or anorak, is without openings except for the face, has an attached hood, and slips on easily over the head and instantly becomes an excellent container for body heat. An Inuit in a nine-pound caribou skin suit could stay outdoors all day fishing or watching at a seal hole in comfort. Our soldiers were bogged down with heavy, difficult-to-move-in clothing. In the Aleutian campaign our soldiers, with forty pounds of bulky wool, cotton, and nylon clothing, were often cold, and many had frostbitten feet because of inappropriate boots.

In 1943 Commanding General Hap Arnold telephoned Stef at the farm and asked him to spend a month with Brigadier General B.F. Giles, who commanded the North Atlantic Wing of the Air Transport Command. Arnold had gotten permission from the Quartermaster Corps to borrow Stef and have him instruct the men about forced landings and rescue work in northern latitudes. Stef enjoyed much of the work but was concerned to find that some of the bases had been built in exactly the wrong places, creating needless danger and work. For example, as Stef pointed out in his report, Frobisher Bay in Baffin Island is surrounded on three sides by mountains that are frequently shrouded in fog. The tide there is one of the heaviest in the world, from thirty to forty-five feet. For two-thirds of the year, freight supply by steamer is impossible because huge ice blocks are tossed about with the changing tides. Ironically, nearby on Hudson Strait were areas flanked by lowlands with longer navigational seasons, lower tides, and flat land ideal for plane landings.

Despite these poor tactics and misunderstandings, some of Stef's instructions were put to good use. In 1943 he and I went to Camp Hale at Homestake Peak in the Colorado Rockies, where Stef was to lecture on Arctic survival techniques, such as how to handle frostbite, how to keep clothing dry, and what to do if one finds oneself stranded in a strange and cold country. With a large group of officers watching,* Stef proceeded to build an Inuit snow house, a marvel of engineering design which two men can put together in an hour and which provides comfortable emergency shelter in the lowest temperatures. He explained how to choose the right kind of wind-packed snow. With a large snow knife, he cut the blocks, talking as he worked, setting them in place, cutting the first tier of blocks at an angle to insure the spiral construction, and tilting the blocks inward. When the snow house was finished we all went to supper. The next day we watched as the hillside sprouted a hundred slightly cockeyed snow houses, built by the officers who had watched Stef's demonstration.†

Our most successful venture with the navy was our book entitled *Sailing Direction for Arctic Waters*. The Hydrographic Office had asked Stef, with his extensive Arctic library, to put together a volume on Arctic navigation, and they sent an expert from the Hydrographic Office to instruct us in the nautical terminology used in such books. I remember with pleasure writing the sections on Labrador and Baffin Island. In the Labrador section, I came across my favorite of all place names: "Windy Tickle," a tickle being the local onomatopoeic name for a small stream of water, usually across a rocky terrain.

---

* As usual, I was the only woman present, taking pictures of his demonstration, in this instance.

† Though the demonstration was a success, Stef, who was so knowledgeable about survival in the cold, had forgotten the force of the sun in high altitudes, and suffered the worst case of sunburn his fair Scandinavian skin had ever endured.

SHORTLY after the war was over, in 1946, the Office of Naval Research asked Stef for his ideas about what was needed in Arctic research for the future. He came up with three suggestions, all of which were favorably received by the navy. The first was a much-needed bibliography of Arctic literature; the second, a roster of people throughout the circumpolar world who had any sort of expertise in Arctic matters; and the third, the compilation and publication of an encyclopedia Arctica. He recommended that the newly formed Arctic Institute of North America, in Montreal, of which he would be a board member, do the bibliography and the roster. He was certain that he and his now-expanded library and staff could best handle the many-volumed encyclopedia. From the beginning, it was an enterprise very close to his heart.

Stef signed a contract with the navy, to be renewed annually. He thought the project would take at least two years, but the deadline could be extended by mutual agreement. The estimated cost was $200,000, exclusive of final editing, and Stef was to do as much of the writing and editing as he could. He would choose the authors of articles and all the staff and translators.

Stef's fame, innumerable friends, and worldwide connections with geographical societies and the concerned governments enabled us to get much priceless information for free. The Hudson's Bay Company, whose records go back to 1670, offered their help, as did other corporations active in the Arctic. Pan American gave Stef permission to use all the pioneering material that he and Lindbergh had accumulated, and many others followed suit. We made a cross-country tour of the United States and Canada, stopping at many universities and other centers of learning. We met with scientists, historians, civil servants, and museum people and were exhilarated by their generous enthusiasm for our project and their willingness to cooperate and suggest others who might want to contribute to the encyclopedia.

On Morton Street the Library expanded into adjoining apartments and took over the space of a ground-floor store. More books were purchased, and more translators, writers, and editors were hired. Stef's knowledge and vision were fully utilized. His enthusiasm enlisted many different kinds of professionals, and we seldom met with a refusal. By this time I was fairly knowledgeable about the north and was able to be helpful to Stef in our travels and in research work back at the library, as well as learning to be something of an administrator as the library expanded and the staff grew. We made a good team. My life was illuminated with happiness as he shared his love and knowledge with me, both of them growing steadily. It was gratifying to be needed and to be able to participate effectively in what was for both of us a grand and ambitious undertaking.

We had been at work on the encyclopedia for only two years when we ran into a problem that in retrospect was inevitable and that had tragic consequences for the project. In addition to getting Canadian and British cooperation, Stef had intended to enlist the Russians, who control 49 percent of the Arctic and three-quarters of the land surface north of the tree line, or the southernmost permafrost line. As Stef wrote, "They were an Arctic-minded, Arctic-inhabiting people. An Arctic encyclopedia could hardly do without them." But in the early days of the Cold War, there was to be no cooperation or sharing of resources with the Soviets. Our staff would have to compile material on the Soviet sphere from our own resources, which were relatively rich.*

As we expanded our staff from ten to twenty, Washington screened each of the new staff members. We had hired as a Russian translator an American citizen who had spent the last years of his undergraduate studies in Moscow. Because of this experience abroad, he was suspect in the eyes of the Office of Naval Research. Stef told them in dis-

---

* As president of the Explorers Club, Stef had been asked by the Soviet government in 1937 to coordinate the search for a missing Soviet transpolar flyer, Sigismund Levanevsky. When Stef refused to accept payment for his services, the Soviet ambassador had promised to send the library everything henceforth published in the Soviet Union about the Arctic. These Russian-language holdings (25 percent of which were not in the Library of Congress) later proved to be immensely valuable to our government during wartime.

Jenö Schwartz, c. 1906.

(*l to r*) Rosalind, Julie, Evelyn, and Bella Schwartz, February 1914.

Evelyn in
Bensonhurst, 1928.

Evelyn (*center*) began working with marionettes while a student at
Washington Irving High School.

Buckminster Fuller next to a model of an early version of his Dymaxion House, 1932. (*Courtesy of Estate of R. Buckminster Fuller*)

Christopher Morley and Evelyn at the Gotham Book Mart on Christmas Eve, c. 1938. (*From* Wise Men Fish Here *by W. G. Rogers*)

(*l to r*) Bil Baird, Rudy Bauss (?), and Evelyn, 1934. (*Photo by Anton Bruehl*)

Evelyn (*left*) posing for Baird, 1935. Years later, when sending her a copy, he wrote on the back of the photo: "Do you think I'd give this one up ifn I didn't have another one?"

At the Romany Marie restaurant in Greenwich Village, c. 1939. (*l to r*) Romany Marie, the dancer Kohana, Vilhjalmur Stefansson, and Evelyn.

Dearing Farm in Bethel, Vermont.

Stefansson and Evelyn supervise the unloading of his Arctic collection in the Baker Library at Dartmouth, 1951. (*Courtesy of Dartmouth College Library*)

Stefansson and Evelyn on the front porch of Dearing Farm. Photo by their friend Margaret Bourke-White.

Stefansson and Robert Frost, 1956 or 1957. The two were often mistaken for one another on the Dartmouth campus.

Owen Lattimore and Stefansson at the Lattimore house in Ruxton, Maryland, 1950.

John Nef and Evelyn on their wedding day, April 21, 1964.

The Nefs leaving Meridian House in Washington, 1964.

Marc and Vava Chagall on
vacation with the Nefs at
Cap d'Antibes, 1971.

Marc Chagall relaxes at Cap
d'Antibes, 1970.

The Chagall mosaic being installed in the Nef's garden in Georgetown,
1971.

Evelyn and John Nef in their garden in front of the Chagall mosaic.

Evelyn and Saul Bellow at a symposium marking the first fifty years of the Committee on Social Thought at the University of Chicago, 1992.

Portrait of Evelyn painted by Alex Katz, 1974. (34″ x 47½″, acrylic on canvas, owned by Evelyn Stefansson Nef, © Alex Katz/Licensed by VAGA, New York, NY)

Evelyn presents the first copy of her Icelandic autobiography, *Evelyn Stefánsson Nef*, to President Olafur Ragnar Grimsson of Iceland in Reykjavik, November 2001. (*Courtesy of* Morgunbladid)

gust that if the young man was suspect, maybe he himself was, too. The navy demanded that Stef fire the young man. Stef was reluctant to lose a valuable staff member and to knuckle under to what he considered nonsense. He appealed to his friend General George Marshall, who backed him up in his refusal to fire the researcher.* Stef thought the problem settled.

Then, in early 1949, Stef was told without explanation that the navy would not renew our encyclopedia contract. We could not find out why. All our queries went unanswered. Dr. Andrew Thomsen, director of the Canadian Meteorological Services, offered to ask his American counterpart, Dr. Francis Reichelderfer, Chief of the U.S. Weather Bureau, to inquire about the reasons for the cancellation. Both men had been participating enthusiastically in gathering materials for us. Reichelderfer reached the key man in Washington and was told the navy had "no comment." The order had come from higher up to cancel the contract, allowing one year to terminate all arrangements.

Stef believed and I continue to believe that McCarthyism was the only possible reason for the cancellation of our beloved project. As part of his work he had subscribed to innumerable publications, including Russian-language and English-language Soviet materials. Always curious about the world, he joined organizations such as *Russian War Relief*, some of which were later declared to be subversive. Stef was certain that he had the necessary wisdom and scholarship to sift through information and decide what was and wasn't true. He hated the growing political hysteria of the time, the pervasive condemnation of people on the basis of rumor and guilt by association. He had never been a communist but thought it undemocratic to persecute people for their beliefs, whether political or religious. He believed even those with unpopular beliefs were entitled to the protection of the law.

Stef had been the target of unfair attacks in connection with his third Canadian Arctic Expedition and had been vocal and effective in

---

* Stef later wrote, "I was crushed later on when I learned that these views of Marshall's, which I had been in the habit of repeating, were used against him when he was himself charged with treason by Senator McCarthy."

defending himself. He enjoyed a good philosophical or political argument and won most of them (all of those with me!). Even though he eventually stopped answering every attack,* realizing how much time it took away from his work to do so, he always felt secure about his ability to convince others of his own point of view.

But in this case, without any reasons given for the cancellation of the contract, there was no arguing to be done, and he was forced to stop the project in midstream.†

We both realized that big changes would have to be made immediately. Stef was always optimistic, but I felt intuitively something that perhaps he could not admit, even to himself—that his grand vision of the *Encyclopedia Arctica* had been dealt a devastating hit. Only later did I more fully understand the extent of the body blow Stef had received with the cancellation of the project. The completion of the twenty-volume encyclopedia would have been the culmination of a lifetime of scholarship and exploration, the crowning achievement of his vast accumulation of knowledge in the field. Great physical skill and stamina are necessary traits in explorers, but Stef was also blessed with a passion for scholarship, a phenomenal memory, and an intellectual ease and grace in his speech and writing. The encyclopedia would have been his monument.

After much discussion, we came to a decision, which Stef describes in his autobiography:

> When it finally dawned on us that the *Encyclopedia Arctica* was going to be sacrificed, I knew that the expense of maintaining my now enormous library in New York was going to be more than

---

* As Joseph McCarthy himself knew well, if you attack someone who is famous you'll get into the spotlight yourself, which is a strong incentive for those—sane, semi-sane, and insane—who crave it.

† Stef later described exactly where we were with the project at the time of the cancellation:
"We had spent more than three hundred thousand dollars of the Navy's money in order to secure more than six million words for the twenty volumes that were to be the foundation stones of our northern polar knowledge. We had shipped the first two volumes to the Johns Hopkins Press. The others would come at the rate of four a year.
"There was nothing to do but reduce our staff, give up what we could of our New York accommodations, and thereafter do practically nothing except type, file and otherwise try to salvage manuscripts, notes, maps and pictures. We found that about a third of our six million words were about ready for the publisher's copy editors."

I could carry. Evelyn and I considered the matter carefully. By thinking first of our Vermont farm, we thought of something else. Following up the thought, I telephoned an old friend, Rolf Syvertson, the dean of Dartmouth College's Medical School. Reminding him that our farm was only thirty miles west of Hanover and that I knew Dartmouth's Baker Library had unused shelf space, I asked him to find out if the college would consider housing my library in exchange for the use their faculty and students could get from it. I also suggested an option to purchase the library at a price to be agreed on, which I assured Syvertson would not be a tenth of what it had cost me over the years.

Dean Syvertson came to New York to talk things over. When he telephoned several days later, he gave us the good news that not only would Dartmouth agree to house the Stefansson Library, but they would be happy to pay the cost of packing and trucking to Hanover.

So, with great courage and grace, Stef accepted the terrible reality of the end of the encyclopedia. He dissolved his staff, some of whom had worked with him for many years, and we moved to Hanover and a new kind of life. He used to say to me, "Never take a chance if you don't have to, but if you have to, take it quickly, and don't look back." That is what he did now. He internalized all the anger, grief, frustration, and sadness that he must have felt and, with cheerful mien, did the necessary and traveled on. He set an example for me that I have never forgotten.

But I am always reminded again of how great a loss he suffered when I read the words from Ecclesiastes, with which he ended his autobiography: "Wherefore I perceive that there is nothing better, than that a man should rejoice in his own works; for that is his portion: for who shall bring him to see what shall be after him?"

CHAPTER XIV

Life in Hanover

DESPITE THE BITTER REASON that necessitated our move to Hanover, New Hampshire, I could not help looking forward to being in the beautiful little town that contained Dartmouth. Never having been to college, I found myself imagining the intellectual delights that might be in the offing, and I was not mistaken. Though tiny compared to New York, Hanover in 1951 offered many advantages, including art, music, drama, lectures, and sports in an almost bewildering array, and everything was close at hand on the beautiful green campus.

We found an apartment on the upper floor of a music professor's house. The owners, Fred and Sophie Sternfeld, became our guides to new surroundings. Shortly after we arrived and were barely settled, they had a large party for us. Fred was fascinated by the relationship of music to the other arts, and when he discovered I could sing asked me to perform at the party. I sang folk songs unaccompanied. He needed an alto in the madrigal group he directed and asked if I would be interested in joining. "Certainly," I replied, "but I can't sight-read music." "That's all right," said Fred. "I'll give you ten minutes before each rehearsal." He did, and I was able to keep up with the group. Some of the happiest moments of my life were spent singing—the *Messiah* or Bach cantatas, for example—with the Madrigal Group and the Handel Society.

Professor Sternfeld introduced me to baroque music, about which I knew little but which became a great love. He invited me to audit his Music I class, which was wonderfully enlightening. The high point of my musical pleasure in this new form was singing the alto part of a lovely William Byrd mass for four voices at Rollins Chapel. To be a necessary part of the delicious sounds we were making in the spacious chapel was as close as I could get to a religious feeling. In addition to singing with these local groups, I joined a Hanover group that played the recorder. They needed a tenor, so I purchased an instrument and became part of the Quartoot, which met once a week to play Elizabethan music. We practiced at each other's houses, and when we tired of recorder playing we would have a drink and sing folk songs.

At Dartmouth I took advantage of every opportunity to learn. It was as if I was at last, in my thirties, going to college. I joined a folk dancing group that met once a week, took sculpture lessons with Winslow Eaves, and studied Danish in preparation for our 1953 trip to Greenland. Dartmouth had an excellent drama department that regularly put on several plays a year. Being an all-male school, they were always desperate for women actresses, which is how I found myself reading for Professor Henry Williams and starting a new acting career. I played several roles, including Portia in *The Merchant of Venice* to Marshall Meyer's Shylock,* Lady Cecily in Shaw's *Captain Brassbound's Conversion*, and Dalilah in Milton's *Samson Agonistes*. I also sang "She's Only a Bird in a Gilded Cage" in a Victorian extravaganza. I loved it. Not only did I get a chance to act, but under Henry Williams's excellent direction each play felt like a course in Shakespeare, Shaw, or Milton. Having to memorize the lines awakened their beauty for me, and many of the best ones have stayed with me.

---

* It was very smart of Henry to get a student who was studying for the rabbinate to play Shylock. Marshall went on to become the chief rabbi of Argentina and played a courageous and dangerous role during the worst of the terror in the days of Peron and afterwards.

SOON after our arrival, Stef was appointed Arctic Consultant to the college at a nominal salary.* One of the first things he did upon arriving was to build an Inuit igloo, or snow house, in the middle of the college green, in the center of town. Surrounded by a group of fascinated students, he talked as he worked, and when he had finished several of them spent the night in the igloo.† Stef loved to substitute for absent professors, whether in the medical school to talk about frostbite and cold-weather survival tactics or in anthropology to tell about his life with the Stone Age Copper Inuit. He was never too busy to listen to a student with a problem, offer reading suggestions, or answer questions. His charisma and enthusiasm for anything to do with the Polar Regions affected a generation of Dartmouth men, many of whom went on to become Arctic and Antarctic specialists in geology, glaciology, oceanography, and anthropology.

Just before we left New York, we called in Charlie Everitt, a famous book dealer in Americana, to make an evaluation of the books in the library. Excluding the valuable, huge pamphlet file, the maps, the card catalogue, and the numerous manuscripts that Stef was donating to Dartmouth, Everitt's estimate for the more than twenty thousand books came to $100,000. Not long after arriving in Hanover, Dartmouth alumnus Albert Bradley donated the money to purchase the library for college. We gave half of the evaluation as a gift to Dartmouth and received $50,000. With it we bought a charming little house, at 2 Allen Lane in town, and Stef split the remainder between us. He, of course, instantly began spending his share. I asked John Meck, a Dartmouth vice president, to help me invest my little pile. It formed the nucleus of a small fund of my

---

* In 1953 the Northern Studies Program was formalized. At that time Dartmouth boasted a distinguished group of faculty members who had worked in the Arctic, including Elmer Harp in the archeology department, Trevor Lloyd in geography, Robert McKennan in anthropology, and David Nutt, who sailed north in his *Blue Dolphin* boat every summer to do oceanographic research.

† One of them, Jack Tuck Jr., later became the leader of the U.S. International Geophysical Year station at the South Pole.

own, which I could spend without asking anyone's permission and which I treasured.

During the war years the library on Morton Street had grown fast in great spurts and was no longer in perfect order. When we moved to Hanover and I became librarian of the Stefansson Library, I had an opportunity to reorganize the shelving plan. Making elaborate plans on paper for the Baker Library space assigned to us, I gave each shelf a number and made two tags for each shelf. Leaving one set in their newly assigned places in Hanover, I traveled back to New York. By putting all the books that belonged together in one box and assigning it its new place tag, I was able, when the books arrived in Hanover, to match the tag numbers up in the new and neat arrangement.

When the Stefansson Collection was safely installed on the ground floor of handsome Baker Library, not far from the controversial Orozco frescoes, Stef was given a desk in the windowed aisle, which became his office. I was given a part-time job looking after the books and helping the students, faculty, and visitors who soon began to use the library. Later I became a full-time member of the Baker staff, eating my brown-bag in the nearby Bindery. We were usually joined by the assistant librarian—elderly, tall, and rangy Harold Rugg—who was a genuine New Englander with a broad New Hampshire accent and an encyclopedic knowledge of books.

My title was Librarian of the Stefansson Collection, but my position was something more. I lectured in the geography department on Alaska, Iceland, and Greenland, using my good colored slides. Unlike most of the faculty wives, I made trips to New York, where I would see Alice Dalgliesh at Scribner's, do a television show for a children's program called *Discovery*, or attend a special meeting of the Explorers Club or the Society of Woman Geographers. I enjoyed dealing with the glaciologists, geologists, aurora borealis experts, archeologists, and anthropologists who came to do research in the library, as well as writers like Farley Mowat, Wilbur Cross, and John

Edward Weems, who was researching the Peary-Cook controversy[*] that seemed to surface regularly every decade. Inquiries about muskeg, pingos (those mysterious dome-shaped earth and ice formations), people writing biographies of Polar figures—almost all the researchers were interesting, and in helping them find what they needed I learned a good deal about their work. It was a happy exchange. Fortunately, I had a good memory and quick recall, and unlike most librarians I was familiar with the insides as well as the backs of the books.

O NCE while I was waiting for Stef outside the Dartmouth Bookstore, I overheard a middle-aged woman say to her companion, "Did you see him? That was Robert Frost." Upon returning to New York after his 1913–1918 expedition, Stef had been befriended by the widow of William Vaughn Moody, the poet whose "Gloucester Moors" had so impressed him and caused him to shift his ambitions from poetry to anthropology. Mrs. Moody's circle included Robert Frost,[†] with whom Stef also became friends. Many years later, when Frost used to come regularly to Dartmouth to lecture, the old friendship was renewed. The two men were both tall and had shocks of thick white hair and on campus were often mistaken for one another.

In 1951 Richard Morin, the librarian of Dartmouth's Baker Library, came across Robert Frost's *New Hampshire* and found a reference to Stef in the title poem: "Just the way Steffanson runs on, I murmured, / About the British Arctic. That's what comes / Of being in the mar-

---

[*] This is a famous controversy regarding who got to the North Pole first. Cook, returning to civilization before Peary, claimed the honor. Peary, who had spend twenty-five years trying and believed he had reached the Pole first, and that Cook never had, was devastated and had a nervous breakdown. Stef believed Peary got there or "as near as makes no difference"and disbelieved Cook, who had lied earlier about climbing Mount McKinley in Alaska.

[†] Frost, like every other poet I have ever met, didn't think much of other living poets. I had inquired about his feelings toward Edna St. Vincent Millay and T.S. Eliot, neither of whom he much admired. Later, when I came to know T. S. Eliot, I found he reciprocated Frost's lukewarm assessment—he didn't think much of Frost either. Poets seem never to have enough praise. Perhaps it is because of the great effort required to make a poem and the slender rewards. Their little volumes never sell as well as the often poorly written bestsellers, and most poets have to resort to teaching, lecturing, medicine, banking, or farming to make ends meet.

ket with a climate." Dick Morin got Frost to inscribe the book and generously gave it to Stef with a note:

> From Richard W. Morin, To Vilhjalmur Stefansson. This volume—which turns out to be a first edition—was acquired in my undergraduate days at Dartmouth. It is for your "vanity shelf" (see p. 3) and comes with my warmest wishes for you.
>
> If you should want to make a retort to Robert Frost he may be reached at 35 Brewster St., Cambridge, Mass. RWM

Frost's inscription in the slender volume is worth quoting because it tells a story:

> For Vilhjalmur Stefansson[*] to remind him of the time I so enthusiastically cheered Mrs. William Vaughn Moody on her campaign to make him President of the University she was then a trustee of, namely Cornell the Great, Robert Frost, at Dartmouth the Great, May 7, 1951.

Mrs. Moody, on the search committee for a new Cornell president, was successful in getting the trustees to agree on her choice of Stef, and he was offered the presidency. After serious consideration he decided his talents lay in writing and lecturing about the Arctic and its future, not in administration, and regretfully declined the honor.

Once when Frost was visiting Stef at Baker Library, he noticed several of the Inuit soapstone sculptures, then obtainable for a pittance compared to today's prices. He inquired about them, and I told him that when I lectured at McGill in Montreal I usually stopped at the Canadian Handicrafts Guild, which stocked them, and bought one or two. "I would like to own one," said Frost, and I offered to make the purchase on my next trip. I was lucky and found a particularly

---

[*] On page 3, where the poem was, Frost had corrected his misspelling of Stef's name (he had incorrectly spelt Stefansson with two "f"s and one "s"), adding his initials and the date.

handsome example on my next trip for thirty-five dollars—not a large sum, but at that time we were poor and living on my librarian's salary. Frost took the sculpture with pleasure and promised to send a check. But to my surprise and disappointment he never did.

WITH the acquisition of a house in Hanover, we were in need of more furniture. Once more Ruth Galey came to my rescue. When I married Stef and was furnishing our St. Luke's Place apartment, she had given me several pieces she no longer needed as well as much useful advice. Her husband, John, had recently died, and she had fallen into a depression from which she would never recover. She stopped having a social life, seeing no one except for two childhood friends and me. She maintained her penthouse on Sheridan Square but was giving up their Seagirt, New Jersey, country house, and was reluctant to sell the lovely old country pine pieces that held so many precious memories of her dear John. I offered to store the furniture that would fit into our Allen Lane house. She was delighted with this solution and said that I could have any furniture I could use, which was a great gift to us. We took an antique fourposter bed, a beautiful pine dresser for the dining room, a lovely walnut round table for the kitchen, and numerous chairs and tables. Almost instantly our little house was handsomely and completely furnished and ready to receive visitors.

Ruth Galey was still a loved and dear figure, though her depression changed her formerly cheerful, sweet disposition into that of an obsessed mourner. The claustrophobia she had always suffered intensified. She stopped traveling altogether. She would talk endlessly, but always about her loss, her beloved and incomparable John. She had been talkative before, but her illness seemed to release an unstoppable flow. When I telephoned to find out how she was doing, she would continue talking, permitting no interruptions, sometimes going on for an hour. In New York I had taken her calls at the library since she seemed to take comfort in being listened to. In Hanover, however, I was being paid by the college and couldn't in good conscience listen for that length of time. I asked her to call me at home. She tried but didn't always succeed. Our relationship developed some strain.

Then suddenly, although she never traveled, she decided she would come to visit us in our tiny house in Hanover, which lacked a guest room. Since both Stef and I were working full-time and had very little money, I suggested that it was not a good time for a visit. Couldn't we postpone it until things were a little easier for us? This brought on an explosion of such fury that I was paralyzed with dismay. "What ingratitude! How dare you suggest a visit is not convenient after all I have done for you," etc. It was a totally unexpected, shocking response, and things were never the same between us afterwards. She decided that I had to pay for the furniture; it seemed that we had never clarified whether she was giving it or we were storing it. There was endless haggling about the price of each thing, which became worse as her anger increased. I offered to send it all back, but that didn't please her. I didn't have the cash to satisfy her but agreed to send a monthly check from my meager librarian's salary, an arrangement she finally accepted. It was plain that she wanted to punish me, for she certainly didn't need the money—she had just endowed a chair at the Harvard Law School in her husband's name. From then on, she seemed to have little else to do but telephone me with her complaints and her sad, depressed anger toward me. I didn't understand how this could have become her whole life until years later when I learned as a therapist about agitated depression and the terrible energy that keeps it going.

I owed Ruth so much. She had saved my life when I was married to Bil Baird and had provided guidance, teaching, affection, and care. She had been the mother I desperately needed, and I was heartbroken when our relationship fell into this unhappy place. When she died in 1964, I was no longer in her will, if I had ever been. She had often promised me things that she proved unable to part with, so I was not surprised. Her friend Elizabeth Macauley, the executor of her will, understood what had happened to our relationship. She telephoned me afterwards and offered me some of Ruth's beautiful blue Stafford-shire china. I accepted it gratefully and treasure it to this day, display-ing it with pleasure on the pine dresser from her New Jersey house. They represent for me all the knowledge and goodness she had made possible in better times.

I MET two women in Hanover who became lifelong friends. When I was appointed librarian of the Stefansson Collection in Baker Library, the college hired as my assistant a young woman named Mary Fellowes, who had grown up in Alaska. We liked each other at first sight. Mary's husband had died prematurely, leaving her with an infant girl who was then about nine. Mary was extremely musical, ebullient, and good-natured. We used to do the messiest book-sorting job at the library while singing two-part songs, making the task light and swift. Mary and her daughter became part of our family. She loved Stef and me, and one couldn't help loving Mary and her darling daughter, Anne. When I began to travel on my own, she would keep an eye on Stef who had suffered and recovered from a small stroke, and I gave Anne her tenth birthday party, complete with a magician who was a distinguished faculty mathematician named Scullion.

The other friend was Ellen Griswold, wife of Professor John Gris-wold, who taught finance at Tuck, Dartmouth's graduate business school. Ellen had and still has one of the finest intellects of anyone I have met, combined with an unusual, exquisite sensitivity. She became my first really good friend, with whom I could share thoughts about everything safely. A graduate of Radcliffe, she had been a pupil of Alfred North Whitehead's and could hold her own in conversations with the most brilliant intellects. She had a pure soprano voice and also sang in the Madrigal Group. She owned a harpsichord, and adding my alto voice to her lovely soprano we often performed duets for our own pleasure as well as for company. We sang Dowland, Campian, and Dufay songs together and Machaut and Bach masses with the group, and thoroughly enjoyed each other's company. Stef admired her, too, and we became close with her and Jack, often dinning at each other's houses.

The Griswolds lived in a handsome modern house, with modern furniture and original works of modern art on the walls, all of which was visually exciting. They drank martinis before dinner and wine with their food at dinner parties. In summer Ellen, a gourmet cook, would invite me for a quick delicious lunch, after which we would go for a swim in a nearby pond—it was freezing cold, but we loved it. Then, lunch hour over, I returned to work at the library. As a Dartmouth insider, Ellen clued me in about the various professors and their wives and the complexities of living in a small town where everything about everybody is known or believed to be known and the unknown is speculated about. Endless gossip attended anything new, different, or strange. I had already experienced something like this during our summers at the farm, but there we had been visitors while in Hanover we were permanent settlers, in the thick of it.

Ellen's and my talents complemented each other. She was thoughtful, learned, and wise. I was quick, enthusiastic, and eager to learn and share. Ellen liked and was knowledgeable about art, and we both loved to go to exhibitions and read about art history. We went together to events that our husbands were not interested in—a great boon to me, since Stef was interested only in his work on polar-related matters and not at all in art, music, dance, or novels. Ellen was being psychoanalyzed and drove to Boston once a week for her sessions. We talked a great deal about psychological problems, not unnaturally, and read the same books so that we could discuss them, including works by Freud and Jones' biography of him. We "analyzed" everybody we knew. Suddenly psychological terms like insight, dream work, complexes, masochism, and aggression became everyday concepts. I grew interested not only in what happens in analysis but in *why* it happens—that is, the technique of the analyst was especially fascinating to me. How does the analyst do it? We judged novels by the amount of good psychological material they contained.

We read our way through all of Virginia Woolf's books. Ellen already knew most of them, but they were new and revealing to me. Virginia was our heroine not only because of her skill with words but also because she articulated many of the feelings we shared but could not express. We were both devoted to Henry James, too, and we gobbled up all the books about them and their fascinating families. The sibling rivalry between William and Henry was fascinating, as was their talented sister, whose only outlet, so common in those pre-women's liberation days, was neurasthenia. We devoured the endless spate of books about the Bloomsbury group—Lytton Strachey, Vanessa Bell, Duncan Grant, etc.—and Dartmouth's Baker Library supplied our nourishment. Like Stef, Ellen knew reams of poetry, and she introduced me to T.S. Eliot.

Soon after arriving in Hanover I became seriously ill, and Stef, who like Bil Baird disliked or feared illness, paid me the least possible attention. It was Ellen who not only visited me at the hospital but had the inspiration to bring E.B. White's *Charlotte's Web* and read it to me in her lovely voice when I couldn't raise my head from the pillow. She had a way of shedding a different light on a problem, making its solution clear, and of gently suggesting advice, offered but never insisted upon. We learned to truly love and admire each other, and to this day she remains my best friend.

CHAPTER XV

The Lattimores and McCarthyism

*I*FIRST MET OWEN AND ELEANOR LATTIMORE in New York in 1939, when they came to lunch at the Stefansson Library. They were just back from one of their numerous Far Eastern journeys and were bubbling with news and good humor. Eleanor was impressive and down-to-earth, a good-looking woman who dressed in very subtle colors of faded green and gold, enhanced by beautiful old Chinese coral jewelry. When she spoke, it was usually to clarify and enlarge upon something that Owen had just explained. What struck me was how well they worked together as a couple. I had met husband-and-wife academic teams working in the same field who, under a cover of politeness, were competitive and sometimes even hostile toward each other. There was none of that with Owen and Eleanor. They were at home in the world and with each other, acting together as smoothly as the two parts of Beethoven's Kreutzer Sonata, each taking the lead when appropriate and harmonizing when they were covering the same subject. They enjoyed each other. They were old friends of Stef's, and after we married they soon included me in their circle.

Owen, who had grown up in China, was a tenured professor and head of the Walter Hines Page School of International Relations at Johns Hopkins University in Baltimore. He and I shared the "honor" of never having been to college. Owen's Asiatic travels and his scholarly books had won him his distinguished place at Hopkins. He was an active and popular lecturer and, like Stef, was enormously productive. An expert on Mongolia and China, he had been the Director of Pacific Operations for the Office of War Information. President Roosevelt had sent him to China as his chosen adviser to Chaiang Kai-shek. He had written both scholarly and popular books, eleven in all. He was younger than Stef, but they shared the same fierce hunger to know "everything" about their respective fields.

As a young woman Eleanor had spent a year in China when her father was lecturing at the University of Nanking, and she had returned sophisticated and grown-up. After a year in New York she traveled, via the Trans Siberian Railway, back to China, where she met and married Owen. They lived in Peking, where Eleanor began to display her gift for making wherever she lived a place of beauty. She knew how to combine colors and place shapes to advantage, and her green thumb always provided flowering plants as the last perfect touch. At her Ruxton, Maryland, house she put antique Hitchcock chairs around a large, round, shiny, Chinese black lacquer table set with unusual plates, silver, pitchers, and serving pieces that came from the four corners of the world. She blended all into what seemed like myriad little masterpieces. She was the kind of woman whose artistic eye could spot the one fine item in a junk shop, and we shared an interest in handicrafts. She knew how to make evening purses out of old Chinese silk remnants and how to cut a new evening jacket from an old Chinese pattern she had learned in Peking. She taught me about houseplants and when to start the narcissus bulbs so that they would be blooming at Christmastime. We found we were interested in the same new books and would sometimes take turns reading aloud when we were a foursome. We spent many joyous Christmases at their Ruxton house, and they became like family to us.

In 1947 we invited the Lattimores to stay with us and then use the farm while we were away on our Iceland trip. It was the first of several summers that we spent together. There in the cool green hills our mornings were spent working. Each of us was writing a book or engaged in some serious research, and every evening we shared what we had learned with each other and indulged in long discussions about geography, linguistics, and anthropology. I once figured out that between us we knew twelve languages. Stef knew Eskimo, Icelandic, Danish, Norwegian and Swedish, Latin, and German. Owen knew Chinese, Mongol, German, French, and Russian, and by the end of his term in Sweden he was lecturing in Swedish. I was studying Russian, Icelandic, and Danish, and Eleanor could chime in with Chinese and French. Owen in addition to all his academic skills was excellent at splitting wood for the stoves and making compost.

Owen was musical and shared my love of folk songs. One of my cherished memories of him was during a summer evening in Cornish, New Hampshire (at the home of George Rublee, a distinguished lawyer and an old friend of Stef's), when he stood up on a hassock and sang to a remarkable group that included Judge Learned Hand, himself an enthusiastic folk singer. Owen's song, consisting of only one repeated line, was "Lloyd George knows my father, and father knows Lloyd George." He sang it with great feeling to the tune of "Onward Christian Soldiers." By the third repetition the entire audience had joined in, and by the end we were all hilarious. Learned Hand then concluded the singing with "Sweet Betsy from Pike."

In the late forties, without consulting me, Stef had purchased the property adjoining our farm to save it from being clear-cut by lumber people. When the Lattimores found that they loved Vermont and living close to us, they agreed to improve the Stoddard property, putting into it as much as we had spent on the purchase, and we became joint owners, enabling them to continue the pleasant proximity that we all enjoyed. In the summer of 1949 the Lattimore's son, David, and a covey of his Harvard college classmates camped out at the farmhouse while they renovated it. They firmed the foundations, plastered, painted, installed water and indoor plumbing.

In connection with his linguistic and cultural Mongol studies, Owen had rescued two Mongolian refugee families fleeing from communist rule, the Onans and the Hangins. Eleanor had found housing for them and their babies, begged needed clothing and furniture from her friends, and found sewing and dressmaking work for the two women; Owen integrated the men into the curriculum of the Walter Hines Page School of International Relations. As soon as the little farmhouse was habitable, the Mongol families moved in to escape the Baltimore heat and humidity. Another Mongolian refugee from communism was the Dilowa Hutuktu, an "enlightened one," the Buddhist equivalent of a high cardinal. He was a near-permanent guest of the Lattimores, and he turned up at Bethel's Fourth of July barbecue in his beautiful yellow robes, to the wonder of the locals.

O N February 2, 1950, Eleanor wrote me with exciting news: "[Owen] has been asked to head a United Nations Mission to Afghanistan, June through September, and he can take me along! He will go out for the month of March to look over the field and then come home and recruit a team for the summer—to work out schemes for technical aid. Doesn't it sound wonderful? I am so excited. U.N. is very keen to have him go, but the reason it still might fall through is that the Afghans might think up some reason for objecting. But I don't believe they will. If they do they don't deserve any technical aid."

Several weeks later, on March 24, Owen was in Afghanistan making arrangements for the summer's work and Eleanor was planning to join him. I had just finished work at 4 St. Luke's Place, where the Stefansson Library was newly installed, next door to our apartment. Turning on the evening news while preparing our simple dinner, I received one of the greatest shocks of my life. For some weeks Senator Joseph McCarthy had been boasting that he would name the "top Soviet espionage agent" who he claimed was heading a communist spy ring in our State Department and who was responsible for our "losing China." In one of his clever public-relations ploys, McCarthy had been repeatedly promising that he would name the villain, creating speculation and discussion.* The person he named that evening was our best and closest friend, Owen Lattimore.

* McCarthy made these claims in hearings chaired by Senator Millard Tydings, before the Senate Internal Security Subcommittee of the Foreign Relations Committee.

We were appalled and flabbergasted. Could this be happening? In the United States? This felt like a Kafka novel in which unimaginable, terrifying, unexplained nightmares occurred. I knew that Owen "was not and never had been a communist," and I thought I knew that he had never even worked for the State Department (and that turned out to be so). Our scholarly friend Owen, the linguist, the businessman-turned-academic, the man who loved the Mongols and their language and culture as Stef loved the Inuit—if it had not been so scary, it might almost have been funny. None of us knew that this was only the beginning of a five-year long "ordeal by slander," which became the title of the book Eleanor and Owen wrote jointly about what followed. No one has ever offered a convincing argument of just why McCarthy chose Owen as his chief target.

On March 25, in Kabul, Afghanistan, Owen received a telegram from the Associated Press: "Senator McCarthy says off record you top Russian espionage agent in United States." In trying to figure out the situation, Owen's first thought was that the charge was the kind of lie that followed the Goebbels formula of the big lie: a lie so big that a lot of people would say: "He couldn't make an accusation like that with nothing to back it up. There must be something in it." Still, he determined not to let the attack shorten his stay in Afghanistan by a single day. He came home exactly on the day planned, having concluded an agreement that was satisfactory to the United Nations and the Afghan government.

On the plane going home, Owen read a letter from Eleanor, dated March 23, which after an affectionate beginning went on as follows:

> I have just learned that the matter is much more serious than I had thought—about as serious as possible—but it is so utterly fantastic and incredible that it may be easier to disprove . . . but I don't know how far they may have gone in manufacturing evidence. I'm going to consult Abe Fortas tomorrow. . . . I'm not being hysterical as this sounds. . . . I never loved you more, darling, I'm sure you'll handle it wonderfully. . . . All my love, and faith.
>
> Hurry home!

March 26th: Darling—no time for a letter—Drew Pearson really broke the story tonight. Papers will probably have it tomorrow. He gave you terrific support.[*]

Owen's first statement to the press upon arriving in New York said that he was "far from being the 'architect of Far Eastern Policy'; [that] I have in fact had no influence on the drafting of American Far Eastern policy; that I am not and never have been a communist, have never advocated the communist cause, and have no communist connections; and finally, that I am an independent expert and commentator and throughout my career have never hesitated to criticize official policy whenever, according to my knowledge and my conscience, I have thought that was the right thing to do. In this connection, ever since the surrender of Japan in 1945 I have been convinced, and many people have agreed with me, that if only the State Department had in fact adopted some of my ideas, and adopted them early enough, China would not today be in the hands of the communists, and the structure of American policy and American interests all over Asia would not be in such a mess."[†]

When brought before the Tydings Committee in 1951, Owen defended himself vigorously and well. He acknowledged that his analysis of our policies "may be partly or wholly wrong, but if anyone says it is disloyal or un-American, he is a fool or a knave." He went on to say, "If the people of this country can differ with the so-called China Lobby or with Senator McCarthy only at the risk of the abuse to which I have been subjected, freedom will not long survive." His words drew thunderous applause from everyone in the hearing room. At the end Chairman Tydings announced that he had seen Owen's FBI file and found "nothing in that file to show that you were a communist or had ever been a communist, or that you were in any way

---

[*] Owen and Eleanor Lattimore, *Ordeal by Slander* (Little Brown, 1950)
[†] Ibid.

connected with espionage." Owen considered himself victorious against a poisonous enemy, but his exhilaration did not last long. McCarthy had no intention of giving up and produced Louis Budenz, a former communist who now saw the light and was making an excellent living testifying and writing about his former colleagues using his imagination to enlarge his knowledge and create sensational charges. He declared that he "knew" Owen was a communist from his own communist days as an editor of *The Daily Worker*.

Despite his courage and his fighting-back spirit, when the Korean War unleashed a fresh epidemic of accusations concerning *who* lost China to the communists, Owen and many other "old China hands" came under attack again, this time from the McCarran Committee. Led by Senator Patrick McCarran, a fiercely militant anti-communist Democrat, the committee called Owen back on July 13, 1951, just when he thought things were easing up. For thirteen horrible days he was interrogated with leading questions of the "have you stopped beating your wife" caliber—long questions designed to entrap, to which he was permitted only a yes or no answer. The committee was determined to get him at least on perjury charges since none of the other charges had held up. He was not permitted to question or cross-examine any of his accusers, but day after day he was accused, insulted, and branded treasonous. Reading the transcript today, one finds it hard to believe that the interrogators could get away with their brazen attempts at entrapment. Fighting back with all his strength, Owen had incurred the anger of his interrogators. He was threatened with being "disciplined" for his "insolent, overbearing, arrogant language and for slandering the Committee's staff." He called McCarthy a "graduate witch burner"and wrote a friend, "Senators can hit below the belt and keep it up day after day; but if he hits back, straight from the shoulder, that is not becoming."

We were helpless. While Owen was still in Afghanistan, Eleanor had begun gathering the material to refute the charges and had the wisdom to approach Abe Fortas, of the law firm of Arnold, Fortas &

Porter, who agreed to help Owen. The whole prestigious firm was soon behind Owen and agreed to do the massive work of organizing his defense pro bono, although the Lattimores had to pay the case's expenses, which wiped out their savings. As a result, they had to turn into cash everything they owned, including their share of the Vermont Stoddard farm. We put an ad in the May 1950 issue of the *Saturday Review of Literature*, offering the farm for sale at $4,500, which would just cover what we and the Lattimores had invested. The ad was answered by Ordway Southard, a man with whom we had a slight acquaintance.

An anthropologist with a degree from the University of Alaska and son of Dr. Elmer E. Southard, a famous Harvard Medical School professor, Ordway Southard had done some reading at the Stefansson Library in New York, as any outsider who qualified as a scholar could. He ran a trucking business on the side to make ends meet and had once trucked some of our furniture and books from New York to our farm. His was the only serious response to the ad, and on June 6, he came to look at the property. Stef, the great debater and persuader, overrode my strong intuition that it would be a mistake to sell the place to Southard, whom I disliked. All too soon my intuition was proved correct. One evening a Hearst newspaper man from Boston telephoned our farm. I answered the phone, and he asked to speak to Ordway Southard. I explained that he was more than a mile away and had no telephone but that perhaps a nearer neighbor, whose telephone number I gave him, might be able to reach him. The reporter persisted and asked if Southard was the same man who had run for governor in Alabama on the communist ticket. "If he was, I never knew anything about it," I said. And was his wife the same woman who had run for lieutenant governor?" Again the answer was that I had no idea.

But I knew instantly that this would be used as a weapon against the Lattimores by the McCarthyites, and I was heartbroken that we should have been involved in anything that would bring more pain to our friends, whom we loved and who had been subjected to more than enough pain and indignity. We learned later that the neighbor had gone to rouse Southard and that he wouldn't take the call. Later he came to see us, but I was so upset that I wouldn't talk to him. He told Stef he was indeed the same Southard from Alabama and that he had not intended to keep his communist past a secret—the subject had just not come up. Stef asked him if he understood what the consequences of his purchase might be for the Lattimores. Well, yes, he said, he had considered that, but he had done nothing that was illegal. Stef had to agree. With his enlightened view of civil liberties, Stef thought it an innocent situation, but I, who by then had become obsessed by the conspiracy against Owen, thought it the opposite of innocent. "They," whoever they were, were out to get Owen by any means, and I agonized that we had been the instrument of one more smear. I was angry and hurt that I hadn't prevailed in not wanting to sell to Southard, probably the only time in our long and happy marriage that I blamed Stef and felt he should have listened to me. It was a serious breach in our smooth relationship, and it took some time for me to get over it.

Stef had heard about Southard being a communist, but his clipping bureau was sending him cuttings from the Hearst and Scripps-Howard newspapers saying that Stef himself was a communist, and Westbrook Pegler was calling our friend A. N. Spanel, President of the International Latex Corporations, a communist or a communist tool, sympathizer, and abettor. However, in June 1950 Stef wrote the following to Owen:

> To me this sort of thing was Salem Witchcraft over again, and I perhaps leaned over backward not to appear to be afflicted with what was increasingly worrying me as mob hysteria. It goes against the grain with me, even now, to take such precautions as many are taking against situations that could involve guilt by association.
>
> Today it was pointed out to me that you are already a victim of a guilt by association frame-up and that I must not let my pooh-pooh attitude become dangerous to you. So I must give you what lowdown I have, mostly hearsay, because of twin dangers: that your selling Stoddard to a "communist" may be used

against you, and that your coming to visit Dearing, contiguous to
Stoddard, the week after the Southards moved in, may be inter-
preted as a suspicious coincidence.

Stef's fears, coming too late in my view, were only too true. Owen
immediately consulted Fortas, who "sensed disaster." He advised
Owen to attempt to cancel the sale, but it was too late. Southard had
a valid contract and could sue if it were broken.*

On July 27, 1950, McCarthy told the Senate, "Lattimore had bought
a half interest in the farm for about $1,500 in 1949 and sold it for
between $4,000 and $4,500. So we find a well-known communist giving Mr. Lattimore $3,000. The communist party often handles pay-
offs/contributions by transfers of property." When reporters caught
up with Owen he explained that he had received only half of the sale
price and that he had sold the property through Stefansson "to a
complete stranger about whom I knew nothing and of whom I had
previously never heard." But the damage was done.†

IN July of 1952 Eleanor sent me a draft of a letter she hoped to cir-
culate among friends. "This is an improved version of the missing
memo I sent you," she wrote. "It is not, at least not yet, for publication
or circulation. You might show it to the Bundys [Robert Bundy was
Bethel's town clerk; Grace, his wife, was our lawyer] and the [Vin-
cent] Sheeans if you see them." I quote the letter here in full:

> *Ruxton, Maryland*
> *July 12, 1952*

Dear —
Several of our friends, here at the university and elsewhere, have
asked for some specific information about the five "matters" about
which the McCarran Committee Report claims Owen "testified

* Robert P. Newman, *Owen Lattimore and the "Loss" of China*, (University of California Press, 1992).
† Ibid.

falsely" and on the basis of which the committee has recommended that the Justice Department conduct a grand jury investigation. I have, therefore, prepared the enclosed memorandum for them—not because we think anyone is going to be interested in so much dreary detail but because it will enable them to say, or write, with more authority what they already know in general, that the grounds on which perjury charges have been suggested are absurdly trivial and immaterial. We can't think that the Justice Department or any grand jury could take them seriously, and we wouldn't pay any attention to them if the publicity given the Committee's recommendation had not already done us a lot of harm.

The memorandum also illustrates the devious lengths to which the Committee went in its deliberate attempts to trap Owen into inaccuracies and inconsistencies. After their eighteen-month "investigation" of hundreds of thousands of "documents" from the IPR [Institute of Pacific Relations] files, and out of hundreds of thousands of words of Owen's testimony concerning hundreds of people and events, it is really amazing that there weren't many more than five instances which even the McCarran Committee could attempt to label as "false testimony." It is also significant that none of the five matters selected involved discrepancies between the testimony of Owen and Budenz, where there were many direct conflicts. Owen had suggested to the Committee that it ask the Department of Justice to review the record and prosecute for perjury whichever of the two appeared guilty. The Committee, in its recommendations, has been careful not to expose Budenz to the danger of cross-examination.

It is typical that the Committee has released a 226-page report containing its attack on Owen and presenting its own flagrantly distorted version of the significance of the testimony but has not yet printed the verbatim transcript of Owen's hearings, concluded almost four months ago; so that open-minded people are unable to go to the record to see for themselves the biased manner in which the "investigation" was conducted, and the full replies patiently made by Owen to endless booby-trap questions. Incidentally the numerous page references in the Report to the transcripts of Owen's hearings show that these must have been in page proof before the Report was printed.

The Report itself is an incredible document. We had expected that it would be as bad as possible, since the whole "investigation" of the IPR had been prejudged from the beginning and the Committee had devoted 18 months to a careful and unscrupulous building up of its case. Since the Committee had worked so assiduously for 18 months to condemn and destroy Owen, ferreting out everyone who because of personal malice or for their own ends was willing to bear false witness, every sentence he wrote which could be twisted against him, every innocent association through his whole lifetime with any person they could claim to be "subversive," it was not likely that they would admit that they had been wrong in any detail. But we hadn't quite realized how bad "bad" could be. The Report is filled with the most flagrant distortion and deceit and its conclusions are completely fantastic to anyone who knows anything firsthand about the IPR. The *Washington Post*, in a July 4 editorial called "McCarran's Revenge," has called it "a shabby piece of innuendo and vindictiveness," and "an attempt to perpetrate another fraud and hoax on the American people."

This editorial also pointed out that "Owen Lattimore was, of course, the subcommittee's chief target—since he had been vocal and fearless in resisting its rehash of Senator McCarthy's exploded charge concerning him. The subcommittee's denunciation of him and its recommendation that the Department of Justice seek to indict him for perjury are naked reprisals. No persuasive evidence has yet been presented to indicate that he has been guilty of anything more than defiance of Senator McCarran's sovereignty."

Since Owen's name appears on almost half of the 226 pages of the Report, it would take weeks of probably fruitless effort to point out and correct the innumerable complicated distortions and misrepresentations of his testimony and of his writings and editorship of Pacific Affairs. Since the picture of Owen they have so diabolically built up is completely divorced from reality it would be more to the point to attempt to counteract it with some positive presentation of what his life, ideas and character really are. Anyway, the immediate, and easy, thing to do now is to show how flimsy the "false testimony" charges are.

Sincerely,
Eleanor Lattimore

IN the little memorial booklet about Eleanor, which I edited,* William D. Rogers, a member of Arnold, Fortas & Porter, wrote the best summary of her role in their ordeal:

The McCarran Committee had just published its report and sent Owen $180.50 as a witness fee. The chilling irony of the check, the prospect of compiling a refutation to the report and the apprehension that McCarran's work would force the justice department to prosecute him—were all weighing heavily on his [Owen's] mind. So he wrote to our firm that July that he had decided, as he put it to " . . . let Eleanor do my homework . . . not because I am lazy or not taking things seriously, but because this is the way Eleanor and I have divided things up for a long, long pull—and incidentally because she is a great deal more competent at analyzing and unraveling than I am.

"By now, I am finding that I am in my own mind dividing this long and skillful persecution into alternating chronic and acute phases. I have been able to stand up under the acute phases only because Eleanor, by doing all the detailed drudgery, has almost completely shielded me from the chronic phases. If I had to take on both, I'd have long ago been in a psychiatric ward or an alcoholic clinic; or I'd have made groveling 'confessions' of things I never said or thought. . . ."

---

* *Eleanor Holgate Lattimore, 1895-1970*, (H.K. Press, Washington, D.C., 1970).

So it had been from the first McCarthy charges in 1950, when with Owen 15,000 miles away in Asia, Eleanor had herself dug the first few hasty trenches and enlisted Abe Fortas, through the Tydings Hearings in 1951 and the triumphant vindication there, followed by the McCarran investigation and Owen's thirteen days of unparalleled inquisition. All this, and Eleanor's incredible labors throughout the 1950–51 period were set out in *Ordeal by Slander*.

So it was, as well, thereafter, through the first indictment for perjury growing out of McCarran's charges, the motion to dismiss, Judge Youngdahl's courageous throwing out of the major charges, the appeal and victory there, the Government's second try. Youngdahl's second dismissal, a second affirmance on appeal, and the Department of Justice's decision finally to drop the persecution in 1955. If the practice of the law comprehends an infinite capacity for detail, then she taught something to everyone who worked with her through that litigation—Thurman Arnold, Abe, John Frank (now of the Phoenix bar), and all of Arnold, Fortas & Porter. She labored indeed, checking dates, cross-referencing documents, burrowing through primary sources for this or that fact, correcting page proofs on briefs, writing notes. Her energy seemed without end.

She shielded him, not only by taking on what he called the chronic phases, but by doing far more—keeping a home to which he could repair, corresponding with friends, arranging their travels, tactfully respecting the fact that the honor of it all was fundamentally his. Though others could watch and labor, no one could live for him "the acute phases," as he put it. And I have no doubt that this was her greatest anguish.

I write about all this in some detail because many people know the word McCarthyism only as an abstraction and cannot imagine the hysteria, the lies, the rumors, the guilt by association, and the smearing that brought out all the latent fury in many otherwise sane people who were infected by the contagion of false patriotism. Owen had tenure at Johns Hopkins so he couldn't be fired, but he was subjected to so many indignities by the academic community that he might as well have been fired. The Page School that he headed was dissolved. He was assigned no graduate students, and undergraduates were advised that it would be a mistake to have him for their adviser. His flourishing lecture business of one hundred per year disappeared. Many who didn't follow the newspapers carefully still believed him guilty of the charges long after they were dropped.*

THE Southard experience "tainted the farm for us," as Stef wrote in his autobiography, and from then on we spent more time in Hanover than at the farm, especially after 1951, when we left New York. The McCarthy madness extended itself to both Vermont and Dartmouth. After the Tydings Hearings, in which Owen was successful in proving the McCarthy charges false, a semi-loony lady named Lucille Miller began to attack Stef in the local Bethel newspaper. She was one of those unpalatable former communists turned McCarthyite informant who sought the spotlight and perhaps money for producing victims. Stef paid no attention to her false charges, and the newspapers dropped the story.

The McCarthy years provided many an aspiring politician with opportunity. In 1954 Louis Wyman, the Attorney General of New Hampshire, an ambitious fellow, set about hunting communists in New Hampshire. One day Wyman telephoned Stef in Hanover and asked if he would cooperate. "Cooperate with what?" asked Stef. "Cooperate with my office and tell them what you know about communists." Stef said he would be delighted. Being the kind of lecturer who improved when heckled, Stef knew he could easily best Wyman in any interrogation. He was enjoying himself. Wyman asked him if

---

* In 1962 the University of Leeds in England invited Owen to establish a department of Chinese studies. He accepted and arrived in Leeds in June 1963 to a warm reception. Unaffected by McCarthyism, Great Britain honored him. The Queen asked him to interpret for her when Britain recognized Mongolia. He was very happy during his seven-year tenure at Leeds. The Lattimores found a place to retire to in Great Falls, Virginia. As they were returning by plane to the States on March 21, 1970, with plans to spend a weekend with me and John Nef in Georgetown, Eleanor suffered a massive pulmonary embolism that ended her life quickly. They had been happy partners for forty-four years. Owen outlived her by nineteen years and died on May 31, 1989, a month short of his 89th birthday. By then he was honored and praised for his courage in defending himself and prevailing against a powerful senatorial committee.

it was true that he was a professor at Dartmouth. "Unfortunately, I don't have that status," replied Stef truthfully. Wyman then said, "I see that you are going to be difficult," and hung up. The next day when Stef went to the post office to pick up his mail he was met by a process server who handed him a summons. Stef reported all this to Justin Stanley, an attorney and vice president of Dartmouth, who took the summons more seriously than Stef did and suggested that Dudley Orr, a Dartmouth trustee who lived in Concord, would be the best person to accompany him to Wyman's office.

When Stef appeared with Dudley at the appointed time, Wyman was surprised that he was accompanied "by the best, legally or socially" that Concord could produce. Wyman asked if Stef knew about communists. "Of course I do, for I am an alumnus of the Harvard Divinity School, where they consider Jesus a communist, and we know a lot about Jesus." That was not what Wyman meant. Did Stef know anything about American communists? He replied that he had lived for years with the North American Inuit, who were all formerly communist, though some were now becoming quite capitalistic.

Stef's autobiography described the scene: "Wyman suggested that I stop play-acting and start telling him about ordinary American communists. I said I knew only one, a classmate of mine named Crosbie. I had seen an interview with him in the *New York Times* telling that he was a communist." Stef had invited him to lunch to find out all about it. Wyman didn't follow up on Crosbie but began to ask him about how old I was when I left Hungary. As far as Stef knew, I had never left, because I had never been there. Wasn't I Hungarian? Yes, in the sense that my parents had been born there. "She was born in New York City." At this point Wyman requested a private conference with Orr. Stef was granted permission to leave the room, and when called back the atmosphere seemed to have cleared. Stef and Orr left.

Dudley Orr told Stef that Wyman was not after him; he was after me. They thought of him as an elderly fool who had been hoodwinked by a scheming wife. While Stef had been out of the room, Wyman showed Orr an informer letter, which was what had interested Wyman in the Stefanssons. I was said to be a high-ranking member of the communist party before I left Hungary and was now indoctrinating Dartmouth students and misleading Stef while masquerading as a teacher of the Russian language. Orr had assured Wyman that my Russian, which I'd learned at Middlebury, was pretty good but that I was not teaching it to anybody. Wyman still wanted to see me, and a date was set for me to appear a week later.

I didn't get much sleep during that week, and suddenly I had a small inkling of what Owen had been through. Here I was totally innocent, but I wasn't eating or sleeping much and was worried that I might be trapped into saying something that might hurt Owen or Stef. Then it was my turn on a lovely summer's day to go to the attorney general's office with Dudley Orr. Wyman himself didn't appear; his deputy took me into his office and began to question me about Hungary. Thanks to Dudley I had brought a copy of my birth certificate, which took the wind out of my interrogator's sail. It was plain that I was too young to fit the description of the informer's letter and that I had not been born in Hungary. I saw that my interrogator was a very ordinary person who was not bright enough to threaten or trap me. The interview was short. I was permitted to leave and hurried back to Hanover.

We were dining with our friends the Rublees in Cornish that night, and, to my delight, on my left I found Learned Hand. "Tell me, my dear," asked the sprightly, genial, revered judge with the extraordinary eyebrows, with whom I had previously traded folk songs, "What have you been doing with yourself today?" In my relief that the worst was over I gave him what I thought was a funny account of my visit in Concord. To my surprise his smile disappeared, and he turned to me with a very serious expression and said, "You are a very lucky young woman." "Why do you say that?" I responded. "Because you were able to prove your innocence on the spot. Many others have not been so lucky." It was a sobering lesson I never forgot.

CHAPTER XVI

Illness and Professional Growth

*A*LMOST IMMEDIATELY AFTER OUR ARRIVAL in Hanover, I was discovered to have an ovarian tumor the doctor thought should be removed. A previous tumor had given me trouble a year earlier—it was a fibroid and fortunately nonmalignant. However, surgeons were quick to perform hysterectomies in those days, and my surgeon, Frank Corscaden, convinced me that it would be advantageous to have one to avoid future troubles. "You are not planning to have any children, are you?" he asked. Slowly and reluctantly I answered, "I guess not." I was thirty-six years old. When Stef and I were contemplating marriage, he had made it plain that he was not interested in having children. From time to time I raised the subject again but never had an enthusiastic response—just the contrary. Much in love and believing that a baby must be wanted by both parents, I became resigned to the fact that I would have to forgo children. Thinking I had come to terms with the situation earlier, I consented to the operation. It went smoothly, and I was soon back at work. But some weeks afterward, when we were at the farm, I was not feeling my usual bouncy self and looked about for causes. The only possibility seemed to be the old lead pipe connecting the well to our kitchen. (I had recently read in the local paper about old lead pipes contaminating water.) My doctor tested me and reported I was not suffering from lead poisoning. Now I know that I had been mourning the children I never had.

Being so new in town, I decided to go back to my familiar New York doctors for the second operation. This second tumor was large but also nonmalignant, and all went according to plan until the day before I was to leave the hospital. Having recovered normally from the surgery, I was suddenly attacked by the most terrible pain. My own doctor was out of town for the weekend, and the resident intern was engaged in a difficult baby delivery. As the pain intensified and the nurse was unable to prescribe anything to help, I grew desperate. Finally, long after midnight, the exhausted resident arrived and decided that I was merely nervous because I was leaving the hospital the next day. He gave me a shot of Demerol and hurriedly departed.

By morning I thought it would be a blessing to get out of this hospital where I felt my escalating pain was not being taken seriously. I dressed with difficulty, and my brother, Myron, picked me up and put me on the train back to Hanover. I spent most of of the ghastly nine-hour train trip in the ladies room vomiting. Staggering off the train, I fell into the arms of our old friend, "Sy" Rolf Syvertson, dean of Dartmouth's medical school, whom Stef (who didn't drive) had sent to meet me. When Sy saw my condition, he took me directly to Dartmouth's Mary Hitchcock Hospital. The Hanover doctors telephoned New York and were told that I was just fine, just a bit nervous about leaving the hospital, so they didn't do any investigatory procedures immediately. But I kept vomiting, and when eventually reverse peristalsis (the medical term is emesis) began the situation was at last taken seriously. They discovered that I had an intestinal obstruction and immediate surgery was imperative. Having had major surgery less than ten days earlier and having been vomiting endlessly for several days, I was a poor candidate for another operation, but there was no choice.

By the time the second surgery was over, I was depleted in body and spirit, and all will to fight had left me. Professor Fred Sternfeld saved my life when he brought to my hospital room a record player and

Bach's *Passion According to St. John*. The beauty of that magnificent work made me weep and helped to ease the accumulated tensions of what seemed like an endless series of agonies. I began to fight and to heal. Bach and Fred had saved me. I was in the hospital for a month.

Once more it was a long and lonely time in the hospital. Again I felt Stef's distaste for anything, myself included, connected with illness. He telephoned regularly, but our conversations seemed limited, per-functory—in any case, they were comfortless. I told myself it was wrong to long for what he was unable to give, but that didn't prevent me from longing for it, all the same. We were new in town and had not had time to make close friends, except for the Sternfelds and Jack and Ellen Griswold, and I cannot remember Stef ever coming to the hospital dur-ing my long recovery. He himself was almost never ill, and he had a deft way of changing the subject when talk of others' illnesses arose. He never went to funerals unless he *had* to and would send me in his stead as often as possible. During the empty, lonely hospital days I thought much about his aversion to thoughts of illness and mortality. Was he threatened, I wondered, by the possibility that I might die, or, worse, that *he* might die? He had been reluctant to make a will and did so finally only at the insistence of a close lawyer friend who emphasized the chaos that would result for me if he didn't. Once, in a lively dis-cussion about our physical states generally, he remarked sharply, "You know, being seventy-three is incurable." Acknowledged for years as an Arctic explorer superman who traipsed across twenty thousand miles of tundra and ice pack, was he loath to be reminded that he could no longer do what he once could? While trying to be an understanding wife, I was nevertheless hurt by his absence. I even dared to think he was selfish in denying me the comfort that visits from him would bring; I might have recovered faster had I been less lonely.

Not long after my recovery from double surgery, Stef woke up one morning in 1952 with a stiffening of his right cheek and a blurring of his speech. We called our friend Rolf Syvertson again, and he sent Dr. Ralph Hunter, a physician at Mary Hitchcock Clinic and a professor of neurology at the medical school. Ralph became Stef's doctor and friend. He said Stef, then seventy-three, had suffered a warning paralytic stroke that fortunately was a small one. Indeed, within a week he was back to normal. His right arm had been affected, but although his handwriting looked different his typing seemed as efficient as ever. Ralph suggested that Stef at 184 pounds was overweight and should lose his excess avoirdupois; he also gave him some drugs to bring down his blood pressure.

Stef cut down on his eating but was feeling headachy and out of sorts. He would lose a few pounds and gain them back, seesawing and watching the scales. Since the stakes were high, he decided finally to return to an all-meat diet. He knew that the Inuit, with whom he had shared that diet, were never obese and indeed that he and Charlie Anderson had been healthier after their 1927 all-meat-diet experiment than before.

So, with my permission, Stef went back on what he called his Stone Age diet, living largely on fat mutton. He lost the excess weight, but I think more importantly the diet reminded him of his more-than-ten happy years in the Arctic, when he had shared the diet with his Inuit friends and expedition members. I always felt that his first little stroke had been the result of the stress that accompanied the failure of the *Encyclopedia Arctica* and having to let go so many of the researchers, writers, and editors who had become our fellow workers. Stef never was able to lay off anyone; he had always turned over that distasteful task to someone else, usually Olive Wilcox.

One of the unexpected dividends of Stef's return to an all-meat diet was that the recent arthritic stiffness in his hip and knee joints disappeared. I often joined him on his diet, especially at the farm where I was the cook, since it simplified my tasks and freed time for writing. Whether it was the disappearance of that arthritic pain or the happy associations of the meat diet, he became more cheerful and was able to make good progress on various writing jobs and his autobiography. He enjoyed campus life and was a familiar figure walking hatless and coatless even in the cold winters.

When we arrived in Hanover in 1951, I was thirty-seven and Stef was seventy-two. He had always seemed young for his years and so vigorous in mind and body that neither of us thought much about the age difference. I had worried about it when we were newly married and thought that perhaps I should assume a more matronly style of dress, but I soon forgot about that. Stef's little stroke made me seriously think, for the first time in our marriage, about Time's Arrow.

Soon after we moved into our splendid new quarters in Baker Library in 1952, the Canadian government discovered that the northeastern tip of Victoria Island was a separate, sizeable island, and decided to name it Stefansson Island. Stef had discovered and named many islands in the Canadian North, but there was no island named after him in the area he explored since among explorers it was considered bad form to name an island after oneself. (Richard Evelyn Byrd got around that in the Antarctic by naming an area for his mother, Marie Byrd Land, no doubt hoping the Geographic Board would eventually drop the Marie.) In any case, we decided to celebrate, and for a week we had parties of several sizes and kinds. It was a signal that a new group was in power in Ottawa and that the controversy that had followed Stef's 1913–1918 expedition was over. I suppose also that many of Stef's ideas about how to utilize and develop Canadian Arctic resources did not seem as "visionary" as they had earlier and the younger generations were more disposed to admire and honor him.

It was about this time that the Rideau Club, the most distinguished of Canadian social clubs, which had blackballed Stef when Sir Robert Borden, the Prime Minister of Canada, first proposed him for membership back in the 1920s, offered him an honorary membership. I made some remark about it being a bit late and supposed he would refuse. He had already suffered a second stroke and walked with a cane. He would never make use of the membership. He replied, "Oh, no, I'll accept. It's a friendly gesture on their part. It would give me no pleasure to refuse, and it will give pleasure to some members if I accept." Stef never nursed a grievance and seldom bothered to answer attacks. His partner on his second expedition, Rudolph Anderson, made a profession of trying to poison people's minds against Stef, but I never heard Stef say an unkind word about him. He was always sad that Anderson, who was a gifted scientist, Phi Beta Kappa, and a star athlete, never lived up to his early great promise.

THANKS to his Icelandic heritage and an intimate knowledge of the sagas, Stef had always been interested in the question of how far the Norsemen had penetrated North America. He collected books on the subject, and I was soon infected with his passion. There was a tower in Newport, Rhode Island, that many liked to believe was built by the Norsemen, and New Hampshire boasted several curious sites and ruins suggestive of Norse occupation. With half a dozen Dartmouth faculty members—Hugh Morrison, an art history professor; David Nutt, an oceanographic explorer; Elmer Harp, an Arctic archeologist, and a few other interested parties—we formed a group called the Early Sites Foundation. We met several times a year at each other's houses to explore, discuss, and socialize.

One of our members, Junius Bird, an archeologist at the Museum of Natural History in New York and an expert on primitive cultures of the Western Hemisphere, flew up from New York for our meetings. Junius was a life-loving, happy type, the kind of man who never embraced you without "sneaking a feel." There was nothing personal in it—it was reflexive, and though most of us females complained to each other about it, we didn't really mind. It was somehow a joyful gesture. Raymond Holden, our poet-writer friend from North Newport, New Hampshire, who was also a member, overheard me telling his wife, Barbara, about my most recent encounter with Junius, and wrote the following limerick:

The wife of a famous explorer
Whose bosom stood well out before her
Said I don't wish my torso
Were less so or more so
But a Bird with ten fingers, Oh, horror.*

One day in 1958 Dean Arthur Jensen arrived at my desk in the Stefansson Collection with the news that Bob McKennan, who taught the Arctic Seminar,† wanted to get back to anthropology. Would I be interested in taking over? I was both thrilled and terrified. I had lectured in the seminar, sat in when someone I knew was lecturing, and taken part in discussions, but to be *responsible* for the course, to teach it, was a new and startling idea. To teach at Dartmouth without even a Bachelor's degree was unheard of. To teach there as a degreeless *woman* was even more far-fetched. At that time Dartmouth never appointed a woman to any department unless they were unable to get a man. I remember only one other female faculty member, a native Russian teacher, Madam Nadezhda Koroton, but she had all the necessary degrees, and I had none. Our friend Raymond Holden sat in on my first class on a visit to Hanover. When I asked him how it had gone, he replied truthfully, "You behaved like a very determined tightrope walker." I relaxed soon afterward and as my confidence grew I came to enjoy teaching.

I cannily enlisted some of the Arctic experts I knew to help out. Walter Sullivan, the science editor of the *New York Times*, who had been to the Antarctic, came up from New York and talked about the new Antarctic Treaty. Sir Hubert Wilkins, a member of Stef's third expedition and a pioneer aviator in both the Arctic and Antarctic, came from Natick, where he was advisor to the U.S. Army's Quarter-

---

* From Barbara Holden, August 8, 1993.

† The Arctic Seminar was a course offered between 1953 and 1962, in conjunction with the Northern Studies Program at the college. It was limited to fifteen selected upperclassmen per year and offered the possibility for in-depth study of the Polar Regions, particularly the study of the area's physical environment and cultural history and the modern Arctic. The format of instruction was lectures by Dartmouth faculty, with visiting guest specialists; students wrote reports and a term paper, supervised by the director.

master Corps. And Louis Giddings, one of the archeologists who had discovered the amazing Ipiutak finds at Point Hope, Alaska, the largest ancient Arctic settlement of its kind, also came to lecture. The Stefanssons usually had open house following a polar expert's talk, giving the students a chance to talk with and question the visitors. The students told me this was unusual as they seldom saw the inside of a professor's house.

One of my secret desires had been to one day march in an academic procession, which always moved me to watch. I loved the parade of the variously colored gowns and hoods, the martial music, and the general panoply. When I became an official teacher, I decided to march in the next academic procession at commencement time. Having obtained a black cap and gown, I looked at myself in the mirror and the result was dull, dull, dull without a hood. So I took a beautiful, handwoven, colorful Thai silk stole from my scarf drawer and, draping it around my neck, made a bow—and felt the effect was much more interesting. On the way to the procession a faculty wife stopped me and said, "What an interesting hood—where is it from?" In a joking mood, I replied, "Oh, the University of Thailand." Of course she took me seriously, and the next day it was all over town: "Did you know that Evelyn Stefansson had a degree from the University of Thailand?" It took a little while to make the necessary corrections. At moments like that I was reminded that Hanover was a small town and a new piece of gossip or news spread far and wide in a short time. A neighbor would cheerily greet you with, "I saw the doctor's car in front of your house. Is somebody sick?" I also learned to "tell all" immediately rather than behave as though I were trying to hide anything, which would be the signal for speculation of every imaginable sort.

WHEN Stef suffered a second stroke, he was not as lucky as he had been the first time. He recovered, but his left leg remained weak and made walking difficult. He began to use a cane and was no

longer interested in going for walks or visiting our farm in Bethel.
Now he would climb the steps one at a time, sparing his weakened leg.
He was happier staying put. I fixed up a study for him in the finished
basement of our little Allen Lane house, which already contained
bookshelves and windows that permitted daylight to enter. He liked it
because he could work at all and odd hours without disturbing anyone
in the house. He stopped going to his office at the Stefansson Collection regularly, instead concentrating on writing his autobiography
at home. He planned to write it as fully as memory permitted "for the
record," knowing that it would have to be cut for publication.

As Stef's physical condition began to deteriorate, our life changed.
Up until then I had been his pupil. He had been in charge of our life
and its direction. He had encouraged me to charge ahead and do new
things, and I had done so with surprising success. I knew that the years
ahead were not going to be easy, but nor would they be as difficult as
friends and family had predicted. We had such a solid relationship. It
was true that as his output of books and articles was declining, mine
was increasing. Loving him as I did and being tuned into his feelings,
it was not hard to ask about his day before telling him of mine and
to dwell on his successes and honors and tone down the account of
my newest achievement. It could not have been easy for him to have his
student, me, asked to make the speech, write the article, teach the
Arctic seminar. He never showed any sign of jealousy or envy, but I
imagined he must have felt at least subconsciously some discomfort
at the new imbalance. I also knew that I would have to take charge of
the direction of our life. He had done so much for me that it was
easy to do things for him. It made the physical difficulties less important, including the waning of our marvelous sex life.

He had always encouraged me to go out when he couldn't, and now
I began to do so. Now I was traveling to the Arctic not as Stefansson's wife but on my own. The *New York Times* and the *Herald Tribune* sent
me polar books to review. The book tours Scribner's arranged for me
took me to cities I'd never seen before, in Canada as well as the States,

and I was asked to do television shows in both countries. I was lecturing at Vassar and McGill, as well as at women's clubs. I had carved a small niche for myself in the polar-affairs world. I loved the new me and feeling my oats and coming back home to tell Stef all about it.

Stef was now disinclined to travel, and when he did I was needed to give him my arm, make travel arrangements, be responsible for the tickets, register us at the hotels, and be ready to supply a missing name or date when his memory failed during a talk. We both enjoyed the little routine when he called on me, sitting in the audience, knowing that I would be able to supply the missing link without interrupting his narrative. The practiced smoothness of it reminded me of the vaudeville acts of my youth.

In 1958 Dorothy Thompson's husband, Maxim Kopf, whom I had always liked, suffered a heart attack and was hospitalized at Dartmouth's Hitchcock Clinic in Hanover. I visited him at the hospital, where he put on a brave show of entertaining his visitors when he was not in an oxygen tent. He recovered and left the hospital with doctor's warnings, which he ignored, about taking things easy. On the Fourth of July he had a second seizure, returned to the clinic, and died two days later. In August 1958 Dorothy wrote her last "On the Record" column, a routine that had dominated her life for twenty-one long years.

In the fall she rented an apartment and moved to Hanover. I think she had expected the Dartmouth students to be thrilled by her presence and to sit at her feet while she held forth about world politics. The young students didn't know who she was, and she found the town's climate and inhabitants cold. She was lonely, perhaps for the first time in her life, and growing more and more deaf. She sought us out and recognized me, it seemed to me for the first time. I found myself feeling sorry for her and took time out from my busy life to cheer her up a little. She seemed dazed by Maxim's death, for they truly loved each other. She was working on her autobiography but not unnaturally was finding it difficult to write. By November she had moved back to New York. In 1960 she flew to Lisbon to spend the Christmas holidays with her son Michael's wife, Bernadette, and her two adored grandchildren. Dorothy was bringing their divorce decree. Toward the end of her visit, she was found dead in her hotel room from natural causes.

Dorothy had left instructions that she was to be buried beside Maxim in Barnard, Vermont. On a cold New England May afternoon I drove over from Hanover for the simple graveside ceremony. Jimmy Sheean, drunk and weeping, was there. Hilda Rothschild and a few neighbors completed the group. It was a small country ending to a large, grand life.

CHAPTER XVII

Paget's Disease and "Dying Order"

*A*T A LARGE PARTY given by Raymond and Barbara Holden in 1959, I was sitting on the floor and singing with a group of people when I rose suddenly and experienced a terrible sharp pain in my left thigh. Involuntarily I let out a cry, and everyone wanted to know the trouble. I apologized and confessed the pain. "You must have pulled a muscle," someone said. "No," said I. "It feels more like a bone pain, as if it is in the marrow." The party continued but so did the pain, which went on long enough for me to consult a doctor. He couldn't find the cause, so x-rays were taken. Then I was told, "You have a hole in your bone, the femur." A hole in the bone—what did that mean? No one would say. But I had read enough to know that that is how metastasized bone cancer behaves. "What do we do about it?" I asked. Take some more x-rays.

Not getting a direct, simple answer from the doctors, I began to worry. After my hysterectomy I had been given the hormone estrogen and almost immediately developed lumps in my breasts. The estrogen was discontinued, but I had to have my lumpy breasts examined regularly. Could those lumps have been an overlooked cancer, and had the cancer metastasized to the bone, where breast cancer usually goes if it isn't treated in time? The pain didn't go away. The doctor said the only way to find out what was really going on was to do a bone biopsy, a process that requires full anesthesia, penetrating the muscle, and drilling out a sample of the bone. I would lose the use of that leg until everything healed. Crutches for six months. I postponed as long as possible before agreeing to the procedure.

I was hospitalized on December 15, 1959. This time, being a member of the faculty, I was entitled to stay in Dick's House, Dartmouth's elegant endowed facility for students and faculty. The hardest part of the experience was waiting for the verdict. I felt like a prisoner waiting to be sentenced. A week passed with no word. I had started physical therapy almost immediately after the operation because I couldn't move the leg that had been biopsied. At long last, after more than ten days of waiting, the verdict was in. I did not have bone cancer—I had Paget's Disease, an incurable but not necessarily fatal condition. Paget's is a chronic disorder that typically results in enlarged and deformed bones in one or more regions of the skeleton. Excessive bone breakdown and formation cause the bone to be dense but fragile. As a result, bone pain, arthritis, noticeable deformities, and fractures can occur.[*] I was lucky in that there was no visible deformation, but who knew about the future. Nonetheless, I was reprieved—Paget's was better than cancer.

After the operation I noticed that the pain, which had been constant before, had departed, and I thought I had been cured at least of that. I celebrated too early, however, for as the bone healed the pain returned in my left leg—not the sharp pain I had first experienced, but a kind of dull knocking and pounding that would radiate down my shin to the ankle or up to my hip. Coming to terms with the pain and not letting it interfere with my work has been a long learning process that continues to this day. I determined at the time that I would never fall into being a professional invalid and that *I* would be the one in control, not the pain. Being fairly athletic, I adjusted to

[*] The cause of Paget's Disease is unknown, but recent studies have suggested that it may be caused by a "slow virus" infection of bone, a condition that is present for many years before symptoms appear. There may also be a hereditary factor since my sister Julie and my brother, Myron, discovered years after my experience that they too had the disease.

the elbow crutches and became expert at using and maneuvering them. Only when the winter streets were ice-covered did I have any trouble. I had to be very cautious and move slowly, which was difficult since I am a precipitous person who moves first and thinks later.

Back at work life settled into its usual routine, except for the slowly escalating pain. When it finally kept me from sleeping, I agreed to a second surgery, which would involve cutting out the hole in my femur and grafting bone from my pelvis in its place. The slices of pelvis bone that were placed in the hole were called "barrel staves" because of their shape. Describing the operation, the surgeon, Dr. Ernest Sachs, explained how lucky I was. Previously I would have had to be in a plaster cast from waist to ankle, but I was just in time to take advantage of a newly developed technique that substituted tightly bound ace bandages for plaster—certainly more comfortable, especially during the summer months.

So, in 1962, I went once more to the hospital. The surgery was successful and provided me with new information. My Paget's Disease was not localized. In the interest of speeding up the operation, the surgeon and his team had wanted to take bone from the right side of my pelvis while another group was working on preparing the left femur for the graft. But they found Paget's in the pelvis (which sounds like some kind of joke) and had to crowd each other and take the barrel staves from the left side, which was Paget's-free. After a long hospitalization, I was again on crutches, and again needed physical therapy. But this time I was expert and fearless on my crutches—I remember even using them while dancing with a partner at a New Year's party. I was disciplined about the physical therapy, determined to rejoin my folk-dancing group when I could leave the crutches behind. I bought a bicycle and learned to ride it, for the first time in my life, in order to strengthen my leg and speed the return to normal life.

After I healed, I went back to folk dancing and have been dancing ever since. The muscles around the site of the operation would atrophy from time to time and produce a limp. But I soon learned to measure the circumference of my thigh and when I lost half an inch or more would automatically get out the athletic boot and start weight-lifting exercises to restore the muscle to its normal size.

BEFORE going to the hospital for the first operation, when I thought I had bone cancer, I put my house in what the New Eng-landers called "dying order," an expression I had learned from a neighbor during our summers in Vermont. The idea is that if you should be killed without warning a stranger coming into your house would find everything in order and very tidy. Something like mothers warning their daughters to always wear "nice" underwear when going out so that if they have an accident or get run over, they would not be disgraced by others seeing the sagging elastic or holes in their everyday underpants. "Dying order" requires tidying closets and drawers, throwing out things that needed to be discarded for myriad reasons, and making a will. It also means thinking in depth about one's death. I have since discovered that you only have to do that once in a lifetime. If you make peace with yourself and those around you about dying, you never have to do it again. I have been "ready" since that time to die if I must and to die well if I could—that is, with a minimum of regret and maximum appreciation for the good life I have been lucky enough to have.

From Stef I had learned that many so-called primitive, Stone Age people dealt with death in a much more realistic and dignified fashion than we do. A Stone Age Inuit no longer able to keep up with the family whose survival depended on movement and migration would ask to be left behind. "I will catch up when I am feeling stronger." Food and drink would be left behind and farewells exchanged, everyone hoping that strength would return to the aged person but knowing, of course, that it was unlikely. This was not considered abandonment, as some uninformed writers have declared it to be, but more like today's aged saying "no heroic measures, please." The leave-taking was always affectionate on both sides, not without poignancy, but there was also acceptance of the common belief that one person's infirmity must not endanger the group's survival.

I believe so many of us have a terrible fear of dying largely because in our culture we do not do enough thinking and talking about it. Prizing youth too much and putting great faith in the medical profession, we may be ashamed or reluctant to bring the subject into everyday conversation. In earlier days, when life spans were shorter, people accepted the reality of death and were better prepared for it.* Having religious faith also prepared people for death and helped them not to fear it. Coming to terms with death enabled me much later to work with terminal patients without fear or dread. It freed me to want to help others because I somehow knew how to make it easier. Because I had to face death, I came understand that it is as natural as birth.

---

* In Elizabethan times people thought more about dying and how to do it well and even with wit, if possible. As the aged Bishop Latimer said to his hangman, "Help me up to the scaffold, Mr. Executioner, please. As for the coming down, I can manage myself."

CHAPTER XVIII

Stef's Death

I N T H E " P O S T L U D E ," A S I C A L L E D I T, to Stef's autobiography, I described the evening of his third and final stroke.* Since I was closer to it then than now, I quote:

On a hot day in late August [1962], an old and distinguished friend of Greenland and Copenhagen days, Eske Brun, was our dinner guest, and we had invited all the Dartmouth polar and Scandinavian folk to come in afterward to greet him. During dinner Stef was in marvelous form, merry and witty, and stimulated by Eske, a veteran of thirty Greenland years, he turned the conversation to medieval falconry (the best white falcons came from Greenland long before Columbus discovered America), to Greenland archeology (Eske brought news of a churchyard discovery containing what was thought to be Leif Eriksson's skeleton) and to the infinite variety of Iceland's literary forms. Flushed with good wine and delight in each other's company, we moved to the living room for coffee. I poured into the old white ironstone egg

---

* Vilhjalmur Stefansson, *Discovery*, (McGraw Hill Book Company, 1964). During his last several years Stef worked on his autobiography, writing down everything he could remember. He knew the manuscript would be too long for a book but wanted to record whatever he could for the archives. He produced an enormous manuscript shortly before he died; indeed, I had the feeling that he was staying alive in order to finish it. After Stef's death, our friend Raymond Holden offered to edit the manuscript and prepare it for publication. Raymond asked me to do an afterword, which I wrote with tears streaming down my face as I recalled our happy years together.

cups we used for after-dinner coffee and passed them. Then, in the silent language all well married couples know, he sent a message, urgent as a cry for help. Following unspoken direction, I rose quietly and, as I approached, discovered that he was silent because he was unable to speak. I offered my arm, and as we staggered out of the room to the hall, I called over my shoulder for Sven Gunderson, who heads our famous Hanover clinic. It was not news when he whispered seconds later, "He's had a shock," using the New England expression for a stroke. Since Stef had just suffered a massive stroke with its accompanying paralysis, it was theoretically impossible for him to have risen and staggered from the room. His enormous dignity, which would not permit him to ruin a perfect evening by collapsing in front of his guests, combined with a strong act of will, had powered his and enabled him to do at the close of his life, what he had often done during it—the impossible! Blessedly, Stef struggled in a deep coma for less than a week, until the early morning of August 26, when he was what the doctors termed dead. For me, the moment of his leave-taking was his poignant call for help, one of the few received in the last quarter-century for which I was unable to provide any aid whatever.

Stef was buried in Pine Knoll Cemetery in Hanover on August 28, 1962; his grave is marked by a huge boulder flown from one of the most northerly Canadian Arctic islands. After his death, I received messages from all over the world in surprising numbers. They included President Kennedy, the prime minister of Canada, and the president of Iceland; the presidents of many geographical societies and the directors of Arctic institutes in Cambridge, England, Leningrad, Copenhagen, and Montreal; the governor of Puerto Rico, Luis Muòoz Marìn, an old friend of Stef's; the Explorers Club; the National Science Foundation; and innumerable friends, students, people he had helped financially, and readers of his books whom he had never met.

The immense pile of sympathy letters weighed on me, and it was six months before I could begin to acknowledge and answer them individually. I had lost a giant of a man who had been a faithful, good husband, lover, father, brother, mentor, and affectionate companion. I went back to work a week after his funeral on the theory that it would help me to get over my depression. But each time another sympathy letter arrived or I saw an annotation in the margin of a book I opened in his familiar, distinctive handwriting, my wound would open. During the day I managed to control myself. Once home in the very empty little house on Allen Lane, I would put on Pablo Casal playing Bach's unaccompanied cello suites and cry.

IN the November 1962 memorial volume of *Polar Notes*, which I edited, Trever Lloyd wrote the following:

> [Stefansson] lived to see many of his prophecies of a half-century before, concerning the Far North, become almost commonplace—and he did more than anyone else to make them so.
>
> His greatest expedition, that for the Canadian Government, lasted for five years, from 1913 to 1918. It changed the map of the Far North, placing on it a series of islands that were the last major discoveries made in the long record of North American exploration. This third expedition confirmed Stefansson's reputation as an outstanding Arctic traveler. He had gone with confidence where others had not dared, and demonstrated that one skilled and observant could live off the resources of the land, doing so even when "the land" was, in fact, the floating floes of the Polar Sea. It was Stefansson who finally took the fear out of the Far North. This expedition ultimately brought recognition of the Arctic's true location—at the center of the world's great land masses, and led eventually to its conquest through the air and under the ocean—modes of travel which he advocated almost a half century ago.

Laurence McKinley Gould, a distinguished Antarctic explorer, also contributed to the memorial issue. He had decided to become an explorer after hearing Stef talk at his university, and in later years became the president of Carleton College, where he often hosted conferences on the Polar Regions. He wrote of Stef:

> Possessed of splendid health and great physical vigor, proper equipment for the explorer, he also had the curiosity, imagination, and the capacity for careful observation which are the necessary characteristics of any good scientist. And so Stef has left us a heritage of great achievement in Arctic exploration, a brilliant record as author, lecturer and teacher, and, as a further permanent record of his consuming intellectual concern, the Stefansson Collection—the most comprehensive library on the polar regions in the western hemisphere. Tradition fades but the written record does not, and in his own works and in his library Stef has left a record of himself which will remain ever fresh.
>
> Stef was provocative and controversial, as indeed most interesting people are. But Stef always provided such stimulating controversy! He was never guilty of the unforgivable sin of dullness. . . .
>
> We shall remember him for the intellectual stimulation of his friendship, for his good humor and his great generosity with his own time, and perhaps above all for his unending infectious enthusiasm.

In preparing that issue of *Polar Notes*, I was reminded that Stef had made original contributions to anthropology, archeology, aviation, bibliography, exploration, geography, geopolitics, history, nutrition, teaching, writing, and linguistics.

Stef once said that if a man is six months ahead of his time he is called a man of vision, but if he is six years ahead of his time he is called a "visionary" (in the negative sense) and his ideas are not taken seriously. By his own definition, then, he fit in the visionary category, for he was often six years ahead of his time and sometimes closer to sixty. He delighted in the world of ideas—original, radical, and thought-provoking—and he percolated new ones as easily as breathing. Those of us who have lived in New England are familiar with the local put-down, "Whoever *heard* of such a thing?" It gives us a clue as to why Stef was sometimes called a charlatan as well as the Prophet of the North, a publicity hunter as well as a great caribou and seal hunter, a faddist as well as a meticulous scientific observer. Many who had never heard of his ideas before rejected them for that reason. He understood that when he wrote, "Man finds it easier to change the face of nature than to change his own mind."

Back in the 1920s many dismissed Stef as a visionary when he advocated using a submarine beneath the polar sea ice. In 1958, when the *Nautilus* and the *Skate* submarines made their transpolar voyages powered by nuclear reactors, everybody had forgotten who had first suggested the idea. Too much time had elapsed between the suggestion and the happening. When Scandinavian Airlines began flying great-circle routes that crossed the North Pole and the Greenland Icecap, the public had forgotten Stef's predictions about how much fuel and time could be saved by flying great-circle routes north instead of east-west.

All the scientists of Stef's day, including the great Fridtjof Nansen and Robert E. Peary, believed that there was no life in the Arctic Ocean once you went any distance offshore. The Inuit believed it, too. Stef persisted in his belief that animal life *had* to be there, saying, "I have examined all the arguments in favor of no life in the Arctic Sea, and it seems to me that they are the kind of arguments that would appeal to a philosopher but not to a fish." On his third expedition he staked his life and that of his companions on this belief and won when far from land on the moving sea ice they found the animals they needed for survival.

He had an uncanny ability to be right. Among his twenty-seven books was one called *Cancer, Disease of Civilization*, published in 1960, which proposed that diet was a factor in the incidence of that disease. There were no reported incidents of cancer among the Inuit while they lived on their primitive diet, and Albert Schweitzer found the same was true of the African natives in Gabon when he first arrived. Fifteen or so years after the introduction of sugar, carbohydrates, and so-called "civilized" food the first cases turned up. The medical world laughed at or ignored the book. The notion is no longer a subject for laughter.

Long before Prudhoe Bay and the Alaska Pipeline came into existence, Stef had written that the polar sea was, geologically speaking, similar to the ancient Mediterranean, and that great stores of oil would be found there. His most famous book's very title, *The Friendly Arctic*, provoked responses like, "friendly, hell." He liked provoking discussion.

I worked with Stef for almost a quarter of a century and learned something new every day. I learned to read not just for pleasure but with passion; to say what I thought (Stef claimed I had a gift for exaggeration because I said a million when I meant at least several); to be a good researcher and librarian; to read, write, and speak Russian, along with some Icelandic and Danish; to write three books; to enjoy making a speech; to consider and sift through controversial materials to find the kernel of truth, and to know that it was *my* truth and that someone else going through the same material might find a different truth; to delight in the accumulation of interesting facts about almost everything; and to sharpen my curiosity and feed it with good books. When people ask me where I went to college, I want to answer that I married Stef. He was my B.S., M.S., and Ph.D.

Stef's own intellectual curiosity was as wide-ranging as Darwin's, whom he greatly admired. It enabled him to listen to a student with the same rapt attention he gave Albert Einstein, Winston Churchill, or the Queen of Denmark, all of whom he met. He generously shared his passion of the mind with me. Indeed, it was a highly contagious thing. If I had to choose the most important thing he taught me, it was that both love and knowledge increase when shared.

WASHINGTON, D.C.

CHAPTER XIX

Mrs. Stefansson Goes to Washington

WHEN STEF WAS ALIVE, Hanover had seemed a delightful, handsome little town with every opportunity ahead for a good life and pleasurable development. With Stef dead, I saw it differently, through my depression. When I had first arrived, I had the naïve belief, perhaps growing out of my own love of learning, that people who taught the young were a nobler and more virtuous breed. During the approximately dozen years we lived there, I discovered that academics were people—good, bad, and everything in-between. They were human, in other words. And while many were gifted in their fields and intellectually stimulating, they were not necessarily friendly. Sometimes they even made promises they didn't keep, like the dean who had promised me faculty status but never followed through. As a couple, Stef and I had made close friendships, which lasted, but when Stef died I understood how insignificant the role of a single woman in a small academic town could be. My only status seemed to be as librarian of the Stefansson Collection. I looked around at the single librarians in Baker Library, and I didn't like what I saw. It reminded me of something my stylish sister Rosalind had stung me with long ago. She had said, "It's bad enough to *be* a librarian—do you have to *look* like one?"

A year after Stef died, I was still depressed and lonely. During that year I had functioned at my work well enough but was like a zombie much of the rest of the time. The Hanover winters were long and cold, and they seemed longer and colder without Stef. Hanover was a man's and a couple's town. Wives didn't seem to enjoy having unattached women around. A single woman was seldom invited to a dinner party except when a partner was needed for a visiting, lone lecturer, and he was usually married. The local bachelors were either homosexual or very ancient widowers. Some married men offered me comfort for their own reasons. I was forty-nine years old, and I felt I had already had the best that life could offer. Somewhere I had to find the strength to live out the remainder of my life in a quiet and dignified manner, but I knew that never again would I find anything like what I had lost.

The following summer, when I was just beginning to hold my head up and smile occasionally, something happened that helped me enormously. Our friends Hugh and Charlotte Morrison asked me to come for dinner on July 24, 1963, which happened to be my fiftieth birthday, at their summer place on nearby Lake Mascoma. Grateful to be diverted from what might have been a depressing evening alone, I drove out to the lake to find a huge surprise party of Hanoverites. I was astonished at the lavishness of the party and the number of affectionate friends who had come to a party for *me*. Up until that time I had thought I was only meaningful to most people as an appendage of Stef's—Mrs. Stefansson. Suddenly the happy thought dawned on me that people cared about me, alone, by myself. This was a true epiphany, and it may have been responsible for ending the acute phase of my yearlong depression. In retrospect, the Morrison's party was a milestone in the return of my self-esteem. I began to stand straighter, to be able to count my successes, and to remember the good things from the past.*

---

* One of the effects of a real depression is that it wipes out even the memory of past pleasure and joy. It also destroys one's energy, which may become so low that making a simple decision becomes difficult, if not impossible. Hans Weigert, a friend who collaborated with Stef on a geopolitical book called *Compass of the World*, had been driving when he had an accident that killed his beautiful, beloved wife. For several years, he was horribly depressed, and once at our house, when I offered him the choice of a martini or Manhattan, he burst into tears, lacking the energy to make the choice.

Not long after that party, another event occurred that changed the course of my life. Gresham Sykes, the head of the sociology department at Dartmouth, was leaving the college to become the executive director of the American Sociological Association in their new offices in Washington, D.C. The ASA was a professional organization of mostly academic sociologists, who met annually and published scholarly journals. He offered me the job of Administrative Officer, second in command, at a much higher salary than I was receiving at Baker Library. I wasn't a sociologist, but I had occasionally run the twenty-member research office of the Stefansson Library before we had moved to Hanover. It occurred to me that Gresham Sykes must be very smart to know that I could do the job. But I was also cautious—I had a lifetime tenure at Baker Library. So I went to see President John Dickey to inquire where the Polar Studies Program at Dartmouth was going and whether there would be any further opportunities for teaching. John Dickey was very friendly. He said that without Stef's presence and adequate funding the polar studies at Dartmouth were waning. There was no plan to continue the Arctic Seminar. Dickey had worked for the State Department and thought Washington would be an interesting and exciting place for me. He also said that while the trustees had recently ruled against professors taking leaves of absence he thought he could manage one for me. "Try it for a year; if you don't like it, you can always come back to Hanover. You have made a place for yourself here that will always be waiting." With that insurance and after conferring with Ellen and Jack Griswold, I decided to take the job.*

I traveled to Washington to look over the offices of the ASA, which were in the annex of the Brookings Institution, at 1755 Massachusetts Avenue, just beyond Dupont Circle. It was a new building and the offices were freshly painted, so we went about furnishing them. When

---

* Erica Parmi, a competent Baker librarian with great interest in the outdoors but no Arctic experience, took over the librarianship of the Stefansson Collection.

the telephones were turned on, Gresham Sykes arrived. He was a weekend painter of huge, colorful abstract canvases, and he lent us some of his pictures to decorate the offices. I brought leftover encyclopedias and dictionaries from the Stefansson Library, along with a fourteen-foot aluminum ladder so we could reach the highest bookshelves. We were to hire a staff of about ten, which we slowly assembled. The first thing on our agenda was to organize the huge annual meeting. There would be nine simultaneous sessions to be headed by the incoming president, Professor George Homans of Harvard. Talcott Parsons was an officer, as were many others with national reputations who had written popular as well as scholarly tomes.

One of my first chores was to go and see the outgoing president, Pitirim Sorokin, a controversial Harvard sociologist of Russian origin. I was told he was "very difficult." He had been elected by a write-in vote of friends, which was unusual, and there was a whispered suggestion that it had been "managed." I was given complicated instructions on how to deal with him and get him to agree to various matters that would take place at the meetings. As soon as we met and I heard his heavy Russian accent, I switched from English to Russian, and from then on we were fast friends. He invited me to stay for lunch, and we embraced when I left. Everyone back at the office was astonished that all matters had been resolved and without difficulty. I knew that what had made the difficult man easy was my Middlebury College Russian.

Because the ASA had always been run by sociologists rather than professional administrators, we found the files in terrible shape. But before long everything was tidy, and I was beginning to rewrite the workbooks, describing in exact detail what had to be done when and how to keep the organization functioning. The office was soon running smoothly, and I was enjoying being in touch with the leading sociologists of the day.

JUST as I was about to leave Hanover for Washington, I received news from my sister Rosalind that my mother, who had been hospitalized for many years, had died. On my way to Washington, driving in my loaded Peugeot, I stopped in New York for her simple, sad Jewish funeral, a family reunion.

After Poppa died and Mother became mute, she still managed to look after herself and keep house. Rosalind married Max Feller in 1932, and they moved into the Eighty-fourth Street house until they were able to afford an apartment of their own. Shortly thereafter I married Bil Baird and moved to our one-room apartment in Greenwich Village. The following year, 1933, Julie married a Broadway press agent, Monte Proser, who took two apartments, installing Julie in one and Mother and Myron in the other. The Brooklyn family house was abandoned for nonpayment of taxes and interest on the $5,000 mortgage. When Julie divorced Monte in 1937, Mother moved in with Rosalind, and Myron went into the army's ski troops. Thereafter Mother alternated between Julie and Roz, according to circumstances. When Julie married her flying instructor, Wallace Stege, in 1945 and they moved to California, Mother moved with them. Julie paid for psychotherapy, but since Mother wouldn't talk it was ineffective. In 1946, when Max Feller was made vice president of International Latex Corporation, they moved to Delaware. Mother's condition had deteriorated by then, and finally she was hospitalized at New York State Hospital in Brooklyn.* Dr. Rothenberg, who had lived across the street from us in Brooklyn, committed her. He had not seen her for years and marveled at how little she had aged and how beautiful she had remained.

All of us contributed to the cost of her care. I had never been to a mental hospital before then, and visiting her left indelible memories.

---

* During this time I was traveling alone to Arctic places with notebook and camera, gathering material for books. I could not consider the possibility of having Mother live with us, and the prospect of leaving her alone with Stef while I traveled was not to be even imagined. Still, I felt enormous guilt when she was hospitalized, as though I were jailing someone I loved.

However, Mama was not unhappy there, and the nurses loved her because she was no trouble and was eager to help them, especially with mending, her skills with a needle never having left her. She was long in the hospital and survived a ruptured appendix, the family complaint. In August 1963, she had a stroke that killed her.

Once more I thought of her wasted life. With four children, no money, and no way of earning a living, she may have seen her illness as a kind of solution. But what a price to pay—thirty-six years, half of her total years on earth, of non-life. I had long thought of my mother as no mother. With my faulty, childish reasoning, I had decided that since she was unable to be a mother to me I had little feeling for her. Tit for tat. Of course, I was wrong. Every child deprived of a mother's love, for whatever reason, continues to long for it. My no-feeling defense was just that—a defense, against the sadness and pain of that deprivation. At the funeral service I dug for and found those buried feelings, and my grief over the loss of Stef and the loss of Mother co-mingled.

WHEN I arrived in Washington at the beginning of September 1963, I moved into a tiny studio apartment not far from Dupont Circle, within walking distance of Brookings. After some weeks I realized that the apartment was too small and moved to a one-bedroom place on the top floor of a new building on Twentieth Street. I went back to Hanover to get my furniture, sell what I couldn't use, and make arrangements for renting the Allen Lane house.

During wartime I had often been to Washington with Stef. But the war was long over, and I knew only two people in Washington. One was Captain (later Admiral) James Calvert, who had taken the nuclear-powered submarine *Skate* to the North Pole; he lived in nearby Annapolis and was heading the Naval Academy. The other was Lisa Sergio, a friend of Dorothy Thompson's. She had lived in Woodstock, Vermont, and we used to see her in summertime at our Bethel farm. An old political hand who knew everybody, Lisa was making her living very successfully as a radio news commentator and a college lecturer. Her distinctive black-velvet voice was perfect for radio. She had a small house on Volta Place filled with beautiful antiques, books, and mementos of her early life in Florence, Italy, where she had grown up. She lived alone and was very helpful to me in learning the Washington ropes. I was eager to take advantage of everything the city offered, including its wonderful museums, symphony orchestra, and vibrant political scene. As a lifelong Democrat, I was excited about the election of John Kennedy. Lisa introduced me to some of her friends, and before long I was at home in Washington and began to feel something like my old buoyant self.

That November Kennedy was assassinated, and the city was plunged into shock and mourning. With half of our staff, I stood at the foot of Memorial Bridge to watch the funeral procession. When Kennedy was first elected, I was reminded of the early Roosevelt days, when young men of talent in every field were called on to rework the machinery of government to pull us out of the morass of the Depression. Kennedy's arrival spurred the same kind of migration of brainy men and women to Washington. Despite often huge salary cuts, they were nonetheless glad to join the brilliant young leader and take part in the new political excitement. To have their brave new leader struck down so dramatically and needlessly affected the whole city of Washington. Just as on the day that Roosevelt died, strangers spoke to each other on the street and many openly wept; we shared a common sorrow and were united by it as we had never been while Kennedy lived. We all felt devastated, but it seemed to be especially hard on the young people who had been engaged politically for the first time by Kennedy's charisma. Rosalind's son, Johnny, was a student at American University, and he looked me up for the first time. He needed someone to listen to his grief.

CHAPTER XX

Meeting and Marrying John Nef

*I*N JANUARY 1964, I RECEIVED A TELEPHONE CALL from a young woman I didn't know named Mary Carswell, who was married to Robert Carswell, a New York lawyer. She said that Anthony di Bonaventura, whom I did know, was giving a Town Hall concert on February 9 in New York. Tony was the concert pianist brother of Mario di Bonaventura of Dartmouth's music deparment, and often came to Hanover to play concerts when Mario conducted the college orchestra. Mary was giving a dinner before Tony's concert. Would I come too? I had been away the two previous weekends and was about to say no, but Mary sounded so warm and friendly that I changed my mind and said yes.

At the Carswell's house on East Sixty-third Street, I found a party of ten elegant people. I sat down on a sofa next to a handsome man, with laugh lines around his sparkling dark eyes and a warm, friendly, welcoming manner, who seemed to be fascinated with *me.* He was Professor John Ulric Nef, who had founded the Committee on Social Thought at the University of Chicago, where Saul Bellow, Hannah Arendt, David Grene, and other intellectuals taught. He knew Tony di Bonaventura's brother Mario, with whom I had sung madrigals at Dartmouth, and his wife Dorothy. He was a close friend of Nadia Boulanger's, the famous French teacher of so many American composers and conductors, and had met Mario when he studied with her.

John Nef had a life both in Washington and in France, where he had been a professor at the Collège de France. In Washington, he was directing a University of Chicago enterprise called A Center for Human Understanding. When dinner was announced, we had to pry ourselves apart and take our places at the table. But at the concert box we were seated together, and between pieces we continued to talk. Mrs. Jock Whitney, Tony's mother-in-law, was giving a post-concert party, to which I was invited. It was very grand, and John Nef stayed at my side throughout.

"When are you going back to Washington?" he asked. "I have to work tomorrow," I told him. "I'm taking the eight o'clock shuttle." "Don't," said John Nef. "There is an 8:30 American Airlines breakfast flight. Meet me there, and we can go back together." I was enchanted and accepted.

I was staying at my brother Myron's London Terrace apartment, and I somehow misunderstood how his alarm clock worked. It didn't go off, and I woke at a quarter to eight the next morning. That nice man, I thought, I'll never see him again. But *maybe*, with a good taxi driver, just maybe, I might make the 8:30. Grabbing my clothes, I finished dressing in the elevator. When I got to the street, snow was falling. I knew that no matter how skilled a driver I found, he wouldn't be able to make it in the snow. I located a taxi, applied some makeup on the way, and felt sad. I decided to stop at American Airlines on the oh-so-slim chance that he might have left a message for me. As the taxi slowed at American, there was John Nef standing outside. "You *waited* for me," I said in astonishment. The flight had long since taken off with his luggage. "I would have waited all day for you," was his reply.

We took the next flight on American and in what seemed like moments arrived in Washington. As we separated, he invited me to dinner that night, saying that the Chilean ambassador and his wife were coming and that he hoped I would enjoy them—black tie, eight o'clock. He telephoned me as soon as I got home from work and asked

me to come early because he wanted us to talk before the other guests
arrived. He gave me instructions about where to park, in his private
parking place.

He occupied two apartments in a handsome old building on California Street. On entering I was thrilled to see original Chagalls,
Derains, Dufys, and Picassos on the walls. Greatly impressed, I recognized each artist as John took my coat and offered me a drink,
until we came to one painting I couldn't identify. I asked who painted
it. Vanessa Bell was the answer. Vanessa Bell, of course, was the sister
of Virginia Woolf, my favorite writer. It turned out that John Nef
knew the Woolfs and had bought the painting through Virginia. I
must pay *attention* to this man, I thought—he is no ordinary man.

Before long our tête-à-tête was interrupted by the arrival of other
guests. During the dinner the Chilean ambassador and I were soon deep
into Chile's problems of Antarctic sovereignty. The ambassador was surprised to meet a woman who knew anything about it, and I explained
my polar connections. John whispered to me to stay at the end of the
evening. He escorted me to my car with two signed books of his and a
box of flowers. When I got home and unwrapped the box, I almost
fainted. It was filled with sprays of the most beautiful small orchids I had
ever seen, not one to pin on a dress, but dozens of sprays, enough to
make a gorgeous flower arrangement. I was stunned with pleasure. Was
this some kind of dream from which I was going to awaken?

With my executive privilege at the Brookings Institution, I had
commandeered a private dining room and asked John Nef to lunch.
Here, five days after our February 9 meeting, he asked me to marry
him. We sat through the serving of an elegant lunch that neither of
us touched. We were busy gazing into each other's eyes, and like
teenagers in love we couldn't eat. The waitress inquired whether there
was anything wrong with the food. We reassured her and waited impa-
tiently for her to leave so that we might continue our star gazing. To
my astonishment I heard myself say, "Yes, I will marry you, John Nef."
A voice in my head screamed, "How dare you say you will marry a

man you have only known for five days!" The riposte came back loud and clear. "Don't be silly, you have just hired a staff of ten people, and there isn't a lemon in the bunch. You know the *important* things about this man. He has a brilliant mind, he is tender, thoughtful, and gentle, and he had a long and successful marriage, which ended with the death of his wife. The things you don't know will not be important." And that turned out to be so.

I found out later that Mario di Bonaventura had written the following to John on November 29, 1963 :

> We have a friend who just moved to Washington from Hanover, Mrs. Evelyn Stefansson, wife of the Arctic explorer who died last year. She is a very charming, intelligent person we think you would enjoy, and we were going to leave it to Kate and Bill Haddad to introduce you had they not at the same time left Washington. Well, perhaps you will meet her in the Washington whirl. She has taken a position at the head of some sociological interest (foundation or research project—I don't know what).

John Nef had been a widower for eleven years. He was very lonely, and although he had been much sought-after in Chicago society, he had never met *the* woman he wanted to share the rest of his life with until he met me. In Washington he had an office in Meridian House, a former mansion that had been turned into an artistic foundation, where he had met and befriended Mary Carswell.* The day John received Mario di Bonaventura's letter, he turned to Mary and said, "What can I do about this? I don't whirl" (referring to Mario's suggestion about trusting to the Washington social whirl to meet me). "Oh, John," said Mary, "I can take care of that." Mary knew about Tony's coming Town Hall concert and thought it would be an appro-

---

* Mary Carswell was a social worker who worked in the Washington International Center. Her husband Robert, a member of the New York law firm, Shearman and Sterling, had come to Washington as special assistant to the secretary of the treasury, Douglas Dillon.

priate moment to arrange a meeting with "the widow." John and Mary agreed that if the widow was a pill, they would not invite her to Mrs. Whitney's party. It seems that I had passed.

John introduced romance into my life at age fifty. This was not only unexpected, it seemed miraculous. John was thirteen years older than I, but at a youthful sixty-three he seemed very young compared to Stef, who had been eighty-two when he died. Boxes of flowers would arrive airmail special-delivery from Hawaii. They contained every variety of orchid—little yellow ones, big brown ones, green fading into white, some on wire-thin stems, others on thick, pencil-fat stems—dendrobiums, cattleyas, phalenaenopsis, and epidendrums. Once when I was researching the flora of Greenland, where tiny, low-to-the-ground orchids are found, I learned that they were the most numerous species of all flowers. That fact was demonstrated again and again as the boxes of flowers from Hawaii continued to arrive. They came not only on monthly anniversaries of February 9 but at random—unexpectedly!

Books also arrived. Some were John's own (he had written ten on topics such as the beginnings of industrialization and the history of war); others were those of his friends and colleagues that he thought would interest me. He took great pleasure in giving me presents, and having had no presents as a child, I was enchanted. With Bil Baird, who was something of a miser, presents were few and almost always reluctantly given, and outside of books presents were simply not in Stef's vocabulary. So imagine my excitement when John said I must have an engagement present and bought me an exquisite, silvery-white mink jacket. Then he asked if I could take a day off from work to go to New York. He wanted to buy me an engagement ring. No one had ever suggested such a thing to me before.

We flew together in time for lunch at Shephard's restaurant in the Warwick Hotel, where John knew the French manager. We had oysters and a bottle of Musigny Blanc, the first time I drank that exquisite wine. "Now what will you have?" asked John. "More oysters and more

Musigny Blanc," I replied, never having tasted such a perfect combination before. John couldn't have been more pleased. For decades he had been traveling to France every year and was a great lover and connoisseur of their wines. Once again I had found a master and became an eager pupil of the mystère of French wines.

After lunch John took me to Cartier's to pick out an engagement ring. I found myself in front of a display case holding hundreds of diamond rings of every size, from pinhead to blockbuster. "Choose," said John. Terrified, I said, "You had better give me some guidelines about size and price." "No," said John. "You must have the one you want." I picked one finally that I thought I could wear in the daytime. It was a round stone, a little over three carats, in a Tiffany setting. When the salesman told us the price, I was aghast. He explained that it was a flawless "gem" stone of the highest quality. I hastily said I didn't have to have a *gem* stone and offered to choose another, but John insisted that since that was the one I had chosen, that was the one I should have. The ring just happened to fit my finger. John had most thoughtfully armed himself with a letter of credit from his Chicago bank that enabled us to walk out of the store with the ring. The next day at work the bright young girls we had hired, many of them from faraway places, who had come to Washington looking for work and a mate, clustered round me oohing-and-ahing over the ring. It seemed ironic to me that the oldest member of the staff should be the first to become engaged.

With the showers of presents and innumerable thoughtful little things that John produced almost every time we met, it finally dawned on me that he derived pleasure from spending time thinking up ways to please me. This was a first in my life. To add to the feeling that "my cup runneth over" John was as interested as I in art, music, opera, theater, and ballet. In my life with Stef, these were all activities I had to pursue on my own. Now at last I had a partner who shared my most intense passions. I apologized for never having been to college, but he insisted that it was *because* my brain had never been pressed into the college mold that it was so remarkable. How could I not love such a man? John Nef thought me beautiful, intelligent, and wise. I knew that he was seeing me through the rosy-hued glasses of love. Nevertheless, his vision of me spurred me to try to live up to that exaggerated high standard.

It was soon apparent to me that John traveled in the highest levels of "society." After I had agreed to marry him, when he was back in Chicago lecturing and we were talking on the telephone, I realized that we had never discussed religion. "There is something that you need to know about me that might make a difference in how you feel about me." "What could that possibly be?" asked John. "I'm Jewish," said I. "What a wonderful gift to bring me!" was John's endearing reply.

JOHN wanted to marry immediately. He had told Mary Carswell that he knew the night he met me that he was going to ask me to marry him. She had warned him not to rush and frighten me off. So he had waited five days! I was a little worried by his haste. It was only February, and I had agreed to take my job for a year, which meant at least until September. We finally compromised on April for the wedding, and I was left to deal with Gresham Sykes. I hit on a plan that made the transition fairly simple. I knew our American Sociological Association budget was tight because of all we had spent on furnishings for the new offices, and I devised a scheme whereby my job could be divided among four of the employees, thereby saving my considerable salary. The workbooks had all been rewritten, nine simultaneous sessions of the annual meeting had gone off without a hitch, and the office routines were now becoming easily predictable. It worked!

When Robert Hutchins, former president of the University of Chicago and a close friend of John's, came to Washington, John asked him to ask his friend William O. Douglas to marry us. Hutchins obliged and returned with the news that Supreme Court justices never married couples. "Besides," Douglas had said with a smile, "If I did there would be a cloud on the title" (he having been married four times). So we got Judge Luther Youngdahl, who had ruled so wisely in my friend Owen Lattimore's case, to marry us in the presence of the Carswells, the di Bonaventuras, my sister Rosalind and her husband Max Feller, and my brother, Myron. We had a luncheon party at my apartment afterwards; John supplied the Dom Perignon and the Fellers provided Lobster Newburg, courtesy of the master chef at the International Latex Corporation, where Max worked.

When John and I became engaged, he had called his lawyer, Thomas Alcock in Chicago, and asked him to change his will, leaving everything he owned to me. His sensible lawyer was greatly alarmed and harbored images of some gold digger getting her hooks into John. Alcock convinced him to at least wait until we were married. On our wedding day at the luncheon reception he formally signed his new will, asking several of our guests to be witnesses. Until then I had no idea how much money he had. I had incorrectly surmised from noticing the worn fuzz on his camel's-hair coat, which was long and old-fashioned looking, that he lived on a professor's salary. It was only as he outlined our honeymoon and the places we would stay that I was able to fathom that he had to have funds beyond a professor's earnings to support such a honeymoon. John was always perfectly willing to answer questions about money, but I seldom asked. Money and its accumulation had never greatly interested either of us.

On every anniversary of our wedding day John always gave me a gift of stock, usually Castle & Cooke, that had the equivalent worth of the salary I had been earning when we married. He thought I shouldn't be penalized financially for marrying him. Neither Bil nor Stef had thought to celebrate a wedding anniversary, much less make me a generous gift. John always seemed to be looking for a reason to do something nice for me. It gave me a delicious feeling of wonder and gratitude.

Gentle John, tender and sensitive, had been alone and sad for the eleven years of his widowhood. A naturally sociable man, he had several lady friends, but none had provided a satisfactory, meaningful relationship. He told me, as he told Mary Carswell, that he knew at our first meeting that he wanted to marry and spend the rest of his life with me. He had affectionate manners and delighted in touching, hugging, kissing, and holding hands. I insisted on our sleeping together before we married, and he was always eager and excited at the prospect of our weekends, when he would join me at my Dupont Circle apartment. I was fifty and John sixty-three when we married, and the fiery intensity of youthful sex had slowed to a calmer and more profound experience. The holding and comforting were now almost as important as the act and went on until John's final illness, when for the first time in our long married life we occupied separate beds.

JOHN's father, after whom he was named, founded the chemistry department at the University of Chicago and was famous for discovering a second valence in the carbon atom. The family was from the Appenzell area of Switzerland, and John Senior had been brought to the United States as a young child. His great love was chemistry, and he was always interested in his most brilliant graduate students. John Junior was an outstanding student throughout his academic life; the only class he had ever failed was Chemistry I.

John's mother, Louise Comstock before her marriage, came from an old upstate New York family. She died of pneumonia at age forty-nine, when John was only nine. His father, no doubt beset by grief and guilt, thoughtlessly told him that his mother had died because he had been a bad boy. I am sure that John Ulric Nef, Senior, had no idea of the hurt and damage he had done in giving voice to such an outrageous statement and no knowledge of the tendency of children to blame themselves when anything catastrophic happens. John had adored his mother, and her loss when he was at so tender an age was multiplied by his belief that he had somehow been responsible. John had retained a feeling of guilt throughout most of his life. When we were married, we talked and talked and talked about the matter until he at last realized that he could not possibly have been responsible for his mother's death.

After his mother died, John's father brought him up in hotels,* and every summer for five years he took John abroad to visit art museums and to listen to concerts that featured the two Richards—Wagner and Strauss, tastes the elder Nef had acquired as a graduate student in Munich. (Perhaps it was no accident that John, when he was able to collect art, was most interested in the modern variety, of which his father so heartily disapproved.)

Elinor Castle, granddaughter of the founder of Castle & Cooke, was heiress to one of the many small fortunes made in the Hawaiian Islands in the mid-nineteenth century. She was one of ten children. She and John married in 1921. Her resources, combined with John's much smaller inheritance, were enough for them to live comfortably abroad in England, Austria, and France for five years after they married, while John pursued research for his first book in the archives of those countries. The rate of exchange back in the 1920s greatly favored the dollar, providing them with the means to buy the paintings, drawings, and graphic works they both loved. John's autobiography states that they were well off "materially, physically, intellectually, socially and spiritually." It was a great sadness to both that they were unable to have children. Elinor had many miscarriages and they finally accepted their childless state philosophically.

I believe that because of his lonely childhood John developed a need and then a genius for friendship. He had the kind of thoughtfulness that endeared and bound him to his friends. He remembered birthdays, he loved to send flowers and gifts, and he wrote appreciative letters to his hostesses after a good dinner party. He enjoyed people and developed his social skills to a high level. This was a man who understood and believed in the power of love. He knew how to give

---

* Because he hadn't had a domestic life as a child, he never learned certain simple things that come from having a normal family home. When something didn't work, for instance, it never occurred to him that he could fix it. I, on the other hand, took pleasure and some pride in being able to change a fuse, rewire a lamp, unplug a stopped toilet, change batteries in a flashlight, or find a leak and stop it—or at least turn off the water if I couldn't. To John it seemed semi-miraculous that I could do all these things and make an omelet as good as any he could get in France. I had a tendency to downplay such tiny successes; he on the other hand overvalued them. But the end result was more love.

and receive it. Conversant with the evils of man throughout history, he was still able to believe in the good, the beautiful, and the true. He once wrote that his ultimate goals were "the strengthening of good against evil, of beauty against ugliness, of truth against falsehood and love against hate." He knew it was impossible to define those words, but that did not diminish the importance of trying to serve those values, which he did throughout his life.

CHAPTER XXI

Honeymoon and Beyond

*H*AVING TRAVELED A GREAT DEAL since early childhood, John loved to plan trips and design itineraries. He
would surround himself with Baedeker and Michellin
guides, get out the maps, and immerse himself in another world. Our
honeymoon plans kept getting longer and longer. He wanted to show
me the places he loved most, and he finally settled on a five-month
journey that included England, Italy, France, and Greece. Wherever we
went he seemed to have friends and former pupils.

Our honeymoon began aboard the French transatlantic liner *France*.
Arriving in our stateroom, I was greeted with an elegant display of
Hawaiian orchids and a separate flower box that contained a lei of
small white flowers, which John explained was reserved for brides.
Before leaving he had shown me two Louis Vuitton wardrobe trunks
and said, "One of these is yours." It now stood opened beside his in
our first-class stateroom. John had taken me shopping (another miracle—he liked to shop with me for clothes), and the trunk was filled
with wondrous new evening gowns to be worn at dinner and suits
and dresses for daywear. I was feeling like Cinderella at the ball, but
without the anxiety that this new world would disappear at midnight.
This was real.

London was our first stop. We stayed at the Hyde Park Hotel in
Knightsbridge, which looked out over the green park of the same

name. It used to be famous for housing conductors and world-class musicians. John had been "introduced" there by his close friend, the pianist Artur Schnabel. "We are going to Tom Eliot's tonight," said John, who was keeping track of our social engagements with his many London friends. About ten minutes later I did what's called on Broadway a "double-take" at the prospect of meeting the greatest poet of my generation. John had told me that Eliot was a friend who had come to the Committee on Social Thought to lecture, and I had been suitably impressed. By then he was newly married to Valerie, his former secretary.

In the taxi on our way to Kensington Gardens, John cautioned me to be careful not to mention where we were going after our Eliot visit. Julian Huxley and his wife, Juliette, were celebrating Julian's seventieth birthday, and we were going to the party. Eliot disliked Huxley. We were both successful in keeping our next destination secret. Tom Eliot looked like his pictures, which could not show his charm. He and Valerie, his young, beautiful, blue-eyed, blond, animated wife, welcomed me warmly and we were quickly at ease with one another. Afterwards, at Julian's, where the rooms were crowded with well-known personalities, I asked myself, does John only know celebrities? The answer, of course, was no. But on this trip there seemed to be so many.

The honeymoon continued like a sweet dream. John's Chicago friend Buffy Ives, Adlai Stevenson's sister, had invited us to spend two weeks with her in Acetri, a suburb of Florence, at the famous Villa Capponi, which she rented every summer. The beautiful sixteenth-century villa was filled with antiques of the period. It boasted a swimming pool in a green dell surrounded by Greek statuary, an avenue lined with lemon trees in huge pots, which Lenôtre might have designed, and a long, breathtaking view below the garden into the heart of Florence. Our bedroom was huge and contained a fourposter canopied bed that required several wooden steps to reach. All the floors were waxed to a high finish, and any piece of clothing that was left about would disappear and return the next day exquisitely laundered. Buffy loved company and had many formal dinners, including a special one for the Queen Mother of Romania, King Michael's mother, whom we all enjoyed. Buffy's husband, a retired foreign service officer, was tall, handsome, and nearly blind. I remember one afternoon reading to him aloud outdoors that magnificent first chapter of Barbara Tuchman's *The Guns of August*.

Buffy knew Florence and was a superb guide. She took me to the couture fashion houses for clothes and knew the best places to buy exquisite hand-embroidered linens. For the first time in my life, I was in the happy position of being able to indulge my taste for beautiful things. With John's encouragement, I shopped for household things of quality. Midway through our visit Buffy became ill, which left us free to wander on foot. We found Galileo's house, where the nearly blind astronomer had been sentenced to perpetual house arrest by the papal authorities. John's old friend Robert Hutchins* was also in Florence during that time, and I remember his description of seeing for the first time the magnificent mosaic-ceiling baptistery. He had apparently said aloud in wonder, "There is nothing like this in Brooklyn or Oberlin," the two places where he had grown up. We also went sightseeing in the areas around Florence. Our well-named, English-speaking driver, Brio, had a relative in every Tuscan village and knew the best restaurants everywhere. He remained our friend and guide in all our subsequent Italian visits.

The Paris I experienced on my honeymoon, escorted by a groom who knew the city well, spoke flawless French, and sported the red rosette of an Officier of the Legion d'Honneur in his buttonhole, was

---

* Robert Hutchins may have been the most celebrated and controversial university president of his time. Six feet two inches tall, handsome, charismatic, and a powerful orator, he was a boy wonder who changed the character of the University of Chicago when he was appointed in 1929, at age 31. He believed passionately in the life of the mind, introduced the "Great Books" course to the curriculum, disdained athletics, and abolished football! He shared with John a belief that universities had become too specialized, narrowing rather than broadening a student's outlook. He encouraged and supported John in the difficult task of forming the Committee on Social Thought, a graduate, Ph.D.-granting department taught by a galaxy of interesting people—including writer Saul Bellow, sociologist Edward Shils, philosopher Hannah Arendt, classicist David Grene, economist Fritz von Hayek, art critic Harold Rosenberg, poet T.S. Eliot, and many others. It was the first interdisciplinary department of its kind in the United States, and more than fifty years later it still flourishes.

very different from the tourist Paris I had previously known. John loved the city and had so many old friends there. He and his first wife, Elinor Castle, had been going abroad each summer since the 1920s, and their friends included members of the French Academy, ministers of state (especially those having to do with cultural affairs), and distinguished scientists, artists, and writers, all of whom were eager to see him and meet his new wife. We were welcomed by a long series of gala lunches and dinners and weekends at aristocratic family châteaux—such food, such wine, such tables sparkling with old silver, crystal, and exquisite flowers, all laced with warmth and affection for John, which soon enveloped me, too.

Among the distinguished Parisians John introduced me to were the former prime minister of France, Edgar Faure, and his wife Lucy, who edited a literary journal; Louis Leprince-Ringuet, a world-famous physicist; Charles Morazé, a professor of history and sociology at the Science Po (Institut d'Etudes Politiques), and his beautiful wife Monique, a writer and translator; and Count Jacques de Bourbon-Busset, a novelist and diplomat, and his wife Laurence, who was a painter and ran the farm at their château in Ballancourt. But the two people I admired most, who were to have the most lasting influence in our twenty-five years of married life, were Valentine and Marc Chagall—but more of them later.

Our morning ritual was to stroll from the Ritz to the Louvre and to spend an hour there looking at paintings. Since my art school days, looking at paintings had been a passion, but for the previous twenty-five years I had only gone to museums sporadically and alone. Now I had a companion who not only loved art, too, but was extraordinarily knowledgeable about the artists and the times that had produced them. Every summer thereafter we returned to Paris and joined the throng who believe it to be the most beautiful city in the world.

Arriving in Greece we spent a month on the island of Rhodes while John finished a piece of writing that was due. We had a windy cabin on a beautiful sandy beach, where we rested up from our social and sightseeing activities. Then on to Athens. Staying at the Grand Bertagne Hotel we soon set off for the Acropolis and the Parthenon. Climbing up the hill polished smooth by the feet of thousands of tourists before us, we were both moved by what we saw. John had taught a course on the Age of Pericles and he unrolled the history of this stunning place as we climbed. Arriving at the top I was so moved I was weeping with pleasure to be in this historic place, one of the few tourist attractions that more than lives up to its reputation. The beauty, the history, and the awareness of my good fortune to be with a companion like John was emotionally overpowering. Neither of us ever forgot the day and that moment.

It was in Athens, too that we met John's old classmate from the University of Montpelior, Georges Katsimbalis, the famous character who Henry Miller immortalized in his book *The Colossus of Maroussi*. He, too, more than lived up to legend as a fascinating character.

Back in Washington after our fabulous honeymoon, I realized that to retain my sanity and to be a proper wife to John Nef I must learn to speak French as quickly as possible. Most, but by no means all, of his French friends could speak English. Those who could did so out of politeness, but when they became excited or enthusiastic they switched back to French, and just when a conversation would be at a most lively turn I would be lost. At the end of a French-speaking evening I would be as tense as a spastic, convinced that if I listened hard enough I could make sense out of what I was hearing. Learning French became my new first priority.

When I told the director of Washington's Berlitz language school that I needed to learn French in a hurry, he asked if I had studied other languages. Upon hearing that I had studied Russian, Icelandic, and Danish, he switched to Russian, and after a short conversation he announced that for $685 and five days of my life, from early morning to late at night, I would be speaking French. "It sounds like brainwashing," I said. "It's not unrelated," he replied and proceeded to describe a new method called "total immersion,"* which derived from what we had learned about prisoner-of-war interrogation and brainwashing techniques. I accepted with a certain grim determination.

The private, forty-minute classes began at 8:30 in the morning and, except for five minute recesses, continued without stopping until 9:15 at night. Lunch and dinner were taken with a professor, instruction continuing throughout the meal. The lessons were given by a succession of male and female teachers of varying ages, all native-born French. At my first class a teacher arrived, extended his hand, and said, "*Je m'appelle Professeur Smit. Vous êtes?*" After a few fumbles I made the appropriate rejoinder, and we were off. He asked me to sit down, stand up, open the door, close it, walk to it, away from it, pick up the pencils, put them down, give them—"*Non, pas le bleu, le jaune.*" After each action he asked what I had done, and until I told him, in French, correctly, we couldn't go on to the next item on the agenda. If I used an English word, or as sometimes happened a Russian or Danish one, the teacher behaved as if he had not heard me. I was told not to speak a word of English at home. Since John was fluent in French, this didn't pose a problem. On the morning of the second day, I was able to say at breakfast, "John, *prenez les assietes, metez sur la table, s'il vous plait.*" John almost dropped the plates, "In one day?!" I explained that those were the only two verbs I knew, that I had been putting and taking all the previous day, and we had a good laugh.

The good thing about this approach is that one begins to think in French and doesn't waste time in translating. On the last day, at lunch with my main professor, we had a small celebration, and I sang him a song I had learned as a teenager from a record of Lucienne Boyer's, "*Parlé moi d'autre chose.*" He said, "There is nothing to correct." My new knowledge also occasionally added a feeling of revelation—oh, that's what that actually means. Wonderful! I had done the equivalent of a year's work in five exhausting days. I knew the

---

* Total Immersion still exists at Berlitz, but it is now two weeks long and the hours are more sensible, from nine to five each day.

numbers, and by using the infinitives of verbs with *avoir* and *être*, I made myself understood.

In France I could telephone and shop by myself. Best of all, I was no longer a prisoner of my ignorance. I carried a pocket dictionary in my purse and had the Oxford French Dictionary handy in the hotel. I began to have an inkling of what was being said at dinner with French friends. While still getting used to breakfasting in bed—the only way you *can* breakfast at the Ritz—we would read the newspapers, *Figaro* and *Le Monde*. I looked up every third word at first, but as soon as my vocabulary increased I became bold about trying to talk, not caring whether or not I was the clown of the group when I made a mistake, like confusing *cheveux* (hair) and *chevaux* (horses). And contrary to popular belief about the French, John's friends were extremely helpful in correcting me and explaining.

CHAPTER XXII

The Chagalls

B<small>EFORE WE WERE MARRIED</small>, John sent the Chagalls our wedding announcement. Marc opened the double page and using colored crayons and ink produced a charming drawing of a woman (whom I later recognized as Vava) offering a bouquet of flowers. He then sent the announcement back to us. Of course, I had the "announcement Chagall" framed, and it still lives in my bedroom beneath a superb gouache of the Purim festival,[*] one of two Chagalls that John had bought before he had met Marc. After meeting me, Marc said, "When you have a house, you must have a *salle Chagall.*" I promised and kept my word: The walls of the master bedroom of our old Georgetown house display only Chagall paintings and lithographs.

Marc and John met early in 1946, when John asked him to participate in a University of Chicago symposium called "Works of the Mind," to which he had invited leaders in a dozen different professions, among them Frank Lloyd Wright, young William Fulbright, and John von Neumann. Then a widower, Marc had never been west of the Hudson River. He knew two things about Chicago: It contained Red Indians and gangsters. He stayed at John's place, where he found not only two of his own paintings, done in Vitebsk in 1915 and 1917, but

---

[*] The Purim painting is a sketch for a huge painting that is now in the Philadelphia Museum of Fine Arts. As often happens, the sketch is fresher and somehow more vital than the large oil, but that may be my prejudice.

also many Derains, Signacs, Dufys, and Picassos on the walls. They conversed in French, found they shared many ideas and interests, and agreed to meet again on John's annual hegira to France. By the time I arrived in 1964, they were old and intimate friends. On our honeymoon visit to France, when I first met the Chagalls, Marc told me that John had "discovered" him forty years earlier, "before I was famous," referring to John's purchase of the two beautiful gouaches back in the twenties. They both believed in the good, the beautiful, and the true and that the single most important thing in life was love.

When I met Marc, he was seventy-seven years old and had curly white hair and bright blue eyes. Of medium height, he was usually animated and has often been described as elfin or pixie-like. When people addressed him reverently as Maître (Master), he loved to say merrily, "*Je ne suis pas Maître, je suis centimetre.*" He would become serious when art or his work was the subject of discussion. He was a remarkable storyteller, and I imagine that he might have been a great actor if he hadn't been a painter. He loved to talk about his early life and act out the scenes with gestures and changes of voice. Very gifted in music as well as art, he knew a great deal about the topic and loved to go to concerts. He could discuss music seriously with conductors and professional musicians, many of whom were his friends. His favorite composer was Mozart, and we would often sing themes from the symphonies, operas, and divertimentos to and with each other.

I spoke no French during our first year in France. Happily, the Russian I had learned during wartime at Middlebury was a bond with the Chagalls, both of whom were Russian. They always spoke that language when they were alone "so as not to forget," Vava explained. Despite his five years as a refugee in the United States, Marc had never learned English. Vava spent the war years in England and spoke it perfectly, with the slightest, charming accent. She commented on my good Russian accent and wanted to know where and why I had learned it. In telling the story, I mentioned that in preparation for a Soviet trip in 1959 I had brushed up with a Dartmouth Russian teacher named

Maria Morozova. Maria and I had read Pushkin poetry and prose together and had become friends. Vava was astonished. She then told me *her* story. She and her wealthy family had fled the revolution and settled in Berlin, joining a colony of like families. Her best childhood friends were Nina Schelemskaya, who became a famous ballerina and married then-unknown Rudolph Bing,* and Maria Morozova.†
Vava was thrilled to have news of her and to discover where she was living.

Vava was Marc's second wife. His first wife, Bella, also Russian and Jewish, had fled with him to the United States in the late thirties in anticipation of a Nazi invasion of France. The International Rescue Committee was responsible for their finding a haven in New York. During this time Bella became ill, and died of pneumonia in 1944. Because neither of them spoke English, they had no access to the city's excellent medical care. He returned to France after the war and there met and married Vava in 1952. Vava, who never told her age, was about twenty-five years younger than Marc. She was taller than him and had long straight black hair, which she wore back severely in a chignon, emphasizing her striking features. She must have been a great beauty in her youth and was still extremely handsome. She came from a rich, cultivated family, unlike Marc, who began life in a Vitebsk *shtetl* and whose father made herring barrels. Marc was a loving and affectionate husband, Vava more dignified and less open. He adored her and was dependent on her to tell him what to do about matters that didn't interest him. Vava handled their correspondence, exhibition business, money, and household matters to keep Marc free to paint.

JOHN and I spent two months of every year abroad. For one month we stayed at his favorite place in the world, the Hotel du Cap at Cap

---

* Austrian-born impresario who was manager of the Metropolitan Opera, 1950-1972.

† Maria Morozova's grandfather, Ivan Morozov, was a rich merchant and an early collector of Picasso, Matisse, Derain, and other early modern painters. The Soviets confiscated his collection, and today the paintings may be seen at the Hermitage Museum in St. Petersburg and the Pushkin in Moscow.

d'Antibes. He had arrived there in 1922 for its first summer season. Previously it had catered largely to Russian nobility escaping from the severe winter cold to the relatively milder French south coast. John liked to say he had discovered Cap d'Antibes before Fitzgerald, Hemingway, and Murphy. In addition to our room high up in the little hotel, we always rented a bathing cabin down at the sea and often invited the Chagalls for lunch and a swim. They lived then at Vence and later at St. Paul de Vence, and kept an apartment in Paris, on the Isle St. Louis. Our friendship grew, and in 1968 we invited them to spend their summer vacation with us at the hotel. We eventually spent about ten summers together.

From my marriages to Bil and Stef, I retained a certain expertise in the care and feeding of geniuses, which turned out to be extremely useful with Marc. Everybody loves a good listener, but geniuses need a rapt one with long staying power. Marc adored Vava and was sometimes uneasy when she was out of sight. She often found it difficult to get away to shop or have her beautiful long hair washed. I would spell her until she returned by encouraging Marc to reminisce about his Russian childhood or his early days in Paris, when he was too poor to buy fresh canvas and would buy very cheap old paintings and use their backs for his own creations. I learned about this particular custom when Marc was visiting us in Washington and we dined at the David Kreegers. David had a large art collection, including one Chagall that was painted on both sides. He believed he had a two-in-one Chagall until Marc disillusioned him and told of his ancient practice.

Our life at the Cap developed a routine. John and Marc both worked in the mornings—John on his latest book, Marc drawing and sometimes working on his autobiography, which he was writing in Russian. Vava and I would meet after breakfast at our little bathing cabin in the pine woods at the edge of the blue Mediterranean. We would gossip, swim, and read. The men joined us for lunch, which was usually preceded by a delicious specialty of the Cap—a large glass of fresh, very ripe, freshly squeezed raspberry juice, with nothing added, so it was sweet and a touch tart. In the evening, when combined with champagne, it became a heavenly nectar, which we often sipped on the hotel terrace as we watched the hot sun set over the Mediterranean.

Vava and John were strong swimmers and liked to swim far out to sea. I knew how to swim, but I liked to have the bottom easily available to my feet and was reluctant to swim in water over my head. There was no beach at the hotel—one swam off the rocks, where the water was already deep—so for the first summer swimming was difficult for me. I was timid about going very far from the ladder and safety. Then I spotted the hotel swimming instructor teaching three-year-old children how to swim in the Eden Roc Pool and decided I had better learn, too. I had a lesson every day for an hour, and by the end of the summer I had added the breaststroke, the crawl, and floating and resting on my back to my old fashioned sidestroke. I completely lost my fear. I remember writing to my darling shrink, Dr. Nathanial Ross (more of him later), telling how at the age of fifty I had finally learned how to swim properly. He reminded me that it was no more difficult to swim in deep water than in the shallows! Marc never learned how to swim, but we would dunk him with Vava on one side and me on the other, and he would thrash around happily.

During these summers with the Chagalls we always celebrated two anniversaries: their wedding anniversary on July 12 and my birthday on July 24. For my birthday the four of us would have a quiet but festive dinner. Marc always gave me one of his colored lithographs, which he would inscribe with ceremony, *"Bon anniversaire"* or some similar sentiment. They were marked in his handwriting *"Epreuve d'artiste,"* artist's proof—these are produced first, before the numbered copies that follow. After several summers, as the numbers accumulated, it dawned on me that he was giving me a very expensive present each year, and I was somewhat embarrassed at his continuing generosity. Realizing finally that he derived great pleasure in bestowing a unique gift, I adjusted! Today I find I have six lithographs of varying sizes; the first, dated 1964, was for my fifty-first birthday. The rest are dated, 1969, 1970, 1972, 1973, and 1975.

Marc's own birthday, on July 9, was also celebrated but almost always on a grander scale. In between the important round-number birthdays there would usually be a celebration at the Chagalls's St. Paul de Vence residence with his daughter, Ida, Pierre Matisse (Henri's son and Marc's New York dealer) and his wife, Fernand Leger's Russian widow, Vava's brother Michel, and whoever of their family and close friends were in the neighborhood. For birthday and anniversary dinners for famous or old clients, the Hotel du Cap in those days would print special menus to mark the occasions. Marc would create a sketch on the menu using the hotel's crest as a woman's headdress or draw a picture of himself and Vava or whatever took his fancy. Those souvenirs, precious reminders of happy times, now hang framed on my walls.

IN time the four of us became a little family, and we saw each other not just during summers but at various times throughout the years. Our meetings were determined by Marc's artistic life and John's academic schedule. In France we were invited to Marc's birthday parties, vernissages (exhibition openings), the opening of his Message Biblique Museum in Nice, and the 1964 unveiling of his Paris Opera ceiling. Marc and Vava provided opportunities to meet André Malraux and other greats of the French art world. In New York they saw that we were present for the Metropolitan Opera's opening of *The Magic Flute*, for which Marc had designed costumes and sets. We also attended openings at the Pierre Matisse Gallery and had dinner with the Matisses in their New York home, which was filled with never-before-seen paintings by Pierre's father, Henri, as well as many huge, rather frightening ones by Balthus.

In 1966 we were with the Chagalls at the unveiling of *Le Triomphe de la Musique* at New York's Metropolitan Opera House at Lincoln Center. These two huge paintings were mistakenly placed in the opposite positions than Marc had intended. (The right-hand one was placed on the left and the left-one on the right, where they remain to this day.) Additionally, they were meant to be viewed from the street below through a huge single pane of glass. Imagine Marc's horror when he saw the piece displayed for the first time and discovered that, because of the excessive cost, instead of a single pane of glass, it was covered with a kind of bronze shoji screen of smaller panes that cut the street view of the two paintings into pieces. Rudolph Bing promised that when sufficient money was found they would replace the front with a single pane, as originally planned. But, of course, it was never changed, nor were the paintings switched to their rightful places.

In 1967 Marc and Vava came to New York for the opening of his exhibition at the Pierre Matisse Gallery, and we spent a week together at the Plaza Hotel before bringing them to Washington. The Rockefeller family had commissioned Marc to do a group of stained-glass windows for their small chapel at Pocantico Hills. These were now complete and installed, but Marc had never seen them in place. Having made arrangements ahead with the clergyman in charge, we drove up together. It was a splendid fall day. Entering the church we were enchanted to see the sunlight streaming through the largely yellow memorial window to Michael Rockefeller, who had died young in New Guinea. The strong blues of the other windows contrasted stunningly with the yellow. The rose window over the altar had been done by Matisse, and Marc later explained that out of respect and honor he had retained the smallish, beautiful round window of the great master. Though we were a group who practiced no religion, we were all very moved and speechless when we saw that little chapel.

I once wrote an article for the Sunday magazine section of the *Washington Post* (January 23, 1972) describing our relationship with the Chagalls:

> As close friends, John and I have seen too many people ranging from nice to nutty, try to enter Marc's private life, using any

pretext, and always wanting something—a photograph, an auto-graph, a signature on an unsigned lithograph, a little sketch for a talented child, or acknowledgment of a distant family rela-tionship. Desire is the mother of fantasy. The unsigned Chagall lithographs are always fakes, and Marc has accounted for all his relatives.

We have, therefore, made it a semireligious practice *not* to ask for anything but instead to take pleasure in doing things for them.

When they visited us in Washington, we were invited to the White House for tea with Lady Bird Johnson and Mary Lasker, who were plotting to beautify Washington from a horticultural point of view. We were received in the oval room of the family quarters and had the treat of viewing the Cèzannes that Jackie Kennedy had moved there and, to Marc's delight, Linda Robb's new baby.

Marc loved the small-town feeling of Georgetown. He liked being able to greet our neighbors and walking to Woolworth's to buy post-cards and an art-supply store to buy more brushes. I gave him my lit-tle sculpture studio,* where he worked until the sun became too hot and he moved to a desk in his bedroom, which had a northern light. One day he said he would do something for the house. But later he said, "No, the house is perfect; I'll make a mosaic for the garden." Delighted with the idea, I visualized an eight-by-ten-inch mosaic that we could place in the garden wall. At the time Marc was being asked by the Vatican to design something for a room next to the great Raphaels; the Lichtenstein Royal family was eager for him to carry out a commission for them; and his friend, Rudolph Bing, was discussing his designing the decor and costumes for a new production of Gluck's *Orfeo and Eurydice.* I thought he would surely forget his promise of our

---

* John gave me a studio for Christmas one year, converting a small porch at the back of the house. I had started sculpture lessons with Professor Winslow Eaves at Dartmouth, but found once-a-week sessions frustrating . . . get-ting started and then having to wait a week to continue when I wanted to keep working on a piece. When the little studio was built, I started again. I worked in direct plaster and then with found objects when I had hand trouble.

little mosaic once he was home. But when we met in France the next summer, Vava said, "Marc has finished the maquette for your mosaic." I didn't know whether to be terrified or thrilled. What would the project involve? Would we be able to afford it? These and other worrisome questions flitted through my head.

In 1969, for the first time since we had known him, Marc invited us into his atelier, the inner sanctum that few persons were privileged to see. On the wall, covered with brown paper, was a twenty-by-thirty-inch something that I rightly guessed was the maquette. With some formality Marc removed the brown cover to reveal a wonderfully colored gouache painting of Orfeo and his lute, the three graces, and Pegasus, the winged horse, all from classical Greek mythology. But on the lower half of the painting was a large group of immigrants and refugees about to cross a wide blue ocean to arrive at the "land of the skyscrapers," a modern theme based on Marc's own experience as a refugee in the United States during World War II.

Also present in the studio was Lino Melano, an Italian artist who was born in Ravenna (which has famous thousand-year-old mosaics) and who executed mosaics not only for Marc but also for Picasso, Lèger, and Braque. He and Marc discussed how many times the maquette should be enlarged. It kept getting bigger and bigger until they finally settled on three-by-five meters—or about ten feet high and seventeen feet wide. We were going to have to build a freestanding, thirty-foot-high wall to house it. My fears that we would have to mortgage the house or sell my jewelry were calmed when Vava told me the mosaic would be a gift from Marc. We would only have to pay the expenses.

The colored sketch was translated into mosaic by Lino and his assistant, who worked in Biot, France, for nine months to complete the work. It was made in ten panels, each of which was carefully housed in a wooden crate, and then shipped by air to Dulles Airport. After a cliffhanger series of adventures, including a feud with the D.C. Fine Arts Commission, the wall contractor's heart attack, the arrival of several master bricklayers combined with the nonarrival of the bricks, and other little crises too numerous to mention, the day of the dedication finally arrived. On November 1, 1971, Marc and Vava arrived, the French Ambassador Charles Lucet made a speech, John made an exquisite, short speech in French, and then we all traipsed out to the garden in the fading late-afternoon light. The artificial lights were turned on and the dazzling display appeared to a hushed silence followed by a roar of applause.*

Since that day many hundreds of art lovers have come from far and near to view this unique masterpiece, the only one of its kind in a private house or garden in North America. It has given pleasure to so many and to me every day. When coming down to breakfast in our dining room, which looks out on the garden, I never fail to notice it. The weather, the time of day, and the kind of light all produce changes in its appearance. When it rains, the wet tesserae are a different, stronger color. The first time it snowed on the mosaic, I wept a little with pure pleasure. The snowflakes seemed to match the mosaic pieces. It seems like a living presence and, of course, it says, "Marc loved us."

The mosaic is the bijou of the small but excellent art collection on N Street, which I tend to think of as John's collection since he gathered most of the paintings, drawings, and etchings it contains. Having been a puppet maker and having taken sculpture classes at Dartmouth, I am responsible for the Maillol, the Frinks, the little Bonnard bronze nude, as well as the Ann Christopher sculptures. There is a story attached to the acquisition of each piece.

---

* Billy and Eleanor Wood-Prince, old friends of John's, came from Chicago for the dedication of the mosaic. They loved it, and the idea of having a Chagall mosaic in the plaza of the new First National Bank in Chicago was born that night. Marc had met the Wood-Princes through John and liked them, and so a large pylon mosaic called *The Four Seasons* came to be. In 1974 we went to Chicago for the gala public ceremonies, which lasted for two days. Mayor Daly officiated at a huge outdoor celebration, complete with speeches, childrens' choruses, and beautiful weather. Rostropovich cancelled a London engagement to be there and played unaccompanied Bach for two hundred people. I met Baryshnikov, then newly arrived from the Soviet Union with almost no English, and we conversed in Russian. It was a grand celebration!

ON July 7, 1973, Marc's birthday, the museum named after him, in Nice, was opened, and we were privileged to be there. Seemingly all of France, headed by the minister of culture, André Malraux, feted the Mâitre. Ceremonies, speeches, and a wonderful Munchinger string concert in the small auditorium of the museum, with its mostly blue stained-glass windows, created many memorable scenes. In his long life of ninety-seven years, there were few artistic techniques that Marc had not mastered. He explored and conquered paint, pencil, etching, lithograph, book illustration, stained glass, tapestry, ceramics, and mosaic. He was probably the most accessible painter of my generation and surely one of the most beloved.

Marc died in 1984, and I flew to Nice alone, for John was already too ill to travel, and drove to St. Paul de Vence, where the funeral was taking place. Cars had to be left below while we all walked to the ancient burial ground on the highest point of land in that exquisite, walled medieval town. Marc was a commander, the highest rank, of the Legion d'Honneur. His colorful medal on a silken cushion was carried at the head of the procession. Jack Lang, the minister of culture, gave the eulogy as the mourners looked around at the 360-degree view of one of the most beautiful countrysides in the world. When the ceremony was over, before the crowd broke, an unknown person began to recite, unscheduled, the Hebrew prayer for the dead, "Yisgadal i yiscadash." No one moved until it was completed.

After Marc's death Vava and I continued to meet on my annual summer visit to France. Sometimes I stayed with her and sometimes I stayed at the Mas D'Artigny nearby. Once she stayed with me in Washington, and I accompanied her to Chicago for the unveiling of a tapestry that Marc had done for Henry Betts's rehabilitation hospital in Chicago. Without Marc, Vava's life became quieter, but she had to deal with the French government to settle Marc's estate, a process which took several years. She also had the thrill of seeing a huge and proper Chagall retrospective exhibition in the late eighties in Moscow, where Marc, once considered a defector to the West by the communist government, was now hailed as a great Russian painter and given his due.

The last time I visited Vava, I was shocked to see, upon entering her handsome living room, bare walls instead of the marvelous early Chagall paintings that were normally there. "Where are the paintings?" I asked. "There have been so many robberies lately that they have been put in the bank vault for safekeeping" was her answer. I wanted to protest that Marc was productive into his ninety-seventh year—surely she could find some drawings, lithographs, sketches, or posters to substitute for the valuable paintings that had formerly lit up the room. But I was silent. It was plain that Vava was depressed and unable to rouse herself from her sadness and pain. She was already beginning to withdraw from life. For the almost thirty years of our precious friendship, we always had so much to talk about—the state of the world, art, music, literature, gossip, clothes, people—but none of that was of any interest to her anymore. She would answer questions with short answers. She no longer had the desire or energy for more. It was a sad leave-taking. I couldn't stop wondering why it haunted me so much. With a flash I realized she was doing what my mother had done so many years ago—she was withdrawing from life—and that recognition made our last encounter especially poignant. It did not come as a shock when some months later, in December of 1993, Bella Meyer, Marc's granddaughter, called from New York to tell me that Vava had died. She is buried beside Marc in the St. Paul de Vence cemetery. Her death left a large empty space in my horizon.

CHAPTER XXIII

A New Home and New Projects

KNOWING THAT WE WERE TO HAVE a five-month honeymoon abroad, John had moved into my one-bedroom apartment on Twentieth Street. When we returned, I began to look for a house. John had lived in hotels as a child and apartments during his married life, but I pictured a house with his beautiful art collection lining the walls. I began the search and eventually found an old house in Georgetown. This was ironic because we had at first decided that Georgetown real estate was overpriced and too chic, but the only real bargain we found that suited us was on N Street in Georgetown. The house was a bargain because its former inhabitants, John B. and Elizabeth Palmer Payson, had committed suicide—first he, then she soon afterward. The house had been empty for a year, and prospective buyers seemed to have a strong prejudice against it. The suicides didn't trouble me; I figured that a house built at the end of the eighteenth century was bound to have sustained births, deaths, and all the usual tragedies of life at one time or another. It had four stories, high ceilings, simple lines, five working fireplaces, and a charming walled garden in the back. Its corner location produced wonderful light from three sides of the double living room. It was perfect.

Furnishing the place was great fun. John had many fine-quality antique pieces, and I had simple old country furniture—Vermont cherry tables and the like. Picking the best of each, we furnished the entire house almost immediately. We filled the gaps with the help of a Hungarian antique dealer, Michael Arpad. We both had silver and china enough, and our friends gave us Baccarat glasses as wedding presents. We bought some good noisy-colored antique plates for the rather dark dining room. John's knowledge of and pleasure in French wine required food that matched. He brought with him from his California Street apartment a cook and a maid, both of whom I was able to befriend.* We began to entertain even before the house was furnished. Just as our two styles of old furniture married well together, so did our friends. Many of John's friends were academic, international in origin and outlook, while mine tended to be scientists. We both also knew writers and artists. People seemed to love to come to our house, and together we produced a happy social ambiance.

In addition to our happy home life, we often went to New York to visit the Metropolitan Opera and the Metropolitan Museum to see a new painting exhibition. Then, in the '70s, the Kennedy Center was built in Washington, and within walking distance we had as much "culture" as we could handle.

When the house was finished and I had learned to give gourmet dinners, I had time on my hands. I began to join women's committees: The Smithsonian Institution, the Corcoran Gallery of Art, the Washington Opera, and the now-extinct National Ballet. I made sculptural table decorations for the Corcoran Ball, one of the important social events of the year. The theme was modern art and I fashioned abstract table decorations of aluminum screening and ruffled aluminum garden edging. I wrote notes for the "Opera News" and became president of the Women's Committee of the National Ballet, which enjoyed a good life back in the '70s under the direction of Frederic Franklin and included an excellent ballet school. I was very

---

* One of them, Lacey Jones, retired and has since died. The other, my beloved sunny Annie Cunningham, who was with me for more than thirty years, was a wonderful cook and, far more important, a devoted, loving friend. She fell and I found her with a broken hip when I came down for breakfast one morning. In the hospital she developed a staph infection that was resistant to every known antibiotic and she died of it after two years of suffering.

busy but felt vaguely dissatisfied somehow. My dissatisfaction grew
and I began to look for reasons for it, but found no satisfactory
answer. That was to come later.

AFTER marrying John, I continued to write polar book reviews
for the *New York Times*, the *Herald Tribune*, and eventually the *Washington Post*. Stef had had an idea for a series of world-exploration books
that would use, wherever possible, the original narratives of the explorers themselves to tell the story. Instead of telling the story of Columbus, use his own journals and writings for the narrative. The editor of
each volume would supply connective tissue as needed. The Delacorte Press had been interested in the idea and in having Stef as the
series editor, but he had died before any contracts were signed. To my
delight Delacorte offered me that post, and we produced five books in
the Great Explorer Series. I had the pleasure of choosing the authors,
seeing the books through the production process, and writing an
introduction for each volume. As librarian of the Stefansson Collection at Dartmouth, I had learned something about editing through
our production of a modest scholarly journal called *Polar Notes*, but the
Great Explorer Series was on a far larger scale. Rhys Carpenter produced *Beyond the Pillars of Hercules*, about the classical world; Earl Hanson, a Latin American specialist, did *South of the Spanish Main*; Owen and
Eleanor Lattimore wrote *Silks, Spices and Empire*, about Asia; and Louis
B. Wright, the distinguished historian and head of the Folger Shakespeare Library, with his assistant Elaine Fowler, produced two volumes
about North America, *West and By North* (about sea exploration and
discovery) and *The Moving Frontier*. It was an enlightening experience to
move in many directions from my familiar polar world. Armed with
my Delacorte contract, I applied at the Library of Congress for special permission to work in the stacks. It was granted and I was assigned
a desk. Before long I was happily ensconced in the great library, educating myself, as the editing of the varied manuscripts progressed.

Another writing project arrived by chance in 1968 when my friend

Dr. Paul Weisberg, a psychiatrist who treated people in group sessions, needed a coauthor to write and edit a book about the group process. Dr. Weisberg was possessed of great charm and charisma in addition to a law degree and medical credentials. He believed that he could write a best-selling book about the group process, but he was too busy to do it himself. He thought me smart enough to supply what he lacked and that together we could manage it. Having no other projects on hand, I agreed.

During this time, group therapy was becoming a fashionable way to treat people with mental illness, and the proliferation of such groups was astounding. The method, born of necessity and a shortage of psychiatrists, had proved effective during and following World War II and had finally caught on with the public. It was less expensive than one-to-one therapy and was extremely profitable for the doctors, who could collect from ten patients instead of one for the hour. Dr. Weisberg had housewife groups, think-tank groups, adolescent groups, every imaginable kind of group. He thought I should sit in on the various groups until I learned the dynamics and could write intelligently and authentically about them. I did so and enjoyed the experience of being an observer. The group could talk about me after I was introduced, but I was forbidden to speak.

One month I was assigned to the adolescent group. They were all very angry at their mothers. Session after session, day after day, I listened to the disturbed young men and women complaining about their mothers. How cruel they were, how uncaring, how sadistic, how mean, how sly, how stingy, how unloving—every imaginable offense was drawn in strong dirty language, punctuated by *you know* and *like*.* After some weeks I began to experience intense strange feelings myself. One day I had to struggle to restrain these feelings until the session

---

* During my apprenticeship in the adolescent group, I had my first encounter with the foul language that during the next decade or two became common, even in some so-called polite society. The teenagers couldn't utter a sentence without *fuck* or *shit*, used as a noun, adjective, adverb, or participle. Shocked at first, I eventually became immune. I couldn't help feeling the repeated use of these words denoted a pathetic absence of an adequate vocabulary, though I understood they were also an outlet for rage and frustration.

was over and the group dispersed. Normally after the session we moved to a smaller adjoining room, where the doctor, his female co-therapist, and I discussed what had occurred and what interpretation should be placed on it. On this day, as soon as I got into the room I burst into an almost hysterical wailing and crying, so unlike me that it was terrifying.

"What is it, Evvie?" the doctor asked. When I calmed down enough to be able to speak, I gasped "Mother!" My own mother feelings—ancient, repressed, rationalized, and unacknowledged—had finally exploded in a bout of abandon that was as surprising to me as it was to Paul and his co-therapist. The collective group anger had roused my own unconscious anger and terrible sadness about my mother and was the beginning of my "working through" these feelings. By the time this dramatic scene took place, I was familiar enough with group dynamics to understand what was going on. Paul congratulated me for controlling myself and not letting go *during* the session.

Normally it is customary for beginning group therapists, co-therapists, and anyone sitting in as an observer to have regular, free supervisory sessions to work through just the kinds of feelings I was experiencing. When I had suggested to Paul that such sessions would be useful for me, he had said, "Oh, Evvie, you are a smart girl; you can figure things out for yourself." Well, it's true, I *am* a smart girl, but I had no background in psychology except from casual reading. Nonetheless, for a month following my outburst whenever I was alone and safe from observation, I would think of my mother, cry, and call her names like the ones used by the adolescents in the group. As a child, I (and probably my siblings, too) had felt a sense of shame about my mother's mental illness. We protected and defended her to outsiders. I will always remember that wonderful line in Albert Camus's autobiographical *The First Man*, referring to his deaf mother, whom he loved most in the world: "All at once he knew shame and all at once the shame of being ashamed." It was a feeling

I recognized.* Now I was able admit how much I had loved her and the terrible, devastating sense of abandonment I had felt when she had tried to kill herself when I was three, when she had stopped talking after my father's death, and when she had finally died as I was moving to Washington.

After several months, I had learned enough about group therapy both from sitting in and from reading that Paul thought we could begin to write. We had agreed to write alternate chapters. I would do my homework, but Paul always seemed to have excellent excuses for not doing his assignments. Using my newfound insight and vocabulary, I realized that Paul had a writing "block." He had hoped working with a published author would unblock him, but it never happened, and eventually I abandoned the project. My belief is that nothing is wasted in life; something good or useful comes from all endeavors, even those that never get completed or that end in disaster. In this case I worked through my mother feelings pretty thoroughly—indeed, I came to understand the process of *working through*. I learned a good deal about mental health problems, both the terms used to describe those problems and how they are treated, and I was pleased with myself for the self-therapy and insight I was able to achieve. John was genuinely interested, too, and benefited to the extent that he gained a better understanding of his own feelings toward his father and mother, which had been masked by conventional politeness. He always enjoyed listening to and sharing my psychological investigations.

* This in turn reminded me of the way that Richard E. Byrd's expedition members would joke about their leader's less-than-marvelous grasp of science and Antarctic history. One joke was that while it was known that Byrd had read the narratives of at least two expedition leaders, Scott and Amundsen, there was no certainty that he had *finished* the Amundsen. But his men also loved him loyally, and they strongly defended him against outside criticism. The strength of the defense is related to the amount of shame.

CHAPTER XXIV

Discovering Psychotherapy

*I*T WAS THE EARLY 1970'S. We had found and furnished our house, established a busy social life, planned and taken winter vacations. I was volunteering for good causes, living with ease, and adored by my husband. For the first time since I was fourteen, I didn't have to work to earn a living. I had what many people would call the greatest good fortune. And how did I react? I became unaccountably depressed! I couldn't believe it. It was inexplicable, but as each day passed my struggle became more painful. Something had to be done. My new and now dear friend Mary Carswell was chairman of the board of the Austin Riggs Center in Stockbridge, Massachusetts, a famous long-term mental health establishment, and I knew she was a good friend of Erik Erikson's, so I asked her for advice. She was instantly empathic and gave me the name of a distinguished New York psychoanalyst who had been wonderfully helpful to many of her friends. Not caring to broadcast to the small Washington world that I was in trouble, I was glad to travel to New York for therapy. Once a week I boarded the Eastern Shuttle, as it was called in those days, had a double session with Dr. Nathanial Ross, and returned home the same day. John supported the plan.

Learning about one's true self is a shattering, thrilling experience, and it proved to be the most interesting adventure of my life. Nathanial Ross possessed what he called "the passion of the mind," which

I shared. We discussed science and literature and the human condition in our intimate relationship. Throughout my therapy with him I
was busy responding on two separate levels. The first was on a level
of discovery. I explored perception and misperception—what really
happened as opposed to what I thought happened; I learned to
remember, report, and eventually interpret my dreams; and I ferreted
out the causes of my well-hidden low self-esteem, which continued
despite my many successes. Dr. Ross was a great teacher. One of the
many important lessons he taught me was that when I was praised,
instead of accepting and internalizing the praise, I tended to explain it
away or brush it aside. For instance, when I told him that I became a
teacher at Dartmouth because they couldn't get a man who knew
about the Arctic, he pointed out that I never dwelt on the key fact that
I *did* know about the Arctic and had some ability and that *that* was the
real reason I had been hired. Given this clue I stopped putting myself
down and with a little practice began to accept praise when it came my
way—well, at least 75 percent of it, allowing room for flattery.

He was a brilliant and bold therapist who made a permanent
impression on my life. Along with what was happening to me as I
steadily recovered, learning en passant the causes and triggers of
depression and what to do about them, was a steady, persistent, and
exciting second line of thought: How is he doing this? How does he
know the exact right moment to plant the seed of a new idea and
when to enlarge on it, sometimes weeks later? How does he make it
take root and flower? Fascinated by my doctor's technique and skill, I
monitored them as we went along. He was impressed with the speed
I displayed in finding, accepting, and putting to work a new insight.
He once said, "If only I had gotten you twenty-five years ago, I could
have made you into a first-class analyst."

By the year's end my acute depression had gone, but I knew that I
was by nature a depressive and that my mother's suicide attempt and
disappearance from my life when I was three was probably where the
depression had begun. At long last I had a name for the lonely, deep,

empty feeling that pervaded my childhood. Every child—indeed, every person, young or old—experiences that feeling from time to time, though only if it is prolonged does it spell a diagnosis of depression.* My father's early death so soon after we had established a happy relationship for the first time compounded and revived the feeling of abandonment that followed my mother's first bout of mental illness. The reason I was unable to cry at his funeral was that I was so furious I couldn't feel sad and permit myself the comfort of tears.

By filling my life with activity I had been able to avoid sad or emotionally trying subjects. As every workaholic knows, keeping busy is an excellent antidepressant. But difficulties arise on long weekends, vacations, or other leisure times. For most of my life, vacations had been few, with Bil Baird because we were poor and working, with Stef because he preferred work to all other activities—nothing was as interesting, he used to say. Upon marrying John, I suddenly had two-month-long summer vacations, as well as winter vacations to warmer places like Martinique and Cozumel, and not enough to do in-between. The chores connected with my new marriage, such as learning to give elegant dinners with appropriate wines for ambassadors and senators, and the regular trips abroad had kept me very busy for awhile. But once I had mastered the skills needed for our luxurious way of life and found myself with time on my hands, I was forced to notice my depression. It didn't have anything to do with John; rather, it was the accumulation of a lifetime of unexplored emotional matters that seemed to be the culprit. So with the end of my therapy came realization that as an old workhorse I was better off busy than idle.

---

*When I was a child, people believed that children never got depressed. Now, thanks to the pioneering work of Renè Spitz, we know that not only do infants and children get depressed in a clinical sense, they sometimes die of what is called "anaclitic depression." Spitz studied infants in orphanages and in prisons, where they were born to female prisoners. In both places the babies were fed and changed, but no one ever played with them or stimulated them. His work resulted in a major change in the way babies in hospitals were treated. Now it is routine for nurses to pick up babies, talk to them, and cuddle them. Tender loving care became part of the treatment of both healthy and sick infants and for the latter had positive effects in speeding their recovery. Margaret Mahler, another great researcher of the early years of life, once wrote that a baby thrives according to the sparkle in its mother's eyes. No sparkle, no growth spurt.

At this time my hands, which had always been busy, even when I was at rest (with knitting or sewing), became very painful, and shaking hands was excruciating. Investigation showed that I had worn out the cartilage between the bones of four of my fingers. Again Mary Carswell came to my rescue with the name of a famous New York hand specialist, Dr. Robert E. Carroll, who would fuse the bones that lacked cartilage to cure the pain. He asked how I wanted the bones fused—straight or curved. "Curved, in typing position," was my reply. He did my right had first. I learned to write with my left and discovered that I could do it almost on the first try. Apparently, I'm semi-ambidextrous. I had learned to use marionette-making tools with both hands, and this training served me well. Six months later the other hand took its turn in the plaster cast, and when it was eventually removed I was—oh joy, oh rapture—free of pain in my hands. I then decided to be on the lookout for something long-term, difficult, and engaging to do—I could not remain an idle lady of leisure without getting into trouble. I was sixty years old and knew that no one would hire me for a regular job, despite my lively mind and body. An idea I played with was psychotherapy.

IN mid-July of 1971, I was at the edge of the landfast ice, north of the northernmost point in Alaska, about half an hour's travel by sled and skidoo from the Office of Naval Research's Arctic Laboratory at Point Barrow. Scribner's had given me an advance to prepare a revised, third edition of *Here Is Alaska*,* and I was gathering fresh data and photographs. Dr. Floyd Durham, a whale biologist, and his Inuit assistant had invited me to tag along while they made precise measurements of the skeleton of a recently killed blue whale, from which the local Inuit had already removed the meat for food. Getting out his measuring tools, Floyd looked up and said, "I shall be at least half an hour—amuse yourself." Comfortably clad in a ski suit plus

* Published in 1973.

Arctic Lab-issue cold-weather boots and parka, I looked about me with a sense of deep pleasure. The open water of the shore lead* appeared almost black in contrast to the snow-covered shore ice. The spectacular sea-ice pressure ridges, piled up by wind and ocean currents, were blinding white, with transparent icy highlights. Dramatically photogenic! My Rolliflex camera was loaded with black-and-white film, the Nikon with color, and I began shooting in an ecstasy of excitement. This was a splendid start to what promised to be a thrilling trip. In the distance I spied an Inuit whaling camp with an upturned, skin-covered umiak drying out beside a tent. The air was clear, cold, and sharp. A fine, light snow was falling gently. Shooting as I walked, I slowly wandered about two thousand yards from my companions and was kneeling down to get an angle shot when I felt myself sinking downward into the icy waters of the polar sea.

In excellent physical shape and with adrenaline flowing, I was confident that by bracing one hand on either side of me I could easily swing my legs up on one side and save myself. But I hadn't reckoned on the extra weight of long ski pants filled with water. It never occurred to me that I was in danger, but I knew that the camera equipment hanging around my neck was. Salt water would not "suit the works," to borrow from *Alice in Wonderland*. With no working cameras, I would be in a pretty fix. Making a cradle of my arms to raise the equipment above the water, I found that the more I struggled to get my legs up and over, the faster I sank and the heavier my legs felt. Throwing pride to the wind, I called out for help. The men didn't hear me. Then I probably screamed. At last I saw the Inuit turn his head in my direction and motion to Floyd. Both instantly dropped what they were holding and ran toward me. In an eternity they arrived and each taking an arm hauled me out of the water. I was wet to the chest, but the cameras were dry! Floyd scanned the horizon and spotted the Inuit whaling camp. Each man still holding an arm, they fast-walked me to

---

* The open water between the landfast ice and the central pack ice.

the tent, which fortunately was occupied by two natives. We told them what happened. They lit their Primus stove. I began to squeeze as much water out of my clothing as possible. One of the Inuit generously offered me a pair of dry heavy socks.

Beneath my ski suit I was wearing an all-in-one jumpsuit. I couldn't remove my wet pants without getting entirely undressed, and it was too cold to risk that. Gritting my teeth, I removed wet socks, substituted the delicious dry ones, put my boots back on, and stood up. By the time we got back to the sled, I was chilled, and we still had half an hour's travel back to the ONR lab. Floyd gave me an old tarpaulin used for hauling specimens. I wrapped it like a Dorothy Lamour sarong round my damp body to keep out the wind, and we started back. There was little feeling in my lower body when we arrived. I returned the tarp and staggered from sled to building. Back in my room, I filled a tub with hot water and peeled off my wet clothes. Only as feeling slowly returned to limbs soaking in the blessed hot water did I realize that I had had a narrow escape. Not testing the snow with a pole or a stick as I wandered off was the kind of dumb mistake that someone who worked on survival manuals throughout World War II shouldn't have made. Striking me like a blow was my late-husband Stefansson's scornful dictum, "An adventure is a sign of incompetence." This is what he meant! Sheepish, ashamed, and guilty was what I felt.

But what does all this have to do with becoming a psychotherapist, you will rightly ask. The answer begins to unfold with the telephone call I made from Fairbanks to my husband, John Nef. In giving him my news, I included, "A funny thing happened north of Point Barrow the other day." For some reason the Inuit all thought it very funny that Stefansson's wife had fallen through the ice. John Nef was unable to see the humor in the event. Death had taken his first wife, and he was certain that the Arctic was going to take his second. Returning home a month later, I found he had lost ten pounds, was extremely depressed, and had great difficulty in believing I was safe, sound, and actually home. Though I protested that the Arctic was no more dangerous than driving on the Beltway in rush hour,* I soon saw that John was genuinely upset. I conceded that I didn't *have* to go to the Arctic, but I still insisted that I had to work. I remembered Dr. Ross telling me that had he known me twenty-five years earlier he could have made "a first-class analyst" of me. I called him, reminded him of his statement, which fortunately he recalled, and asked, "Can you do anything for me today?" "Are you serious?" He asked. "Never more," I replied. "Let me think about it and call you back," he said. And he did.

---

* Ironically, I had never thought of the Arctic as dangerous. Hadn't I been married for a quarter of a century to the author of *The Friendly Arctic*?

CHAPTER XXV

A New Career Late in Life

A FTER OUR PHONE CONVERSATION, my former analyst Nat Ross arranged an interview for me with the director of the Institute for the Study of Psychotherapy in New York, Dr. Gertrude Blanck. Knowing that most institutes require a master's degree in social work or a medical degree for admission, I was anxious. But lacking these advanced credentials was the least of my worries. I didn't even have a bachelor's. I had never been to college, and even my high school diploma from Washington Irving might not be considered legitimate, since I had taken primarily art courses. So I went to the interview armed with anything I thought might help—my *Who's Who in America* entry, copies of my three published Scribner's books, the journal *Polar Notes*, which I had edited when I was librarian of the Stefansson Collection at Dartmouth. I even remembered that having taught the Arctic Seminar there for two years I was entitled to call myself a lecturer and truthfully declared that while never having *been* to a college, I had taught at one!

Ironically, none of the things I thought might impress weighed very heavily with Dr. Blanck. She told me later that what had tipped the scales was that, thanks to Stef's being an anthropologist, she thought I probably knew a lot about how primitive Inuit brought up their children. Child development, both normal and pathological, was the major part of the first-year curriculum at the institute, and Dr. Blanck thought my knowledge of Inuit child-rearing practices would be useful. She said that the school could provide a certificate of attendance, but without an M.S.W. there would be no diploma. I said I would take the chance. Regardless of whether or not I ever practiced as a psychotherapist, I was still interested in learning all I could on the subject. So, starting in 1974, for three years I commuted to New York on the Eastern Shuttle once a week, spent the night, and returned the next day. I was sometimes late but never missed a class because of weather.

Soon after I started school, Dr. Ross said, "You must get some experience in being with and observing really sick people." That was easier said than done. It is virtually impossible for an unqualified person to enter the locked floors of a psychiatric ward or hospital. Then I remembered Dr. Zigmund Lebensohn, an old friend and the head of psychiatry at Washington's Sibley Hospital. I telephoned and told him what I was doing and that I was willing to do almost anything to have a chance to work with mentally ill people. He knew I was serious, good with my hands where sculpture, painting, and crafts were concerned, and that I wasn't a sensation seeker. We worked out a scheme whereby I would become a volunteer candy striper and he would arrange assignment to his department. I became assistant to the professional occupational therapist and began by keeping the supply closet tidy and helping to set out materials for leather tooling, macramé, painting, needlepoint, and so on.

After some weeks the therapist trusted me to work alone and to open and close up shop. I observed that when occupational therapy was most needed—on weekends and holidays—the department was normally closed. As anyone who has had a long hospitalization knows, home and families are missed most during these times. I offered to come in on the days the department was closed, and for the next year I was there on weekends, Thanksgiving, Christmas day, New Year's, and Easter. The patients really appreciated my presence. Making myself generally useful, I taught the exercise class occasionally, learned

which patients to touch and which not to, and most importantly lost
any lurking fears I may have had about being close to seriously psychotic people.

Around this time, a paying job opportunity opened up for a technician on the floor. Counting my two years of institute schooling
and almost a year as an assistant occupational therapist, I felt qualified
and applied for the job. To my surprise, I was turned down. I was
puzzled, since I had proved myself in many capacities on the floor. I
discovered by chance that when consulted my boss had not recommended me, saying I was "overqualified." Because of me, she had been
able to boast of the only hospital occupational-therapy department
in Washington open seven days a week; it had never occurred to me
that she might arrange to have me turned down in order to have such
services continue.

One night at a dinner party I sat next to Dr. Tom Nigra, chief of
dermatology at the Washington Hospital Center. He told me of a
new, highly successful ultraviolet-light and drug treatment called
PUVA that was being used to treat severe cases of psoriasis, a debili-
tating skin affliction that affected the mind as well as the body of its
sufferers. "Who is investigating the psychosomatic aspects of the
disease?" I asked. "Why, no one," he replied. "Would you be interested?" I leapt at the chance. Within days I switched hospitals and
was enrolled as a volunteer in the dermatology department of the
Washington Hospital Center. I began to learn about psoriasis and
other skin diseases and was treated as a professional for the first time.
Soon I donned a white coat and was helping out in the treatment
center, talking to the patients, making appointments, assisting in the
treatments. Then I became a technician and was trusted to do the
actual treatments. My previous experience as a photographer came in
handy, because we photographed all patients before and after their
treatments. Handling the Hassleblad camera* was great fun, and even-

---

* An extremely expensive camera used commercially for fine definition, especially good for medical photography.

tually I could do it alone. From the beginning I had volunteered to do counseling and here got my first professional experience listening and talking to patients with skin problems.

After some months of working as a technician and doing research whenever there was a lull in the treatment center, I had learned enough about the disease to think up a study designed to prove or disprove the presence of a psychosomatic factor in psoriasis. Dr. Nigra, to my delight, welcomed the idea and made helpful suggestions. He introduced me to Dr. Elmer Gardner, chief of psychiatry at the hospital and an experienced medical researcher, who critiqued my plan and instructed me in scientific jargon as well as the mysteries and protocol of foundation grant applications. After spending six months writing and rewriting the application, I took it to the Jeremiah Milbank Foundation in New York. To the delight of all of us, it was approved and we were granted $45,000. We set up quarters in the George Hyman Research Building of the Hospital Center. I was suddenly a paid research director with a research assistant. Dr. Gardner did the psychiatric evaluations and acted as consultant.

The Psoriasis Social Adjustment Study, which began in October 1977 after I graduated from my institute, divided into two groups eighty-four patients who were receiving the new PUVA light and drug treatment. All patients had interviews with Dr. Gardner to eliminate any psychotic or untreatable types. All were subjected to a battery of well-known psychological tests before, during, and after their treatment, but only one group, one half of the patient population, received eight counseling sessions, each with me. I had been skeptical about having any lasting effect on a patient after only eight sessions, but to my surprise I happily turned out to be wrong. By the end of the study we found that patients who had received counseling cleared faster and had fewer recurrences of psoriasis. In more than half a dozen cases, especially where patients had formerly made no connection between stress and outbreaks of their illness, the awareness of such a connection, along with suggestions for coping, enabled them to help themselves in real ways.* Knowing I had only eight sessions with each patient, I developed a fast bold technique that had lasting influence on my career as a therapist. Although classically trained in psychoanalytically-oriented psychotherapy, I became much more interested in short-term, speeded-up treatment, and remain so to this day.

What I loved best about working at the hospital was going on rounds with Dr. Nigra, surrounded by his team of residents and interns. They would look at the patient's lesions; I would always look at their faces. They would ask about skin outbreaks; I would ask about feelings and what had been going on emotionally at the time. Dermatologists seldom have time to ask about what their patients are feeling, but I was now certain that in many cases those feelings were a part of the illness. I became the department shrink. The nurses would call me if they found a patient to be difficult or hostile. I would often discover that he or she had just split up with a partner, that a family member had recently died, that they had just lost their job, or that they had recently moved and were friendless in a new city. Giving them a chance to ventilate was always helpful. Overall, I learned an enormous amount about skin diseases, differential diagnosis, and psychosomatic medicine through my work at the Hospital Center.

MEANWHILE back at school in New York, at age sixty I was the oldest in the class and not unnaturally worried in the beginning about whether I would be capable of learning and digesting the huge amounts of new material that would have to be assimilated. I had learned that brain cells were the only cells in the body that were not renewable, and we lose them steadily as we mature. I soon realized that I needn't have worried. However, I had some reason to be worried about having to present a case history in a thesis during my third year of training—no trouble for my classmates, all of whom were practicing social workers, psychotherapists, or M.D.s.

---

* Today the understanding of this connection between stress and psoriasis is utilized by treatment centers throughout the country.

Tentatively, diffidently, I let drop in conversations with friends that I was looking for private patients. Almost as if he had read my anxious mind, Dr. Nigra telephoned one day to say he had a friend, not a patient, who was in trouble. Would I be willing to see her? I said, "Certainly," and shortly thereafter she was sitting on our living room couch telling me her troubles.

This woman was my first private patient, and I was very lucky—she was acutely depressed and she recovered completely. She also became the subject of my required thesis, called *First Case*, which began with my favorite Emily Dickinson poem:

> The Brain is wider than the sky,
>   For, put them side by side,
> The one the other will include
>   With ease, and you beside.
>
> The Brain is deeper than the sea,
>   For, hold them, blue to blue,
> The one the other will absorb,
>   As sponges, buckets do.
>
> The brain is just the weight of God,
>   For, lift them, pound for pound,
> And they will differ, if they do,
>   As syllable from sound.

In my preface, I attempted to convey the excitement, the anxiety, and, ultimately, the joy of exploring this new realm of the mind and heart:

> This is the narrative of a voyage of discovery made by a beginning psychotherapist with a first patient. Like most accounts of exploration into unknown territory it contains standard in-

gredients: New land found, certainly, wrong turnings taken, encounters with unfamiliar primitive beings and the finding of an oasis called déjà vu where fresh experience joined learned memory in a happy marriage. As a virgin expedition for this explorer the accompanying emotions were fraught with anxiety close to terror at one end of the horizon and unbelievable satisfaction at the other. During the course of the campaign, familiarity with the strange terrain improved and so did the confidence of the investigator. At journey's end, despite mistakes en route and vast quantities of still unknown surrounding territory, there were sweet rewards of new knowledge gained and the synthesis of scattered bits of learning into a single almost solid entity and a feeling of accomplishment beyond the ordinary.

Perhaps the most thrilling single moment in my life occurred when I received my thesis back. On the last page in the handwriting of Dr. Blanck, the director, I found, "A very superior paper indicating talent and skill that promises to flourish with experience." Gertrude Blanck had warned me at the beginning that I would not earn the graduate certificate but only a certificate of attendance. To my delight the faculty decided, in view of my valuable participation in the class and the excellence of my thesis, that an exception would be made; I would graduate with my class and receive the hallowed piece of paper, a certificate in recognition of completion of a course of study in the theory and technique of psychoanalytic psychotherapy, chartered by the Regents of the University of the State of New York. So on June 20, 1977, at the age of sixty-three, I graduated and received my first Social Security check!

One of the most important results of my working at the Hospital Center was that I developed a good working relationship and then a warm friendship with Dr. Elmer Gardner. We had worked well together during the psoriasis study, and when it was finished I asked

---

* Dr. Gertrude Blanck was my first, and later Dr. Ernst Ticho, formerly head of the psychiatric services at the Menninger Clinic, also served in that capacity.

him to be one of my three supervisors.* A fine teacher, he introduced me to brain chemistry and psychotropic drugs. Since I am a believer in the biochemical causes of many mental illnesses, it was important for me to have a close relationship with a psychiatrist who could prescribe medication for my acutely depressed patients or those with manic-depressive illness. Having Dr. Gardner as my supervisor enabled me to work with seriously ill patients who I would have otherwise been unable to treat. Twice so far in my practice I have had suicidal patients whom I wouldn't have dared to treat without his supervision and the knowledge that, thanks to him, these patients could be hospitalized immediately if necessary.

My first three private patients were all women in their early thirties who had marital problems, and I began to get the feeling that therein was my fate as a therapist. But then came an obsessive-compulsive male and then a phobic woman, and soon I had a full schedule and an interesting mix, with slightly more women than men. (When mental illness strikes, women tend to seek help from their gynecologist, G.P., or pediatrician while men go to the nearest bar and talk it over with friends or the bartender.) My patients have ranged in age from fourteen to late-seventies, with problems that ranged from adolescent rebellion to midlife crisis and age-related depression, from marital and sexual difficulties to work-related and career issues.* With very few exceptions I have liked all my patients and have loved some. Washington is a small town in a social sense, and it is not uncommon for me to meet former patients at social gatherings, where we are friendly and polite. More than several have wanted to be friends after the therapy is over, but I do not encourage that. I try to eliminate the last vestiges of dependence *before* termination.

IN learning to be a good therapist one must, of necessity, improve one's own character. For example, at home I was known to my

---

* The most common problem, of course, is depression—from my own observation, I would estimate that one in four persons will during their lifetime experience what we call a clinical depression.

French-speaking husband as "La Rapide," after the super-swift French train. My responses are quick, immediate. If I know something, I can usually tell it immediately without having to go through the usual journey of making the right connections. This gives me a tendency to speak first and think later. Perhaps the most difficult discipline for me to acquire as a therapist was curbing that natural response. It's important to have the responses and to define them, but then instead of speaking, telling, teaching, the therapist needs to be silent, to remember, to file for future use, to wait for the exact right moment before speaking.

It seems to me that the art of the therapist (and I am certain it is an art and not a science) lies largely in an accurate, sensitive sense of timing. You need to know when a patient is "ready" to discover what you have known perhaps since your second session. Just telling it would bounce right off the psyche of the average patient. But after, I hope, subtle questioning, a little leading, and a lot of listening on the therapist's part, the *patient* begins to make connections for him-or herself. Previously unasked questions emerge—why and how do you suppose it could be? Hidden feelings are discovered, especially anger, envy, hate, jealousy, and other socially unacceptable feelings that well-brought-up civilized people are not supposed to have. When there are perhaps a hundred pieces of the mental jigsaw puzzle, some of them already matched and connected, then and only then does one diffidently offer a suggestion of the possibility of what the final missing piece might be—the piece that will lock into place and make the real picture appear. As every teacher knows, if a pupil "discovers" an important insight for himself he makes it his own, one hopes forever.

It is sometimes said that those of us who choose to be psychotherapists do so because of our need to solve our own emotional problems. It's true that becoming a therapist not only enriched my present life but also illuminated my past life in a new way. So many of the feelings I was unable to understand as a child and an adolescent were clarified and became comprehensible, and I often found myself thinking, "So *that's* what must have happened." But being a good psychotherapist also requires talent, like being musical. If you are able to do it, if you enjoy doing it, and if most of your patients get well, therapy is one of the most rewarding professions out there.

I often have the feeling that all of my busy and extremely varied life was preparation for doing psychotherapy. The oddest pieces of information may provide the exact metaphor that will engage a patient. For instance, I had a thirty-year-old phobic patient, the eldest of ten children, who was robbed of most of her childhood playtime by having to look after the innumerable new babies that came along with distressing regularity—one a year. She survived thanks to a rich fantasy life, which she was unable to share with anyone in her lower-middle-class family. She was deeply interested in the Antarctic, and she read library-borrowed narratives of exploration, accompanying her heroes to the southern Polar lands to comfort herself. I was the first person she had ever encountered who knew the name of the explorer Ernest Shackleton, and when I was able to talk about him from firsthand knowledge a bond was created that enabled her to trust me. Then we began to work together to resolve and dissolve her numerous phobias.

My first adolescent patient was a very intelligent young girl, ahead of her classmates and occasionally her family intellectually, but far below her peers emotionally. She hated everything and everybody and had only two sources of pleasure in all the world—horses and photography. Having been a professional photographer, I was able to engage her interest and once in a while offer her a technical suggestion. Then she was able to listen, trust, and use the therapy.

Sometimes I am a role model for a patient. A woman in her forties suffering from the "empty nest syndrome"—all her children have grown up and departed, the house is terrifyingly quiet, and she has "nothing to do"—once asked, "How can I, at my age, begin to look for a job?" I told her that I had been sixty years old when I began to study to be a psychotherapist and that that choice had enriched and colored my life, so that at seventy and then eighty I completely forgot my age and only felt the pleasure involved in solving difficult and challenging puzzles.

I firmly believe that my most important therapeutic tools are my own life experience and my natural optimism—my honest belief that I *can* really help someone. To a depressed person that optimism often feels like a lifeline thrown to a non-swimmer in the ocean. Of course, to be helped, a patient must be willing to help himself. I can only give someone a map, a pocket compass, suggestions about emergency rations, and new modes of transportation, which may make the journey possible and certainly less painful.

People often ask me, "Doesn't it wear you out and depress you dealing with so many sick people, listening to trouble, trouble, trouble all day long?" Strangely enough, it doesn't. I usually arrive home after six, slightly exhilarated, sometimes physically tired but usually with a strong feeling that it has been a good day. A good day to a therapist may mean finding a hidden nut while a very good day is cracking it and a splendid day is discovering the sweet meat inside. I became a therapist in part because my husband didn't want me to go off to the "dangerous" Arctic. Though I was, of course, extremely interested in psychotherapy from the beginning, I didn't know at the time how rewarded I would feel when a sick person got well or how happy it would make me to discover a small gift that could aid people in trouble. The most treasured compliment I ever received was from Tom Nigra: "Evvie, you are a born healer."

CHAPTER XXVI

John Nef's Death

NOT LONG AFTER I TOOK those swimming lessons in the mid-sixties at Cap d'Antibes, we had reason to be grateful that I had. One fine day during our annual summer stay, John and I were swimming off the hotel rocks when I looked across at him and saw instantly that he was in trouble. There was a rigid, frightened look on his face, and he was gasping for breath. Closing the space between us as swiftly as I could, I soon saw that he was unable to swim or speak or help himself. I held him up with one arm and swam with the other until we were able to approach the ladder, where another swimmer helped to get him up. Very slowly John seemed to recover and was eventually able to move and then to speak. When I asked what had happened, he replied, "I don't know. Suddenly I couldn't move and would surely have drowned if you hadn't rescued me." We went to the little village near St. Paul de Vence where Marc Chagall's local doctor lived for an examination, but the doctor could find nothing wrong with John. He suggested that he have a thorough checkup when we got back to Washington. He did so, but the checkup revealed nothing.

Then, in December 1972, we were in Santa Barbara, where John was giving a lecture and participating in discussions at Robert Hutchins' Center for the Study of Democratic Institutions.* During the ques-

---

* Someone once wittily characterized the Center for the Study of Democratic Institutions as "the Leisure of the Theory Class" since the scholars congregated and lived in palatial quarters that housed the richly endowed center.

tion-and-answer period following John's lecture, I realized that something was wrong; instead of answering the questions that were being asked, he kept repeating, "That's an interesting question." The chairman closed the meeting, and I hurried over to John's side. He greeted me with "What am I doing with these papers in my hand?" Answering reassuringly "you have just given a talk for Bob Hutchins," I realized that he had suffered a mental blackout. He didn't know where he was or what he was doing and was grateful to have me tell him what to do as I led him back to our quarters, where I telephoned our close friends Jim and Ethel Douglas for information about medical help. I took John to the local hospital, where he stayed overnight and was thoroughly examined. The next morning the doctor told me that John's memory had returned and he seemed to be completely recovered except for a mild suggestion of Parkinson's disease. This explained the Cap d'Antibes muscular freezing in the water. I also remembered an incident in an elevator when John had lost the use of his legs and slumped down on the floor until I and a fellow passenger got him up and walked him out. In a few moments he was able to move again, and we were on our way. And once after a swim, while we were changing in the bathing cabin, John had confessed that he had "lost his memory"—he didn't know where he was and was disoriented. Again memory slowly returned. These were the first symptoms of what was to become a gradually accelerating illness.

John's Parkinson's increased with time, and the medications, which had been so startlingly helpful in the beginning, became less and less effective. But his spirit remained high, and we learned to use wheelchairs at airports and my arm as support when we walked. The difficulty was getting him started. He would decide to take a step, but the message going from his brain to his muscle lacked a neurotransmitter—dopamine. I discovered that a repeated strong rhythm could often help to get him going, so I would sing a few bars of the Marseillaise or "Onward Christian Soldiers." After the first difficult step it got easier and easier. Old nursery rhymes were called into play, like

"One, two, button my shoe, three, four, shut the door." When we came to nine, ten, John would triumphantly shout "a big fat hen," and we would have a big laugh. This technique enabled us to go to the theater, the opera, and the symphony, well beyond what he would have been able to negotiate alone. I arranged for seats on the aisle or in a box so that we wouldn't inconvenience others and could leave quickly at the intermission or any other time if John got tired. One of my friends once said, "Evvie, you *willed* John to walk." Of course, I did, for his sake but also my own.

When I was commuting to New York and psychotherapy school, John had a stroke and could no longer walk. We then had to utilize wheelchairs indoors, too—one on each floor. Several years later another stroke scrambled his brain and confused his thinking. He lost his sense of time and place and was no longer able to organize his thoughts. He had little short-lived fits of paranoid anger, which were generally displaced onto his caretakers. It is not uncommon for strong men to become angry when they are seriously ill and to turn on those who are closest to them. Thankfully, he remained loving and affectionate with me to the end. But my old John was gone! No real conversation was possible now, only pleasant automatic niceties: "Good morning. How are you? Did you have a good night?" He would tell me his speech for a nonexistent television appearance was ready and ask what time he needed to be ready to go out to dinner, though he hadn't been "out" to dinner since his first stroke.

During this time, Gerry, John's wonderful night nurse, would take him downstairs for breakfast bathed and smelling sweet, dressed in a fresh shirt, pants, and sweater, and seemingly thrilled to see me. We would embrace. He would get into his wheelchair with help, and once at the table he would attack his breakfast voraciously, often before Gerry could get his plastic apron in place. His formerly exquisite table manners became primitive. He would spill, dribble, butter his coffee, sprinkle the floor with his blueberry muffin, and be thoroughly engaged by these activities. Sometimes he would fall asleep with his spoon halfway to his mouth, and sometimes his full coffee cup would fall, but he remained good natured, and so did we. Spills would be wiped, crumbs vacuumed—the goal was to keep him as happy and content as possible.

When John had his third and final stroke, he did not lose consciousness, and he begged me not to let the doctors hospitalize him. I promised and, thanks to our being able to afford private nurses around the clock, was able to keep my promise. He could stay at home and die in his own bed in the "Salle Chagall" surrounded by the beauty that was so essential to his life, and with me nearby. Parkinson's gradually reduced all motion. Finally, in December 1988, when John was no longer able to swallow or to cough, his wonderful doctor, Robert Langevin, and I conferred and decided not to treat the recurring pneumonia. He became sleepier, and about ten days later, on Christmas Day 1988, at the age of eighty-nine, he died. I was dressing to dine with friends (John always encouraged me to go out). I had found a magazine article about André Derain, one of his favorite painters, and said I would be back in a few minutes to read it to him— though I wasn't sure whether he could understand the article, I knew that the sound of my voice was comforting. Minutes after I had left his room, the nurse called me back, and I found John dead, with the same sweet expression on his face as when I had left him. The nurse, who was Romanian, seemed to feel it was very necessary to light a candle and did so while I telephoned the doctor. Astonishingly, though I was interrupting his Christmas dinner, the doctor came right over to sign the death certificate, telling me that district law required that without a doctor's signature the police would have had to be notified, which would have involved a great deal of red tape at a very difficult time.

Every year since we had married, John and I had had a New Year's Eve party in honor of Bob and Mary Carswell, at whose house we had met. When John died, the invitations were already out to about thirty of our closest friends, many of whom had come year after year to our black-tie celebration. My first instinct was to cancel the party. But thinking of what John would have wanted, I made the difficult decision to have the party, only six days after his death. There was to be no funeral, and the memorial service would not come until later; the party would give us all a chance to talk about John and his death. And I needed the support of my friends. So I held the party, without the customary music and dancing, and we did talk about John and cried a little together. It was a therapeutic experience for all of us. I still have that party every New Year's Eve. As one friend said, "Evvie, where would we *go* if you didn't give your party?"

Later a beautiful memorial service was held in the auditorium of the Corcoran Gallery of Art, where I had been a board member for many years. The Cleveland Quartet played Mozart and Beethoven, and our old friend Bobbie de Margerie, the French ambassador, spoke, as did Bob Carswell and Paul Wheatley, the director of the University of Chicago's Committee on Social Thought, which John had founded.

FOLLOWING the death of John's first wife, Elinor, in 1953, after thirty years of marriage, his world had fallen apart. Her loss seemed to "place all my principles in jeopardy," he wrote in his autobiography. He felt defenseless, with a desperate need for something firm to take her place. His friend and colleague, the philosopher Jacques Maritain, lauded Roman Catholicism, with the enthusiasm of a convert, as a source of comfort and healing. In Paris John's friend Nadia Boulanger introduced him to the Père A.M. Carré, a charming, intellectual Dominican who baptized him and looked after his spiritual needs for the decade before he met me.

When John and I first talked about a marriage ceremony, I declared that a Roman Catholic ceremony was impossible for me. My agnostic feelings were too strong. My belief that man invented the religions he needed to fulfill his fantasies and calm his fears had been confirmed and strengthened during my time with Stef, who had studied comparative religions at Harvard and had come to the same conclusion. I love the music associated with all religions and can be moved to tears by the sound of a cantor's voice singing an excerpt from the Orthodox Jewish service or an aria from Bach's St. John's Passion, but I could never believe in the divinity of Christ, the Immaculate Conception, or the various miracles depicted in the Bible.

After we were married, John used to go to Mass at a church on Dumbarton Street, around the corner from our Georgetown house. The church had a service in French, and many diplomats and their wives attended. In the glow of our first year together, I would accompany him, enjoying the Gregorian chant singing and imagining beautiful words being spoken in a language I couldn't understand; it was like going to the opera before surtitles. But by the second year of our marriage, after Berlitz, I had learned a considerable amount of French. When I could understand what was being spoken and sung, I was horrified by the amount of *sin* and *guilt* and negative ideas the service contained. I told John I preferred to spend my Sunday mornings in ways that were more profitable to me but urged him to continue going on his own. He began to skip Mass, at first occasionally and then often. When I asked him about it he said, "Since I have you, I don't need to go to Mass. It only makes me sad now." I had a twinge of guilt, but he seemed so happy it didn't last very long.

With my patients I often hear, "I'm not afraid of death, it's fear of a long and painful illness that troubles me," or "I'm not afraid of my own death, but I can't bear the thought of my *mother* dying." It usually turns out that these are displacements or covers for their own fear of dying. One has to confront the idea nakedly and be able to face death with courage and without strain.* The death of John's mother when he was nine and then his father thoughtlessly telling him that she

---

* I had initially made my peace with death back in Hanover, when I thought I had cancer. I had gone through some but not all of Kubler-Ross's stages (denial, anger, bargaining, depression, and acceptance), and when I was told I had Paget's Disease, an incurable but usually nonfatal bone disease, I felt I had been given a miraculous reprieve, a great gift of life. After that experience, I knew with certainty what my priorities in life were: love, family, friendship, and the life of the mind. Things—wealth, jewelry, clothes, social position—none of them really mattered; they were worthless if you weren't well and alive.

had died because he was "a bad boy" had left John with a terror of abandonment augmented by a strong sense of guilt. By the time we met this psychological characteristic had merged with and strengthened his fear of death. Thanks to my insisting that we talk through these fears, before John died we had talked often, easily, and sensibly about both our deaths and our choices for how they were to be handled. We had both chosen cremation over burial, and neither of us wanted any religious ceremonies. John suggested that his ashes should be buried at the foot of the Chagall mosaic in the garden. I told him I thought that was a good idea, that it would suit me, too, and that I would join him there.

John had been terminally ill for more than two years, so I had done what people in my profession call "anticipatory mourning." I felt blessed having found an engaging and satisfying new career, one which enabled me to think about the pain of others instead of my own. So I was unprepared for the sharpness and depth of my sorrow when John actually died. I was grateful that my patients needed me—after a week of paralysis and weeping, I forced myself to go back to work. Most of my patients did not even know of my loss. The *Washington Post* obituary was sparse; the larger one in the *New York Times* escaped them. The routine of having to get up and dress and walk to my office, about four blocks from where I lived, forced me to think of things besides my depression.

Soon after we married John had published a history book called *The Conquest of the Material World.* Its dedication read: "*A Evelyn Stefansson Nef—Qui m'a delivré de la tristesse.*" He always made me feel that I had rescued him from an eleven-year depression. We had twenty-five years of happiness. But I well knew that older survivors of a long marriage were at risk. Many survivors die within a year of their partner's death, and they are sixteen times more vulnerable to illness than the average person of similar age. So I did all the things I would have advised a depressed patient in my position to do: I made myself exercise regularly, go to cheerful movies and the theater, and see people even though what I most wanted to do was to isolate myself and weep. The text-books say that theoretically acute depression following the loss of a mate lasts three months, but it was more like three years before I could spend a day without hurting. The lighter pain never does go entirely away but becomes interwoven with one's psyche in a safe, hidden place.

How lucky we had been to find each other. John, a widower for eleven years, was sad and lonely when we met. I had thought my life was over and was instead granted twenty-five happy and romantic years with a loving husband who wanted to take care of me and did. He made a carefree happy life for us. I'm not saying that our life was a cloudless dream. Every marriage has difficulties and differences of opinions, though we had relatively few. We did have illness and scares and narrow escapes of one kind or another, but looking back how grateful I am that we spent no time quarreling or on hurt feelings. We empathized with and comforted each other. John's thoughtful-ness via flowers and gifts was startling at first, but I soon learned to reciprocate and do things for him that gave him as much pleasure. This is not Pollyanna-the-glad-girl speaking, for I had two interesting pre-vious marriages with which to compare ours. I always thought it was the greatest good luck to have romance *late* in one's life, when one can truly appreciate it, not take it for granted. Looking about me, I saw many marriages that had lost that valuable ingredient.

John had always maintained a strong interest in the Committee on Social Thought, the interdisciplinary Ph.D. department he had founded. After we married, he continued to lecture, and I often trav-eled with him to Chicago and thoroughly enjoyed meeting and befriending department members like Saul Bellow, Alan Bloom, Edward Shils, Hannah Ahrendt, and Harold Rosenberg. Before John died, when he had already had several small strokes, I established a John U. Nef Professorship at the University of Chicago's Committee for Social Thought. I wanted to do this while he was alive and could enjoy the thought that his name would be perpetuated in the depart-ment he loved. It did cheer him. Since then I have played a sort of godmother role to the committee, visiting now and then, arranging scholarships for gifted students and providing a lecture fund to bring distinguished speakers from other universities, continuing a tradition started by John.

CHAPTER XXVII

Philanthropy and Life in 1990s and Beyond

*I*N THE EARLY 1990S the insurance company that had provided malpractice insurance for my whole class at the institute went out of business, and I had to find another company. To my horror, I was unable to find one that would insure me. The institute had taken my teaching experience at Dartmouth, my publication of three books, my editing experience producing *The Great Explorer Series* for Delacorte Press, and my knowledge of how primitive Inuit brought up their children as the equivalent of bachelor's and master's degrees. The insurance companies were not so liberal and insisted that no degrees meant no insurance. My lawyer, Mike Curtin, advised that it would be foolish to practice without, since I was working with people who were not always emotionally stable and the resources I had accumulated might be tempting to a litigious client. He said, "Look, you have had a good run—almost twenty years; it would be sensible to retire." I didn't feel like retiring, but I respected Mike Curtin's advice. So I took the rest of the year to "finish" my patients, with all but one satisfied that they had completed their therapy.*

It was sad to give up practicing. The therapist-client relationship is an intimate, meaningful one that if successful brings pleasure to

---

* One gentleman was nervous about terminating despite my assurances that he was ready, so I told him he might telephone at any time if he encountered difficulties. He did call me about six months later to tell me I had been right about his being ready.

both parties, and I knew I would miss it. I had had a success rate higher than average and had thoroughly enjoyed the feedback from patients who had been ill after they became well. It was not long, however, before I was involved with several new enterprises that engaged both my time and my emotions. When John died, for the second time in my life I believed that my life was, practically speaking, over. The first time I felt that way occurred when Stef died. I was wrong on both counts. In some ways the years following John's death, once I recovered from the acute depression that was bound to follow, turned out to be the most interesting of my life.

W HEN John became disabled by his second stroke, I was forced to think seriously about finances. Round-the-clock private nurses are not inexpensive. Like it or not, I needed to look into money matters. My first move was to subscribe to the *Wall Street Journal*, which I read religiously, at first without much understanding. But in time I accumulated enough knowledge to feel capable of making informed and sensible decisions. Previously, John had left all his stocks and bonds in the hands of his Chicago lawyer friend, Tom Alcock, who cut the bond coupons and forwarded the dividends as they arrived. The stocks consisted mostly of huge chunks of Castle & Cooke and Alexander & Baldwin, two Hawaii-based stocks inherited from his first wife. For sentimental reasons John would never sell any of the stock. As long as there was enough income accumulating to cover housing, food, entertainment, vacations, and gifts to the University of Chicago, he was content. Even when Castle & Cooke suddenly stopped paying dividends, for the first time in its history, and our income was halved overnight, it never occurred to John to sell the valuable stock and invest in other, dividend-producing stocks. Fortunately, Alexander & Baldwin prospered mightily about that time and took up a good deal of the slack.

Then Tom Alcock died, and suddenly I was in charge. Emptying all the safe-deposit boxes, I moved everything from Chicago to Washington. I looked for and found good financial advice and began to take a genuine interest in my inheritance, vowing to put any excess where John would have wanted it to go. Within several years both my holdings and my income had quadrupled in value. Having been a poor girl and then a working girl until I married John, I had to *learn* how to spend money. It occurred to me that I could now purchase a painting or a piece of sculpture without asking anyone's permission, or buy a Mary McFadden evening dress without having to wait until it was marked down for the third time, or fly up to New York for an interesting dinner party without calculating the cost.

The 1990s happened to coincide with a fantastic rise in the stock market, which made many young people multimillionaires and some of us older folk more prosperous than we had ever been. Since neither John nor I had children or needy relatives, I began to look around for worthy causes in which to place my surplus. There was no need to look long or far. The National Symphony Orchestra, the Washington Opera, and the National Gallery of Art were all near at hand. Now that I was able to make substantial contributions, I was sometimes asked to join the boards or inner circles of these organizations. In this way I became in touch with the workings of a great orchestra and had the chance to meet its musicians and its gifted conductor, Leonard Slatkin. The same happy circumstances prevailed with the Washington Opera, which is now directed by the great tenor, conductor, and entrepreneur Placido Domingo. My passion for music is thus *almost* satisfied.

I also came to know the director and several curators at the National Gallery. Some, like Andrew Robison, Senior Curator of Prints and Drawings, became my friends. Andrew became a mentor as well. He had the bright idea that instead of my simply making the usual annual contribution to the Gallery, he would find a small work of art in an area that particularly interested me and I would supply the money for its purchase. Then, whether on exhibit or in the archives, it would always carry my name as donor. We were both pleased with this approach.

I loved being invited to formal openings of the new exhibitions, meeting other collectors, and visiting foreign curators. On one such happy evening I found myself sitting next to Dr. Albert Kostenevich, the Curator of Modern European Painting at the great Hermitage Museum in St. Petersburg, which had lent numerous pieces to the Gallery for its *Matisse in Morocco* exhibition. He was interested to learn that a Marc Chagall mosaic colored my garden and wanted to see it. Once in my house he wanted to see the rest of my holdings, and it was with the greatest pleasure I showed him through the entire house. Later, on a visit to St. Petersburg, I had the thrill of his guiding me and my little party through the Hermitage's twentieth-century paintings, many of which had come from Maria Marosova (my Russian teacher at Dartmouth)'s grandfather's collection, which had been taken over by the Soviet government. Kostenevich told one unpublished fascinating story after another about the Matisses, Picassos, and Derains. Later, when he and his wife, who is also a curator, specializing in ancient Greek art, were visiting scholars at the National Gallery's School for Advanced Art Studies, they both came to dinner, and we had a jolly reunion.

At the Corcoran Gallery of Art, where I had earlier been a board member for many years, I established a fund called "Still Working" for under-recognized older artists. It enabled an artist who had devoted himself to his art for a lifetime to have a one-man show, with a catalogue and a formal opening at a famous museum. Having been an art student myself and knowing many artists in Greenwich Village during the thirties, I understood something of what it means to an artist to be "recognized" and appreciated.

My dear friend Mary Carswell was the executive director of the MacDowell Colony, the oldest artist colony in America, from 1987 to 1996. Founded almost a hundred years ago by the composer Edward MacDowell on the site of his summer home in Peterborough, New Hampshire, the colony has housed many distinguished artists. Leonard Bernstein wrote *Mass* there, Thornton Wilder *Our Town*, Milton Avery painted there, and Aaron Copeland not only had been a colonist but also was a board member for thirty-six years and president for six. Mary tried successfully to interest me in their activities, and I visited the lovely green place for their annual Medal Day, meeting both officers and colonists, and was enchanted by the setting and the interesting poets, painters, sculptors, musicians, and composers who inhabited the studios. I was invited to become a member of the board. Because the colony's photographic studio was old-fashioned and dated, I decided to give them a state-of-the-art space as well as the scholarships necessary to keep it occupied. It was MacDowell's first new building in thirty-five years and happily set a precedent that was followed by others' giving a new sculptors' studio, with the necessary equipment for large-scale creations, and a new writers' studio. I enjoy the quarterly meetings in New York, headed by Chairman Robin MacNeil, formerly of the MacNeil-Lehrer news program, who now spends most of his time writing novels.

Soon after marrying John Nef, I had a flareup of my Paget's Disease and poor luck in finding an orthopedist or endocrinologist who knew much about it. Finally, I asked Dr. Robert Butler, a friend and famous gerontologist, "Who is the world's best authority on Paget's Disease?" Dr. Butler did some homework and told me there were two—one in California, Ralph Singer, and one in New York, at Columbia Presbyterian, Dr. Ethel Siris. New York being closer to home, I called Dr. Siris and arranged an appointment. She turned out to be a delightful as well as a learned person. She explained that the medicine I had been given was not a bad medicine but that it had to be taken on an empty stomach in order to be effective—a small detail that my Washington doctor had neglected to tell me. Dr. Siris was doing research on a new series of drugs that were being explored for Paget's and managed to get me into one of the early trials. Like magic my pain diminished. After thirty years of chronic pain, I was soon almost pain free. My gratitude to Dr. Siris was enormous, and we became friends. She asked if I would be interested in joining the board of the Paget Foundation. I was, did so, and thereby learned much about the newest methods of treating the disease. One fascinating aspect of recent Paget's research is that the medications developed turn out to be valuable also in the treatment of osteoporosis and cancers that metastasize to bone, like breast and prostate, eliminating some of the agonizing pain that often accompanies the late stages of the diseases.

For decades my friend Bob Butler has been trying to educate the country about the worldwide longevity revolution that has taken place. Most of us are living more than twenty-five years longer than our grandparents. Bob feels passionately about the need for establishing gerontology departments in our medical schools to look after the problems of our aging population. There are pitifully few—only three in the entire United States. In 1990 Bob established the International Longevity Center in New York City, a nonprofit, non-partisan organization devoted solely to the study of longevity and population-aging and their impact on society. The center has branches in Japan (now with the oldest population in the world), France, Great Britain, and the Dominican Republic. The center is affiliated with the Mount Sinai School of Medicine. I was honored to be asked to join the board and love our meetings, where I have the opportunity to learn from its distinguished members, each concerned with a different aspect of the problem—medical, social, ethical, and economic.

Discovering how enjoyable it was to put money where it was needed for a cause one believed in, I decided that the next logical step was to establish a small foundation, with limited funds to give away during my lifetime and then more later. It seemed sensible to establish the paths of giving in a modest way while I was alive in order to ensure their continuance later. The Nef Foundation has only five board members, all female, all friends, and all qualified in some particular area. Mary Carswell, trained as a social worker, was experienced in directing the MacDowell Colony and was invaluable in teaching us some of the basics of foundation-building. Elaine Kurtz, a successful practicing artist who had been an art teacher in her youth, was knowledgeable about the New York art scene. Sheila Platt, married to a diplomat, had lived in many parts of the world, where she had used her skills as social worker-psychotherapist to learn as well as teach. Linda Yahn, my assistant for twenty-five years, gifted in handling numbers, is the secretary of the foundation.

We meet four times a year in New York City, usually at Elaine Kurtz's studio near Union Square. None of us is paid, but we usually have a splendid lunch after our meetings downstairs at the Union Square Café. The bylaws state that our mission is to give in the field of mental health, especially new approaches, and to all branches of the arts. We only give to organizations that are personally known to our board members—we don't accept solicitations from outsiders. We make site visits occasionally and do further research when necessary. All of us enjoy each other and the satisfying work we do.

O N a pleasant summer day in the Berkshires, weekending with Mary and Bob Carswell, Mary voiced her concern about a body of land just opposite theirs that had suddenly come on the market. Developers in hovering helicopters were flying back and forth, tying plastic ribbons around more than a dozen possible house sites where soil tests were to be made. She feared that the wonderful peace and quiet of their country weekend and vacation haven would be destroyed if the projected townhouses were built just across the road. Remembering that any means I had came from my marriage to John Nef and that if it hadn't been for Mary we would never have met, I decided it was really my duty to rescue the Carswells, and I announced that I would try to buy the land and save their precious privacy. With luck, a good lawyer, and considerable cash money (which the developers fortunately lacked), we were able to purchase the 147 acres of prime real estate a few miles from the town of Great Barrington. There were no buildings on the land.

Back in Washington and pleased with myself for my good deed in rescuing Mary and Bob, it occurred to me that at the age of eighty-two the time would soon come when I would no longer be able to traipse abroad so easily when Washington became impossibly hot and humid in July and August. Why not have a house where the summers are cool and the landscape green, with close friends across the road? I then turned to my old friend and neighbor, much-honored architect Hugh Newell Jacobsen, who had constructed innovative and beautiful structures around the world, and asked him to look at the site and design a small dream house useful in both summer and winter.

Hugh loved the setting, chose the specific site, and designed a prize-winning modern house. Constructed of cedar wood, painted white inside and out, with blue stone floors and mat aluminum roofs, it looked like a typical house in a small New England village from the front. The back of the two-story-high living room, which faced the green Berkshire hills, was glass from floor to ceiling. I rented an old frame house a mile up the road and spent the next summer watching the new house grow. It was an exciting, terrifying, pleasing, worrying, and eventually comforting experience. The house was so beautiful. I moved all but one of the abstract Elaine Kurtz paintings from my Georgetown house and commissioned four more. These were the largest paintings Elaine had ever painted up to that time and today grace the entrance gallery. Ann Christopher, a young British sculptor friend, came up to the still-unfinished house, took measurements, made a scale model of the terrace facing the pool, and designed a fourteen-foot-high, bronze-and-stainless-steel abstract sculpture, which adds the perfect finishing touch to the house. We planted an arcade of sixteen blossoming pear trees for the approach to the front door, which was painted red on one side, a signal that I was at home, and white on the other, which, when closed signaled I was not. Hugh furnished the place, mostly with pieces of his own design, borrowing a little here and there from Corbusier and Mies van der Rohe. I named the house Ultima Thule, the medieval geographer's name for the farthest land, and so far have enjoyed four wonderful summers there.

Mary had grown up in nearby Lenox and with her usual generosity introduced me to her old friends and to the doctors at the Austin Riggs Center, a famous mental health facility in nearby Stockbridge, where she had been chairman of the board for many years and where Erik Erikson had worked. Tanglewood, where the Boston Symphony Orchestra summered, was nearby, and I soon became involved with the music makers and the Kousevitsky Center, the summer school for young professional musicians. In a surprisingly short time I was pleasurably surrounded by a circle of new and interesting friends. Near Lee was Jacob's Pillow, founded long ago by Ruth St. Denis and Ted Shawn and ever since a gathering place for the dancers of the world as well as for neophyte and would-be dancers, which provided another source of aesthetic and spiritual nourishment.

The house is comfortable in winter, thanks to radiant heating and two fireplaces in the living room. I usually go up for Thanksgiving and Christmas, sharing festivities with the Carswells and their son, Will, and daughter, Kate, who is my godchild, and her new husband, Tim. I am always back in Washington for the New Year's Eve party that has occurred every year since I married John in 1964 (except for one winter when I went to the Antarctic). The twenty-five to thirty folks who gather to toast the new year, dance, and sup in black tie have grown old with me. Some of the group have been lost to death, and new, young blood comes to keep the event healthy.

BEFORE I started this book, I applied for admission to the MacDowell Colony and wrote the rough draft there. There is nothing to do at MacDowell except work, and the colony has only one rule: No one visits you without an invitation. Breakfast and dinner are served in the main colony hall, and lunch is brought to your door in a basket and left. In the evening writers may read a chapter of a book (I did), play a newly composed piano piece, or take a trip to town to go to the movies. The colonists usually report that aside from the blessing of being able to work undisturbed, the friendships formed between people of differing disciplines are meaningful and often lasting. Like most colonists I had a profitable and exciting time.

During the seven weeks I spent in Peterborough, I decided to drive over to Hanover to look up material in the Stefansson Collection. I arrived at the Hanover Inn, the scene of many a pleasant evening spent in the dozen years Stef and I lived on campus. I set out on the familiar walk across the green to Baker Library, with notebook and my favorite pen, and when I arrived I inquired about the whereabouts of the Stefansson Collection. I knew it had been moved from the spacious quarters we had occupied in the past. Directed to the library's Treasure Room, I was there introduced to the Librarian of Special Collections. Most of the people I had known when working there from 1953 to 1963 were gone, but Ken Cramer and Virginia Close, the remarkable reference librarian, were still there. Ken warned me that there were surprises awaiting me at the Stefansson Collection, but that did not prepare me for what I found.

When Stef and I arrived in Hanover, the collection had consisted of about 25,000 books and an extensive pamphlet file (Stef had particularly valued pamphlets because they were often lost or thrown away but often contained valuable and unique information). The books now numbered 2,500, and there was no pamphlet file. Miraculously, all of Stef's voluminous correspondence and manuscripts had survived and, thanks to a grant from the U.S. Department of Education, were meticulously catalogued, cross-referenced, and computerized. Nobody offered any good explanations for the changes, at least from my point of view. Stef and I had done without many things to keep up the library, and we brought it to Dartmouth thinking that there it would be preserved and kept up. I could understand that with Stef's death and the migration of the arctic-minded professors to other universities they might cut the budget for the collection, but it never occurred to me that they would destroy it. But we had no contract with the college—our understanding of what would happen was verbal. So as

I recovered from the initial shock, with my Pollyanna-the-glad-girl defense I began to count my blessings.

The photographs had been preserved, including the ones I had taken to illustrate my northern books. The computerized catalogue of the correspondence would help me date events, something I was notoriously bad at doing on my own. The kind librarian, Philip Cronenwett, assured me I could have copies of anything I might need. I stayed only a short time, postponing any real research until I had completed the first draft of my book, glad of a reason to leave quickly. Summer school was in session, and there were women students now, a welcome change from the formerly all-male student body. Still, the Hanover visit revived painful memories of Stef's death and my medical episodes at the Mary Hitchcock Clinic.

In the summer of 2000, about a decade after my last disappointing visit, I received an invitation from Weyman Lundquist, acting director of the Institute of Arctic Studies at Dartmouth, to meet the new president, attend a luncheon, where I was to say "a few words," and visit the new library where the Stefansson Collection was housed. At first I decided to "regret" but on second thought believed the invitation would be an opportunity for me to voice my indignation at what had happened to the Stefansson Collection. As Robert Burns once said, I had been "nursing my wrath to keep it warm."

The morning after the pleasant dinner, where I was seated on the left of the new president, James Wright, I was taken to the Rauner Library, where the Stefansson Collection was newly housed in a handsome setting, and was greeted by Philip Cronenwett, the librarian. I was delighted to learn that he was genuinely interested in polar history, and he told me the astonishing good news that 90 percent of the original collection had been reconstituted. Philip Cronenwett had managed the resurrection of the Stefansson Collection with funds from the Lincoln Ellsworth Foundation*, the

---

* Lincoln Ellsworth was a wealthy explorer in the 1930s who participated in several polar expeditions. He died in 1951.

Dirlam Fund, and the Stefansson Fund, which included the Vilhjalmur Stefansson Memorial Fund, formed at the time of Stef's death.
Cronenwett said there seemed to be a greatly renewed interest in
Stef's work. The new Vilhjalmur Stefansson Arctic Research Institute, established at the university in Akureyri, Iceland, was in almost
daily computer contact, and there was also new interest in Stef's diet
studies in the medical profession. Philip Cronenwett had miraculously found the old, previously discarded pamphlet file, managed to
rescue it and place it all in archival boxes, and intended now to re-
catalog it in its entirety.

At the Dickey Center luncheon, where I was scheduled to speak, I
told the truth about my old feelings and how I had come prepared to
be highly critical and had to change my tune since I was thrilled with
the resurrection of the library in its handsome new setting and the
care that was being taken of even Stef's old lantern slides, which had
been cleaned, wrapped, and catalogued, available for consultation by
anthropologists. It was a tremendous relief to have a happy feeling
about the library, and with good conscience I could once again add
to the holdings of the collection.

Later that same year I stopped off in Akureyri, Iceland, at the Vilhjalmur Stefansson Arctic Research Institute to participate in the
Stefansson Memorial Lecture and a three-day conference concerning
the problems of all circumpolar peoples of the north. How pleased
Stef would have been to see this gathering of natives from Siberia,
Lapland, Greenland, the Canadian Arctic, and Alaska. The conference was opened by the president of Iceland and ended with the opening of *The Friendly Arctic* exhibit at the art museum. I came home in an
emotional, intellectual glow.

In my twenties, when I began to work for Stefansson, I was the only
member of the staff that didn't have a college degree, and some of the
Ph.D.s made me feel self-conscious about it. It stopped being a matter of concern after publishing my Alaskan book, which was a bestseller. I would have loved to have gone to college, and in the early

days I used to envy those who had. So it was both a surprise and delight to go back to the University of Alaska at Fairbanks on May 10, 1998, to receive an honorary Doctor of Law "for significant and lasting contributions to the State of Alaska." Curiously, just two years later the Corcoran School of Art, now the Corcoran College of Art and Design, presented me with their "highest academic honor, the degree of Doctor of Fine Arts, honoris causa."

W HEN John died, our art collection had to be evaluated for probate purposes. I was shocked to discover the huge sums assigned to the Picassos, Chagalls, Signacs, Dufys, Pascins, and Derains. John and his first wife, Elinor Castle Nef, had bought most of the paintings in Paris in the twenties, long before they brought the astronomical prices of today's art market. A little money and great taste had produced a small but impressive collection, which had been augmented over the years by my passion for sculpture. The eighteen-inch-high bronze Aristide Maillol nude which I had found and John had given me, now had a six-figure evaluation. The set of fourteen Saltimbanque Picasso etchings John had bought from Ambrose Vollard back in the twenties for $100 were now almost priceless. One of them, *Le Repas Frugal*, sometimes called "The Absinthe Drinkers," is said to be the most famous etching of the twentieth century and alone has commanded a high five-figure price at auction. The etchings hang in the hall of my Georgetown house and continue up the stairs to the second floor. They had been framed before we knew about the necessity of having acid-free mats, so I have since had them restored, re-matted, and re-framed, and they now look clean and fresh.

For my sixty-fifth birthday John had given me a bronze sculpture of a nude woman, only about six inches high, by Pierre Bonnard. Like most art lovers I was familiar with Bonnard's paintings, especially the magnificent large oils in the Phillips Collection here in Washington, but I had not known that he did sculpture and was deeply touched by the gift and its beauty. I often thought that if I hadn't had to earn a living I would have been a painter; now I know that sooner or later sculpture would have captured me.

I was blessed in having Dame Elizabeth Frink, a well-known English sculptor, for a friend. I visited her often in Wooland in Dorset, England, and lent one of her pieces to the great one-woman show she had at the Women's Museum for the Arts here in Washington. Over the years I was able to purchase more than half a dozen of her bronzes and was devastated by her early death at the age of sixty-three from cancer. A dividend of our friendship was getting to know Ken Cook, who was in charge of Liz's bronze castings for many years. His handsome young wife, Ann Christopher, was a budding young sculptor, who has now come into her own. Ann and Ken live near Bath, at Merryfield, England. At first I bought several of her smaller abstract pieces, but when John died I asked her for a memorial piece, something larger to stand outdoors as a marker. She made the stunning, tall bronze that stands in the front garden beside the door to the house in Georgetown. And when I built the house in Great Barrington, I commissioned Ann to do the piece described earlier.

My eighteenth-century Georgetown house has four stories. From the downstairs hall to the top floor, where Linda Yahn, her assistant Terry Scanlin, and the computer reign, the walls are lined with the art treasures that John acquired and that we augmented together. Their names are a kind of music for me: Braque, Callot, Chagall, Corbusier, Dufy, Grosz, Kandinsky, Leger, Pascin, Picasso, Rouault, Signac, Utrillo, and Whistler. As I travel up and down the stairwells, which I do many times every day, I greet them all as old friends. Sometimes the light changes and an etching or a watercolor suddenly looks different, and I stop to find out why.

I N my eightieth year I began to work with a gifted personal trainer named David Keller. From the days of my surgery for Paget's Disease, I had been disciplined about exercise, but never before had I worked steadily, five days a week, with an experienced and talented trainer. Friends have often commented on my sprightly step and my ability to rise quickly from a deeply upholstered chair, run for a taxi, and dance every dance at a ball without tiring. I always credit David. Having worked steadily and slowly increasing my stamina, I can now do 300 sit-ups easily. When possible I enjoy walking instead of riding and climbing stairs instead of taking the elevator. Exercise keeps me healthy and cheerful; it's an antidepressant cheaper and less toxic than pills. In summertime I continue a routine designed by David utilizing the heated pool at Ultima Thule in all weather for both exercise and swimming. Older people are bound to fall, but if you are in good physical shape you are often able to catch yourself before you fall, and you don't fall as often. When I was eighty-five, the heel of my shoe caught in the carpet and I fell down a whole flight of steps, landing on my hip. To the doctor's astonishment, I didn't break my hip—the usual result of such a fall at my age—but only bruised the bone. Regular exercise made the difference. It's never too late—ninety-year-olds can develop muscle with exercise, and it can be life-saving and life-prolonging.

Staying slender helps. Watching my diet keeps me at 125 pounds, the same weight I carried in my teens, albeit differently distributed today. I avoid sugar entirely, except for an occasional birthday cake, cut down on fat—no butter or margarine—use olive oil for cooking, avoid carbohydrates, and never touch the diet sodas and other sugar-laden drinks advertised so heavily. The terrible statistic that 50 percent of our population is obese is surely due in large measure to the junk food and sodas that comprise lunch for our children as well as for too many adults. Children watching TV instead of playing outdoors also contributes to the problem.

Although I don't think about it unless necessary, reality tells me that at eighty-eight death may not be very far off. I feel ready to meet it without anxiety. Like most of us, I wish for a swift and if possible dignified end with no heroic measures utilized to keep me alive artificially. I agree with Stefansson's belief that man created his gods according to his needs, so I don't believe in an afterlife. The title of this book says truthfully that most of my life has been lived "finding my way," in trial-and-error fashion. Now it is safe to say that despite losses and setbacks during the dozen years since John's death, I have *found* my way. I am still mentally and physically healthy and have a busy social life with persons of varying ages. I still respond to music, theater, art, books, natural beauty, and especially people, with enthusiasm. I am content.

ACKNOWLEDGMENTS

Warm thanks to:

Sarah Baldwin for her editorial support;

Barbara Bristol who started this book on its way;

Philip Cronenwett, the gifted librarian of the Stefansson Collection at
   Dartmouth College's Baker Library;

Ellen Melrose Griswold for her friendship, letters, and memory;

The MacDowell Colony for its oasis of calm and nourishment;

Robert P. Newman for his excellent book, *Owen Lattimore and the "Loss"
   of China*;

George Nicholson, literary agent and friend;

Terry Scanlin for secretarial help;

Dr. Ethel Siris, Paget's Disease specialist, who kept me relatively pain
   free; and

Linda Yahn, my able assistant for every kind of help.

INDEX

Vendl.
1964

Felicitation
et voeu